RICHES UNDER YOUR ROOF

RICHES UNDER YOUR ROOF

HOW YOU CAN MAKE YOUR HOME WORTH THOUSANDS MORE

JIM BELLIVEAU
WITH MARY BELLIVEAU

A PRINT PROJECT BOOK

HOLT, RINEHART AND WINSTON
NEW YORK

Library of Congress Cataloging in Publication Data
Belliveau, Jim.
Riches under your roof.
"A Print Project book."
Bibliography p.
Includes index.
1. House selling. 2. Dwellings—Remodeling.
3. Dwellings—Maintenance and repair. I. Belliveau,
Mary. II. Title.
HD1390.5.B44 1983   333.33'8   82-15420
ISBN Hardcover: 0-03-053016-4
ISBN Paperback: 0-03-0533301-5

First Edition

Design by Sonja Douglas
Illustrations on pages 162 and 163 by David Lindroth
Printed in the United States of America
1 3 5 7 9 10 8 6 4 2

We wish to extend special thanks to the following for contributions
in their respective areas of expertise:
Bill Kelly of Central Hudson Gas & Electric Corporation
Leland Bookhout, SREA—MAI
Congressman Hamilton Fish and staff, Poughkeepsie, New York
Doris Tieder of John B. Tieder Real Estate, Rhinebeck, New York
Mel Jones of M and D Painters, Red Hook, New York
Tom Regna of The Rug Den, Kingston, New York
Lyn Murphy, Rhinebeck, New York
Steve Schrieber, Rock City, New York
The National Association of Homebuilders, Washington, D.C.

ISBN 0-03-053016-4 HARDCOVER
ISBN 0-03-053301-5 PAPERBACK

To THE AMERICAN DREAM OF OWNING YOUR
OWN HOME . . .
FOR SOUND INVESTMENT, PROPER MANAGEMENT,
AND MAXIMUM PROFIT.

CONTENTS

Riches Under Your Roof

1

THE RICHES-UNDER-YOUR-ROOF PHILOSOPHY
HOW YOU CAN MAKE YOUR HOME WORTH THOUSANDS MORE

Your house is the place in which you live; the place where you and your family eat, sleep, play, love, laugh, cry, and hide from the rain. Your home is your island of safety in the bustling world, the center around which everything you do revolves, your nest.

But your house is much more than a place to live. It's probably the best *investment* (and the biggest) you'll ever have. In these inflationary times, the prices of new and used housing rise monthly. Your house is actually like a second job, earning money as it stands, silent and still. A house can increase in value a tiny fraction every night, even as you sleep.

Whatever its value, your home can be worth more—much more—with a minimum of effort on your part. The key is to treat it as the investment it is. Spending relatively little, you can turn your biggest asset into one that's worth thousands more.

All you have to know are the tricks of the home-improvement game—savvy culled from builders and developers, brokers, professional renovators, people who know, people who've done it. As a professional, I've made it my business to learn everything—I mean *everything*—about this fascinating subject. And in this book I intend to pass the information on to you, so that you too can profit from the real estate you own.

You're going to learn *why* houses increase in value, *which* houses increase in value the most, *what* are the most important factors in determining house value, and, especially important, *how* you can make your house increase in value much faster than you ever thought possible. You'll learn what to do and what to avoid. (Do you know, for example, that most homeowners invest far more in their kitchens and bathrooms than they'll ever be able to recoup when it comes time to sell?)

I've learned—as have most professionals—that there are many surprisingly simple improvements you can make that will boost the value of your home, and boost it out of all proportion to the actual cost of the improvements.

It's possible, for example, to add $1,000 to the market value of your home by investing only $100 in shrubs—if you know the "investment rules" of landscaping. It's possible to create visual or aesthetic improvements, as well as vastly increase functionality, all with relatively small expenditures of money and labor.

Most techniques are simple and low cost. And all of them depend not on learning some deep mystery of the realtor's art, but on developing a certain point of view, a certain philosophy.

The major theme you must grasp from this book is also the "secret" principle from which all things (extra profits) follow:

> The way to upgrade the value of your home is to know what other people want when they're house hunting—what they think they need as well as what sort of total image they're going to respond to on an emotional level.

These two factors, *market demand* and *total image*, are at the heart of *Riches Under Your Roof*. Plant the RUYR principles firmly in your brain as you read on.

THE VALUE OF YOUR HOUSE IS NO ACCIDENT

To understand your house as an investment, you first have to understand the nature of houses in general as things of value. No matter how prominently your house may figure in your dreams or feelings of identity or security, the fact remains that at bottom it is a thing of greater or lesser value in the economy. And it stands in a hierarchy of values compared with other houses, different as one may be from another.

You may think of your house as your home, but if you want it to increase in value you must begin to think of it as an object with a worth in dollars. In that sense, a house is no different from a bar of gold or a diamond necklace or a fur coat or a Hummel figurine. It is a rather large thing, but it is still a thing. And in the economic world, people exchange money for things.

Logs sell for one price; kiln-dried two-by-fours sell for another. The market decides. Factories in a certain condition sell for so much per square foot. A car of a given make and model has a certain value in dollars. Whether it's bubble gum or Boeing jets, there is a market-determined price for everything.

And the price depends on all the features of the object that the buyers in the market deem important—the specifications, as it were. Excellent conditon is worth more than good condition, good condition worth more than poor condition, and so on.

To estimate the dollar value of any object, you must know what buyers seek when they are buying and how much they will pay for every feature they seek.

You can't assume that what the market wants is necessarily rational. Most car buyers, for example, will pay a lot more for a clean and polished car than they will for a dusty one. As often as not they'll wind up paying far more than it would cost simply to clean the dusty car. But buyers are human, and the marketplace is subject to human fears, weaknesses, insecurities, greed, and ego.

No matter how much you may love your house, you've got to learn to envision it as an object in the marketplace. Only then will you see clearly how to make it worth the most for the least expenditure. Once you know what buyers want in the marketplace—and this book will show you that—you can estimate value, and you can take action to make the value grow.

Most homeowners never get the correct perspective on the house-as-investment because they don't think of the marketplace until they are actually ready to sell. By then it may be too late. Costly and self-defeating decisions have already been made. The time to start thinking of your house as a thing-in-the-market is *now*, when you're also living in it, not later, when you may have done irreparable harm to your asset.

Value, as you have perhaps begun to see, is a tricky subject. Analyzing value is an art as well as a science. In determining value you may not be able to achieve absolute certainty all the time, but with the principles in this book you'll become an expert, able to make solid, educated judgments. You need only teach yourself to analyze all the elements that create value. Once you learn to analyze, it's a relatively short step to learning the practical ways you can put your analysis to work. And these two things—analysis and practical application—are exactly what *Riches Under Your Roof* will teach you.

Let me give you an example of what's possible. In the process I want to illustrate two key principles that you will encounter throughout this book: (1) *the value of a house is a matter of the sum of its parts*, and (2) *the higher the value of a house today, the better investment it will be tomorrow*.

I improved a house for two clients—both newspaper writers—in 1976. This house was sound and good-looking on the outside, but the interior was somewhat shabby. It had been bought for $50,000, quite a bit below the average market price for a similar-sized house on similar land. We gave the kitchen simple but nice counters, papered and replastered all the rough walls in the house, added a little front vestibule/mud porch which gave the exterior more interest, and converted a garage that was really a bit tight for even one car into an office or study that could double as a guest room. Total renovation cost was $5,000.

When the work was completed the original broker came back—three months after the sale, now—and told us the house would fetch *at least* $60,000, probably more. It had been brought "up to market." With its RUYR improvements it would now appeal to a much greater number of people.

My clients weren't interested in a quick resale, though. They saw themselves as *investors*, not house traders. They were interested in having a nice house to live in *and* having the best possible long-term gain on their money.

Recently they had the broker return for a reappraisal, and the result was interesting.

ORIGINAL HOUSE	
Cost	$50,000
Value in 5 years at 10% per year*	73,200
Profit	$23,200

WITH RUYR IMPROVEMENTS	
Cost	$50,000
Cost of improvements (financed†)	5,000
Total cost	55,000
Instant improved value	60,000
Value in 5 years at 10% per year*	96,620
Profit	$41,620

*A 10% per year compounded home value inflation is assumed.
†Finance charge not included. Interest rate varies.

Inflation does its work on houses year by year, and the idea is to bank on this knowledge. If your house is worth $60,000 unimproved and it gains 10 percent each year through increased prices, it only stands to reason that you'll have a lot more at the end of five years than if you start with an unimproved property valued at $50,000. This is the best argument for making your improvements *now* (plus the fact that cost of improvements is rising continually and will be higher later). As you can see, at the end of five years my clients' $5,000 investment added an extra $18,420 to the value of their house! When you realize that the cost of the improvements was paid through a financed loan costing just about $100 per month, you can see that you're looking at quite an effective investment/savings program.

Where else can you get such a good investment? The $5,000 had its fabulous building power only because it *didn't stand alone*; it was coupled to the ever-increasing price inflation of the underlying house. The $5,000 by itself didn't grow the extra $18,000 in five years; *the entire improved house* grew in value. A true sum that's greater than its parts.

A BASIC ATTITUDE

Your attitude toward your property is your foundation as an investor. You can't afford to treat your house simply as a place to store the garden hose and watch television. Your house gives you the chance to be richer than you are.

You must make, as we'll see later on, a conscious choice. Do you choose merely to live in your house and enjoy it? If so, read no further.

"Well, of course I want to make my house worth more," you say immediately. But the choice is not as simple as might appear on the surface. We have grown up with certain ideas and attitudes about houses that aren't always easy to break. And our attitudes are often not oriented toward investing. On the contrary, common attitudes can work against sound business judgments you might otherwise make. Perhaps the most damaging is the idea that your home is your castle and that you can set it up just exactly the way you like.

I've done a lot of work for a wealthy stockbroker in my area—we'll call him Richard R. He's a prime example of someone with excellent business judgment in one realm of life, and wretched business judgment when it comes to investing in his home. I've tried many times to explain his errors in house investment to him, but it is like talking to a stone wall. I'll never know why someone who can analyze the value of billion-dollar companies can't do the same with his own house.

Richard picked up a marvelous Federal-style brick house in mint condition eight years ago. Compared with some of the estates (now of faded glory) that line the Hudson River in our Upstate New York area, his may not qualify for mansion category, but with fourteen rooms, four bathrooms, two porches, and a broad river-view patio, you can accurately say it's a big house.

Now, would it surprise you to learn that Richard is a confirmed bachelor? He is. But anyone has the right to live in as big a house as he pleases—nothing the matter with that.

But Richard proceeded to alter this perfectly maintained period house into a sybaritic bachelor pad. On top of the $175,000 he paid for the house, he had me do another $158,000 worth of renovations! A highly successful lawyer and his family had lived here before Richard bought the place; it didn't exactly need a new roof! Most buyers would have been delighted to move in "as is."

First, Richard had me tear out all the walnut wainscoting and trim in the master bedroom. "Richard," I told him, "pardon the pun, but walnut woodwork doesn't grow on trees." "Bah," he said, "it's stuffy." So I pulled it out, as he instructed; sheetrocked over the ornate ceiling plasterwork, as he also instructed; and bit my cheeks as I installed mirrors covering all four walls and the ceiling. That's right, mirrors everywhere. I like mirrors, but . . .

Then he saw a kitchen he liked in one of the decorator magazines. "That's it. Do it exactly," he said. The kitchen was designed for a sunny California beach home, but that made no difference to my client. He soon had, for $42,857 in United States currency, a sparkling Malibu kitchen in his dignified brick Federal.

Next he had me rip out two bathrooms that were placed back to back in the upstairs hall. The new single room thus created was perfectly square, and he had me install fluorescent lights recessed into the ceiling. Richard, you see, liked to play billiards, and he wanted his poolroom close to the bedroom. "I need it for when I get up in the middle of the night wrestling with an investment decision," he said. Some investment decision, I thought.

Need I go on? To make visiting clients feel right at home, Richard decorated the smaller bedrooms in a style I'd call neo-Holiday Inn, complete with Wall-tex on the walls and a new bathroom for each bedroom. It was hell getting all those waste pipes in without spoiling the downstairs, and it cost him a pretty penny. I won't bore you with details about the swimming pool or the paddleball court or the wine racks built in the basement (plus climate control, naturally).

Here, in extreme form, you can see a problem that I'll be discussing throughout this book. Richard wanted his house *just the way he wanted it*. His house fantasy—we all have our own house fantasies—included lots of delirious Hollywood-type extra features. But how many future buyers will want the same? Few, if any, I fear.

And it is future buyers—no one else—who determine the value of your home.

A house functions on the free market, and in any market the existence of someone, somewhere, with taste eccentricities similar to your own is possible. But we as investors don't want the possible; we want the probable. By definition, you're much more likely to get a good price for your house if it appeals to a *large number* of buyers rather than a rare individual. Think of the marketplace as an auction: the more buyers, the better the price.

As a thing of value, then, a house will have its greatest worth if it is basically conventional—appeals to the greatest number of people— and has relatively minor details that make it *stand out against other, similarly conventional houses*. It's a fact of life in the real estate market: Buyers like something a little different, or done with good taste, or done better, and they will pay a surprising amount more to get that. But they want it only *a little* different. People don't like to rock the boat. They don't like to stray too far from the straight and narrow. At times when their lives are being upset—when families are being uprooted and moved to new states, new jobs, new lives—people become surprisingly rigid. These are the times when they most want the reassurance of the familiar.

This is a primary concept for us: the idea of Conventionality Plus. As a general rule, improvements should take the house a step further, not a leap. For the serious investment-minded improver, what could be more logical? The house need not appeal to every buyer alive, but it should appeal to the greatest possible number of buyers who will be interested in that kind of house. I can't think of many people who'd want a mirrored bedroom in a nineteenth-century brick Federal with the river and the blue Catskills stretching out behind it.

We'll delve deeper into the details of Conventionality Plus later on.

PLANNING

By now you've gotten the gist of the Riches-Under-Your-Roof philosophy: Improving the value of your house is not something that can be done willy-nilly; it must be carefully thought out if you want to be successful. My client Richard, for example, probably won't get back a penny for his investment come selling time. I wouldn't be surprised if he had actually decreased the value of his home from the original purchase price.

And selling time will come, sooner or later. While you live in your house you enjoy the rooted feeling of homeyness. The last thing you want to think about is moving. But life has its twists and turns; change happens. You get a better job or a job in another town. You get a divorce. Your spouse dies. Your kids grow up and move out. In this country, owner-occupied houses change hands on the average of every 4.9 years, according to the National Board of Realtors. Some 5 percent of all existing homes are sold each year. Sooner or later you too will become one of these statistics. You must ask yourself, before selling time comes, Do you want to make a small profit or a big one?

The answer is obvious. And the route to the answer is obvious, too. *Plan now. Plan now for gains later.*

INSTANT RETURN VERSUS RETURN-OVER-TIME

Recall my earlier example of the profits that can be gleaned from careful, cost-efficient improvements. The wealth-building power of these improvements is clear; yet it's difficult to attribute the profits to the improvements alone. For the improvements are always coupled with the house itself.

As investors, of course, we would like to know precisely what our investment return is going to be when we improve our houses: 100 percent over three years? 50 percent over two years? 400 percent over five years? Of course, no investment is a certainty. A buyer of IBM stock doesn't know for sure if it will go up or by how much. During the 1970s and early 1980s, even buyers of U.S. bonds have lost money.

The housing market, remember, operates subjectively. But you can put the investment odds in your favor by studying and analyzing the subjectivity of the market and by making the lowest-cost investments in improvements that appeal to the greatest number of buyers' subjective desires.

When you undertake this process shrewdly, you can be reasonably sure that your home improvements will show a better return than any other investments available. (Ask any stockbroker. He'd be overjoyed if his IBM went up 277 percent in five years.) And, at the same time, you can enjoy the greater practicality, space, beauty, and pride of ownership that home improvement brings. Fixing up your house is a lot more satisfying than staring at the gold bar you've got hidden in your winter boots.

In the long term, you can count on an outstanding return on your home investment for several reasons. First, inflation raises the total value of your improved house each year. Second, it raises the value of each improvement you've made, as material and labor costs rise each year. Just about everything has doubled in price in the last five years, and that's true of the *replacement value* of your improvements. Today's greenhouse window at $500 will be worth $1,000 in five years, and buyers will pay for it. Wisely chosen RUYR investments are bound to be profitable in the long run.

But your investment has short-term as well as long-term value. What will your improvement do for the value of your house the instant it's completed? That depends on your house and what the improvement is. If your house looks old, weathered, and peeling, and you scrape and paint it, you may show a profit on the day you're done—as well as more profit a few years down the road. The same is true for fixing up a ratty lawn or any other improvement that brings the house up to market.

On the other hand, if you add special features—say, spend $5,000 on refurbishing the kitchen—it may take one to three years before the increase in your home value recoups your investment (depending on the cost of the house and your area). From then on, though, you'll be earning a profit. And all the while you've profited personally from your new and delightful kitchen.

Because there are so many variables and intangibles—every house and area is unique—this book will consider investments from the point of view of their return in *five years or more*. This is our *investment-holding period*, as it were.

You'll see some exceptions pointed out along the way (like the exterior paint job mentioned above), but generally, when you see an analysis of the investment value of a given home improvement, do not think that the investment necessarily bears fruit instantly.

First you have to plant the tree (after selecting the right tree); then water and feed it; then let it grow. The fruit comes automatically.

2

HOUSE IMAGE:

OR, I'LL GIVE YOU A HOUSE
YOU CAN'T SAY NO TO

STYLE

A surprising number of houses are clean, well cared for, and even expensively furnished, but lack one important quality: style. A house that lacks style doesn't speak to you. A house without an image is a house the potential buyer walks right by.

On the other hand, you know about the house with charisma. Even when it is not the one in which you feel most at home, this is nevertheless the house that communicates. The force of someone else's imagination and energy has created an effect, and that effect pulls you in. Perhaps it is an unusually handsome Mexican rug that first attracts you. Then the deeply cushioned rattan couches. Everything contributes to a harmony of colors and textures—white adobe-finished walls, large clay pots filled with flowers and *Ficus* trees, sheer muslin curtains at the windows. There are the usual homey artifacts: a basket of knitting, a magazine rack, ashtrays, and pipe collections—objects that might add up to a feeling of chaos in another house, but not here. Some principle of order prevails here and subtly dominates the look and furnishings of the house: An aesthetic *style* has been captured.

Style is doubly functional. It's pleasant and stimulating to live in a house with style. And when the time comes to sell, a house with style will move off the market much faster—and fetch a far better price—than its indefinable neighbor. People *want* style. They want to feel that after they've laid out the down payment and started sending the mortgage checks, the house they'll be feeding such a large portion of their income will exude personality.

It has to do with the personal image we want to communicate. When people are house hunting, they look for image more than any other single factor, even more than the quality of the structure itself. The quality of the structure—including the strength and durability of its materials and appliances—depends a great deal on how much the house cost to build. But a house can be valued at $1 million and lack the sort of defining image called style.

Image is intangible, and for that reason it doesn't necessarily cost anything to create. The cheapest, dinkiest little house can have a winning image. Image begins in the mind of the owner; it evolves out of the owner's inventiveness and creativity. But it is also a sensitivity you can learn to develop. Building a strong house image may, at first, seem an elusive concept, but it's worth your thought and energy because *image will make you money*. Moreover, it doesn't cost a cent more than you'd have to spend fixing and furnishing your place to begin with.

Let's try to get a better understanding of why it is that house image touches such a deep chord in people. Why is it that we long to own a certain house, daydream about how we would look and feel living in it, imagine how our friends would feel when visiting?

WHAT YOUR HOUSE SAYS ABOUT YOU

A house is the mirror of its owner's soul. More than anything else that's associated with you—more than the clothes you wear or the job you have or the people you know—the place you choose to live in reveals you to the world. Your home tells anyone entering it how you live. And how you live goes a long way toward describing who you are.

As a contractor, I probably have more experience than most in examining people's houses, and after one look at a house I can generally tell you whether or not its owners have a place to store newspapers and mail, if there's an ash drawer on the woodburning stove, where the dirty laundry gets sorted, whether sandwiches are made on a chopping board or the kitchen counter, whether grocery shopping is done daily or weekly, where the animals are fed, and how large the owners' wardrobes are. I can come pretty close to the mark when guessing whether the children are allowed to snack in the living room, who has a job outside the house, who in the household smokes, whether the family likes to play games together or watch TV, what kinds of music are played.

To a greater or lesser degree, everyone gets clues about the resident's life-style when entering another's abode. We are unrelentingly curious about our fellow beings. And we search their surroundings as closely as we search their faces for signs of who they are. Knowing this as we do (and everyone knows curiosity is a universal trait), we care about how we come across to others. Consequently, we care about what our homes communicate—the warmth, the liveliness, the serenity reflected by their proportion, their decor, and their order. This personal involvement in how our houses make us feel, as well as the image they create about who we are, is the psychological underpinning of that elusive but potentially so lucrative concept: *house image*.

THE HOUSE WITH NO IMAGE

Think of the houses you've been in that you wouldn't give a fig for. They may have been sizable, well located, tightly constructed, but with nothing special, nothing unique. The house without an image is the dull repository of all those conventional features we have come to expect in a house. Nothing distinguishes it from all the other three-bedroom, two-bathroom, double-garage houses on the block. The house without an image has no niceties, no carefully thought out conveniences—wet bar or flower-potting counter or mirrored walk-in closet—that make us feel special and cared for, and that, yes, add a kind of status to our surroundings. Such a house—ordinary, conventional, undistinguished—will, you may rest assured, fetch the lowest possible price for a house in its particular category in the local real estate market. If you own such a house, you may eventually make a small profit simply because inflation will nudge the market value of your house up a notch or two. This will happen even if you do nothing but stay in bed for four years.

On the other hand, if you take the most ordinary, conventional four-walled structure and work up an image for it, the value of your property will soar accordingly.

There are no standardized figures on these things. Only individual examples will show you the ultimate worth of thinking and planning and making the right kinds of changes and additions to your house. My favorite example of what can happen when you take the time and energy to create a house you can't say no to involves two families— we'll call them Jones and Brown—who bought very similar dwellings within several months of each other. As a matter of fact, Joe Jones and Tom Brown worked for the same supercorporation, the kind that moves its middle-management personnel to different jobs in different parts of the country every few years. Both these families purchased $55,000 houses in 1977. They were located in an area not far from me that still had some wonderful Victorian structures available at bargain prices. As it happened, both the Joneses and the Browns consulted me about making some changes in their houses. Jones consulted me, hired me, and told Brown about me. But Brown and his wife, Angela, ultimately decided to leave their place untouched. It was a perfectly nice old house, but nowhere near what you would call "top of the market." I remember Angela saying, "It doesn't make sense to do anything to this place. The woodwork is beautiful. The floors are beautiful. The big old Victorian porch is beautiful. We'll just live here and enjoy all this space. When Tom gets transferred in a few years, there's no way we'll have trouble selling a beauty like this."

Angela was a city girl, you see, and her eyes opened wide at all that space and pristine oaken woodwork. What she didn't recognize was that not everyone interested in buying a house (when hers was eventually put on the market) would hail from the same small, thin-walled city apartments as she had. Which brings me to the fundamental approach in creating an image for your home. You can't think simply in terms of what satisfies *you*. There's a whole world out there, and you have to reckon with it—with others' needs, others' tastes, others' backgrounds. Victorian may have its charms, but it can also be damned inconvenient. Most people, as the Browns would eventually discover, want *convenience* along with their charm.

Now the Joneses took a very similar house—same period, same size, same location—and approached it more realistically. "Jim," they told me, "we've got to get some light into this place. Victorian is beautiful, but it's too dark. Also, we want a laundry room, and we have to have the kitchen made functional."

Their budget was tight, so we planned carefully. A skylight was put into the roof above the stairwell, allowing light to spill down through the dark center portion of the house. A large, rectangular opening was cut into the wall between the first-floor hall and the living room, preserving the feeling of "hall" but increasing the sense of space (Victorian parlors can be tight) and allowing the new light to have its greatest effect. This and a glass sliding door I installed while "functionalizing" the kitchen banished that ominous Victorian gloom.

In the kitchen, my goal was to modernize while leaving intact the charm of the original setting—specifically the mahogany wainscoting and the wall-hung, glass-doored cabinets. The mandate was to effect this kitchen renovation as cheaply as possible. I simply installed a work island, complete with countertop stove, so that it formed an L with the kitchen-sink counter. The extra space at the far end of the room was given over to a small round wicker table and chairs. New glass sliders allowed a spectacular view of neighboring woods and fields and opened onto a small but ideally located patio of dry brick set in sand by Joe Jones himself. A part of the large and space-wasting mud porch on the back of the house was turned into a laundry room, tying into the existing plumbing.

The most expensive part of the work I did for the Joneses was constructing the kitchen work island, which needed special wiring and some relatively fancy cabinet making. Everything else involved breaking holes into existing walls and roof, which is one of the cheapest and most cost effective ways you can transform the interior look of a house. For the whole job—including the skylight, the cutout in the living-room wall, construction of a simple laundry room, and functionalization of the kitchen—the Joneses had to pay me $5,100. The bank gave them a five-year home-improvement loan, which added $90 a month to their $348 mortgage payment.

Three years later, when Joe Jones's corporation informed him he was being relocated to the Northwest, the value of that $90 a month had dropped to an inflation-chopped $75. And in the meantime, Jones had gotten several raises. But most important, through careful planning and good real estate sense, the Joneses had vastly increased the worth of their asset. Come time to sell, in 1981, the Joneses asked $78,500 for their "modernized Victorian"—and quickly got it, thereby snaring for themselves a tidy profit of over $17,000.

When the Browns had to relocate, they found they were unable to sell their house in the two months allotted them. They had no alternative but to sell it to the corporation Brown worked for, realizing not a penny more than they had paid. "No loss," you might say; but in fact it was a loss. The $55,000 the corporation reimbursed Tom and Angela was worth 17 percent less than the $55,000 they'd paid out three years earlier. And in the meantime, real estate values had soared across the country, so that when they moved to the outskirts of Boston, they hadn't enough cash to purchase a house in the same category as the one in which they'd been living, but had to scale down to a smaller, less handsome place. So Angela and Tom's reluctance to get involved in some fairly minor improvements ended up costing them. The lack of modernization made their house hard to sell on the 1981 market. In addition, Angela herself had long been peeved by the inconvenience of cooking and serving meals in their big, poorly laid out kitchen, and Tom had come virtually to hate the house for its darkness. So not only did the Browns lose money on the house, they didn't even really enjoy living in it.

The Joneses followed RUYR principles. For a modest outlay, they created a pleasant house with all the modern conveniences and features buyers want today. They also retained the Victorian image of their house. The new buyer got a house that *works well* and also has Victorian charm. The Browns' buyer, on the other hand, got an old Victorian house with all its *disadvantages*, unremedied and untouched—all its inconveniences. The Joneses' buyer can think, "I live in a Victorian," though it's now really a modern home with a Victorian look. The Victorian image was preserved, and enhanced, with modernity. And that means value in the marketplace.

THE THREE RULES OF CREATING HOUSE IMAGE

RULE 1: GIVE YOUR HOUSE A THEME

A first rule in the business of creating house image is *give your house a theme*. This will help you to get a handle on what kinds of improvements will add to a total image and what will take away from it. Just as a successful party is often organized around a theme, so too can the theme principle work in helping you to develop a strong look, style, or image for your home.

If your house belongs to a noteworthy architectural period, then by all means go with the look that's already been established. You can do wonders accentuating, say, the simplicity of a 1940s farmhouse or a little country cottage done in the style known as Carpenter Gothic. If you own a Victorian you may want to do some research in the library and decorate the parlors as authentically as possible. (All it takes, along with the research, is energy, patience, and paint.) Of course, you can and will want to modernize; but retain the flavor, the nostalgic charm of the original.

If your house is very old, you'll likely need to restore it to its original condition. (See Bibliography for books detailing how properly to restore an older home.) Very old houses in prime condition, however, are absolutely at a premium in this plastic-sated culture. People want antiquity. They want history. They want roots. So if the idea of restoring that seventeenth-century stone house with the wide plank floors challenges you, go to it. As for the profits to be made, you can probably do proportionately better by fixing up a newer house with less character. Restoring an old house really soaks up time, energy, and materials, as anyone who's ever attempted such a job will be happy to tell you. To some extent, restoration is a labor of love. But if you have an old house in a prime location that you were able to buy at a good or bottom-of-the-market price, and if you are careful in your planning and in choosing a contractor (see chapter 10), you can turn a tidy profit when you sell. (I will confess right now to a hopeless affinity for very old houses. I will also tell you, however, that *consistently easier and larger profits can be made on the house that's less than 100 years old*—and it is this younger house toward which most of the information in *Riches Under Your Roof* is aimed.)

If your house lacks a strong architectural style, there are other ways of conceptualizing a theme for it. The question, Who and what is this house for? will quickly bring things into focus. Is it a family house? If so, How big a family? Is it a first home for newlyweds? A retirement home for "empty nesters," as real estate people call them? Is it a country house or a vacation place to be used primarily on weekends? Will a lot of entertaining be done there, or work of a solitary or creative nature?

Thinking clearly about the function of your house (and about its potential function for possible future owners) will help you to make sensible decisions about improvements. If you develop the plan carefully enough, working from a strong sense of a house's functionality can create its image as effectively and clearly as any other theme or concept.

Here is an example of how functionality is transmuted into image. A country home for a family that lives and works (and whose children go to school) in the city will need sleeping quarters for everyone and for weekend guests as well. If the house is to be used in winter, money may have to be spent initially to provide features that keep heating costs down. Thought should be given to ease of maintenance (weekending family members won't want to spend any more time than necessary cleaning and straightening). Unless someone in the family is a major cooking enthusiast, the kitchen can probably be kept simple (as long as you provide enough electricity to supply the appliances of later owners). A feeling of luxury is not as important to most urban vacationers as a view and a sense of quiet space. Monstrous walk-in closets would probably not be necessary; a fireplace or setup for a woodburning stove would be.

After working through the solutions to practical problems, we come to something that's still very closely related: decor. When I think of creating a country-home image, certain things come to mind as appropriate, while other things fall quickly from the picture. French antique furniture would be out of place in a weekend home that will ever accommodate children—yours or anyone else's; early American primitives, on the other hand, might do just fine. Maintenance-free floors are a must. They don't have to be vinyl; polyurethaned wood is cheaper and prettier, as is fieldstone if it's locally available. Furniture should be comfortable but minimal. Large couches slipcovered in pre-shrunk cotton, a large pine table for dining, a few colorful, easy-to-clean rugs (hooked or braided cotton, or sisal or woven straw for summer). Nothing at all at the windows if they are well proportioned and attractive to look at, and if you don't have neighbors looming too nearby. Add a few wooden benches for magazines, plants, and cocktails, and what more do you need but a roaring fire in winter or breezes in summer?

If you have trouble conceptualizing a theme or image for your house, try imagining the newspaper ad you will one day write when ready to sell your chief asset. That ought to help you begin seeing your house in a realistic and marketable light. Mary and I were not long in the second house we owned when we began mulling over the ad copy:

> Charming, three-story *farmhouse* on 4 lush acres less than
> two hours from Manhattan. Barn with studio. Private road.
> Deer.

Imagining the calls an ad like that would generate when placed in *The New York Times*, Mary and I were able to charge full steam ahead in developing our "charming farmhouse" theme. We patched and spackled and whitewashed walls. Striving consciously for stark simplicity meant we could get away with applying expensive, Colonial-type stenciled wallpaper in halls and bathrooms only. We refinished the old spruce floors and stripped the darkened shellac off the wormy chestnut woodwork with denatured alcohol. The place was bedroom-heavy and bathroom-shy, so we made a second bathroom out of the smallest bedroom, leaving its nice wood floor and installing an old sink and a footed tub bought at auction. In short, we let the fact that our home was originally built as a farmhouse carry us—no extra ornamentation, no fancy tile in the kitchen or bathrooms. (The old pine wainscoting in the kitchen we thought beautiful in itself, though not the linoleum the farmer had put down. That we ripped up to expose the plain pine floors beneath.) We hewed to the image suggested by the original function of the house, believing this would enhance its marketability when the time came to sell. And indeed it did. A lot of elbow grease and $2,200 sunk into materials and new plumbing for the added bathroom turned our asset into a $65,000 house five years after we bought it—at $47,000. And that was before inflation hit the real estate market!

The fact that theme sells houses is not lost on building developers, by the way. They sometimes go to hilarious extremes to imprint "theme" on the minds of potential buyers. One California builder, trying to sell expensive "customlike" homes, gave each of its town-house models a different theme. One town house was decorated in hot, tropical colors and had jungle music playing in the background. Another, emphasizing "olde English" decor, had taped madrigals accompanied by lutes in the background. "We wanted prospective buyers leaving our complex to know they'd been somewhere special," the marketing director told me.

Rule 2: KEEP IT SIMPLE

This story brings me to the second rule of creating your house's image. It's an idea that may strike you as obvious but that is overlooked time and time again in the homeowner's misguided efforts to make the house impressive: *Keep it simple*. Whatever type of house you're

working on, don't make the mistake of adding a lot of false ornamentation. If the house was originally built with gingerbread hanging
from its eaves, fine; if not, don't add any. Ditto such "improvements"
as plastic tile in the bathroom, Astroturf on the back-porch floor, and
latticework sheds for the trash cans.

Use real materials that will hold up: solid, well-cut woods; genuine
quarry or ceramic tiles; and for kitchen and bath appliances, the simplest no-frills models from top-quality manufacturers. Buyers know
cheap when they see it and definitely won't be impressed by imitation
artiness. As we'll see in later chapters, your materials don't have to be
absolutely the best money can buy. They do, however, have to be real.
In our artificial culture the real becomes worth more every day.

Keep the line of your house and outbuildings (garage, barn, pool
house) clean—no drooping antennas or tacky, add-on cupolas. Tuck
any work or gardening sheds neatly against the back corner of the
house. When buyers approach your property, they should be presented with a clean, pleasing arrangement of land, gardens, and house,
with any additional buildings organized so as to *enhance* rather than
detract from what is central in this total scene: the house.

The keep-it-simple rule means avoiding decor that will disturb the
potential buyer: vivid, offbeat paint on the walls; a fountain in the
foyer; bizarre, melodramatic lighting schemes. Such artifice does
nothing to help the house's image; it really destroys image, just as
attention-getting behavior obliterates a person's true character. I remember an elegantly modernized farmhouse located at the end of a
beautiful lawn with a stand of tall pine trees on either side. The one
false note—it stood in jarring contrast to the rest of the house—was a
circular pit in the middle of the living room, the center of which was
occupied by a round, open fireplace over which hung a blinding red
hood. This bit of visual folly destroyed the entire living room, making
it difficult to entertain more than four people at a time and conjuring
up the atmosphere of a singles resort—not at all what the owners had
in mind. When ready to sell, these people could not get their house
off the market until they disposed of the pit, which meant ripping out
the fireplace and hood and replacing the flooring. They installed a
glass-doored woodburning stove against a wall at the end of the living

room and arranged some comfortable chairs and a low couch facing it. Soon after this transformation the house was snapped up. (Unfortunately, this family would itself have had more pleasure living in the house if only that initial urge to be creative had been ignored.)

RULE 3: ADD FEATURES

This brings me to the third rule of image creation: *Add features to your house*. People may not be attracted to a garish firepit in the middle of a living room, but that doesn't mean they aren't interested in special features. They are. *Well-conceived* extras (throughout the book we'll try to clarify the difference between useful features and money-wasting extras) will add a great deal to a house's image and thus to its worth. They distinguish it from the ordinary house, make the potential buyer feel that he or she is getting something special, and inevitably lend greater status to the house.

Features mean convenience. They also imply an added functionalism—something you'll be able to do or feel or enjoy that you couldn't before the feature was there. You'll notice that real estate ads always highlight any special features a house may have. Check the listings at the back of your local paper and note how quickly your eye is drawn to such tantalizing extras as "mature plantings," "French doors," "pond and fruit trees," "solarium," "Ping-Pong room," "greenhouse off kitchen," "health spa adjacent to master bath." (Some of these you'd pay for; some you wouldn't.) Features stimulate you to imagine the rich life, the comfortable life, the mellow life. A personal health spa may be the last thing you care about, but "adjacent pasture with cows" might be the touch that absolutely knocks you out. People *want* special features, will look for them, and will pay extra, over and above what the features cost, for the houses that have them. (But beware: While many people will pay extra for fruit trees, for example, few will pay for a hot tub.)

An independent study commissioned by Maywood, Inc., a major manufacturer of specialty wood products, showed how the simple addition of wooden shutters and bifold closet doors drastically changed people's opinions of what a house was worth. Before additions, the people surveyed valued the house at $78,000, and after, at $89,000—a value increase of $11,000! (Materials cost only $780.) Even more amazing, almost a third of the people who saw the house after improvements gave it higher marks for neighborhood attractiveness. When the house looked better on the outside, so did the neighborhood in general.

Certain features are considered prime by people in the real estate business and will add considerably more to the value of your house than you pay in materials and labor to install. The following list of prime features has been gleaned from our RUYR board of realtors, real estate trade journals, and my own experience and that of other contractors.

THE MASTER SUITE. Buyers all over the country have shown an upsurge of interest in the master suite—a bedroom that lies away from the madding crowd, preferably with its own bath and dressing area. If your house hasn't a master suite, do what you can to create one. A feeling of warmth and security is what buyers want, according to a survey conducted by *Housing* magazine. Developers noted the selling power of such features as bedroom fireplaces and glass sliders leading to private outdoor living spaces. Among the hints they gave for "putting sell" into the master suite are:

- Create the feeling of a private living room.
- Add a touch of glamour with an opulent bath.
- Play up spaciousness with a large dressing area.
- Tie it in to private outdoor living areas.
- Let the bedroom serve a lot of different functions.
- Stress luxury when space is inflexible, and emphasize architecture when space is flexible.

EXTRA BATHROOM. Any house with three bedrooms should have an extra bathroom, or a powder room (toilet and sink), or at least an extension of the family bath.

A house buyer with a family big enough to occupy three bedrooms or more will be grateful for an extra bath and will likely prefer the house that has one to the place next door that has a marvelous gazebo but no extra bath. Be clever in the installation of this feature. Do not turn it into a major construction project unless your house is worth an awful lot of money to begin with. Tuck the extra bath into a corner of the master bedroom (a fiberglass shower stall and a toilet will add great convenience if there's not enough room for a full bath) or under a stairway, or add it to the back of the house so it can tie in to the main plumbing.

The "extended bathroom" is a new and highly marketable idea. Some developers have found that if the one bath in the house is extensive enough—perhaps with a nearby dressing area—the extra bath can be omitted. Many young couples, for example, are perfectly happy as long as they have two lavatories. As Mike Engel, vice-president of marketing for a builder in Long Beach, California, says, "We put the second lavatory in a separate dressing area glamorized with a skylight and mirrored closet doors. The dressing room area expands the usability of the bath enough that we feel comfortable not offering a powder room on the first floor."

Another way of extending a single bathroom is to compartmentalize it; for example, a family bath in which parents and children share the tub but have separate toilets and lavatories. The big advantage? Space saving. Sometimes there are things you'd rather do with space than give it to a second bath. "If we had to squeeze two full baths into the 728-square-foot second floor of this development house, we would have to shrink closet space in the master bedroom," Henry Zuckerman, a New York architect, said of the compartmentalized baths he installed in a development in Rocky Point.

LAUNDRY AREA. A laundry area is appreciated by everyone, newlyweds and empty nesters alike. If it's in a family home, be sure to provide enough space for folding, sorting, and hanging large quantities of clothing.

Big, drafty bathrooms or kitchens in older houses can be divided off to provide adjacent laundry areas. Many people find it convenient to have laundry equipment on the same floor as the bedrooms.

Cellars are frequently used for laundry equipment because you can cheaply tie into existing plumbing in space that's otherwise wasted. Good lighting and a colorful paint job will help lift a cellar laundry area out of the gloom.

LANDSCAPING. Gardens and special landscaping are always a boon in the marketing of a house, especially if you're lucky enough to be selling your property in spring or summer. Flowering perennials are cheaper over the long haul than annuals. As a dollar-for-dollar investment, the installation of gardens may not always bring back more than what it costs in time and labor, but it's possible that no other single feature will move your house off the market faster than scads of riotous blooms.

PORCHES, PATIOS, DECKS. Extending living space to the outdoors is highly desirable in all parts of the country except the Deep South, where people stay inside air-conditioned houses unless they're situated near swimming pools or water. Any outdoor extensions should be located and landscaped for privacy. Materials should be weather- and termite-proof, but can be roughly and simply constructed to great effect. Be sure the shape and size are in pleasant proportion to the house itself and to any nearby garden areas. It would be hard not to double or triple your money on porch, patio, or deck, *unless* you have gone way overboard on materials and labor. Again, *keep it simple*. A cedar deck and some large clay planters can do magic—and can cost as little as a few hundred dollars if you do the work yourself.

Here's a lesson in the wisdom of simplicity. An old friend, Henry Wistler, made an interesting improvement on his Southern California home. Like many houses in that area, his was built on a hill overlooking less expensive development houses. Beyond the housing tract, however, was an inspiring view of the San Gabriel Mountains. Wistler's task was challenging: how to block out the unattractive cluster of houses beneath him and still see the rising landscape.

Starting with the continuous redwood porch already in existence on the side of the house with the view, Henry built a 10-foot wooden extension out over the ledges beneath and added a double, 4-foot-high redwood fence and wall, 40 feet long, between which he sandwiched specially made flower boxes and filled them with an assortment of native cacti. The effect was stunning; moreover, it neatly accomplished the task of blocking out an unattractive view. But what do you think old Henry paid for his "small" improvement? A whopping $5,859.

If Henry were to try tacking $6,000 onto his asking price, most buyers would consider his price out of line and look for another place to invest their money. The average buyer simply doesn't place as much value on the improvement as Henry did, even though his addition was certainly appealing—functional, in good taste, and an asset to the marketability of his home. But the *value* of his home was hardly changed.

The more you pay for outdoor enhancements, whether it be a new porch or patio or an outside fireplace or electric grill, the less likely you'll be to see your dollars return. Improve your yard in simple, clever, *low-cost* ways. Use your imagination rather than your checkbook. A "seven-way patio," for example, really moved a bunch of West Florida condominiums. The tract's developer used a simple patio—basically, an open slab attached to the back of the house. But it was showing buyers how that slab could be improved in seven different ways that really sold those condos, according to developer David Yorra.

EXTRA ROOM. An extra room—one that can be used as library, den, sewing room, guest room, or artful combination of all of these—is always a plus. Psychological studies have shown that people need to be able to get off by themselves sometimes. Real estate studies have shown that most buyers want one extra bedroom that can be used as a den/library or a guest room. People shopping for a detached home consider a family room a "must have" in every area of the country except Florida, a haven for empty nesters.

KITCHEN CONVENIENCES. Kitchen aids impress, though they need not be top-of-the-line. A general rule in buying appliances is *the fewer the buttons the better*. Extra gadgetry tends to add cost out of all proportion to the extra convenience.

Whatever you can add to create order and convenience in a kitchen will pay back. Cute or elegant decorative items (French baker's racks, glass-doored refrigerator units, track lighting) will not. Nor will top-of-the-line hardwood cabinets pay back. Or kitchens with two of everything—except for a second oven, which surveys show has become a very popular extra. (One interesting fact uncovered by developers' studies is that even in the highest-income categories, shoppers won't spend an extra $300 for ceramic-tile kitchen countertops, but they're willing to put that much or more into an upgraded oven—microwave or self-cleaning, say.)

Here are some general rules of thumb on added features that will develop a strong, functional, and highly appealing image for your house.

1. Don't let anything you add be too expensive, too large, or too elegant for the rest of the house. A $20,000 swimming pool on a $35,000 house will just make the house look silly. Always, always *keep things in proportion*.

2. Try to adopt features that have common appeal. These will almost always be practical in nature. Things like storage improvement, built-in cabinets, zoned heating, or a remote-control device for the garage door are more compelling to the *average* buyer than hot tubs, poolrooms, and bidets.

3. As you live in your house, be on the lookout for small improvements that would make your own living more convenient: closet organizers, kitchen-cabinet organizers, good lighting and large mirrors in the bathrooms and dressing areas, easy storage of household cleaning equipment—all these will help make your house the sort buyers can't say no to. In fact, as you will see in chapter 8, convenience features can add up to a big leap in the value of your home on the real estate market.

4. Don't assume that anything and everything you add to your house is sure to come back to you in the sale price; it isn't.

In this living room elements of decor and design are tastefully blended into a unified thematic whole. Note the stained-glass inset in the door; it was found in a junk shop. The fireplace mantel was stripped to expose the beauty of its natural wood. Toward the rear we see an additional room created by enclosing a ramshackle porch. A skylight gives it a lovely light, and its new floor complements the adjoining original floor in style—exact matching isn't necessary.

You can do wonderful things with wallpaper, as these two adjacent rooms demonstrate. Style, feeling, and sense of space can all be radically altered by wall treatments. In this case, both wallpaper patterns enhance the tasteful country charm of the house.

Top: This country farmhouse look was created for a few dollars. Floor, door, and wainscoting were cleaned with denatured alchohol; then varnished. The stove was purchased at a country auction for $15, the chair for $10. The spice box was found in the basement. Paint and a 1-inch pine countertop completed the existing cabinet.

Bottom: A visual demonstration of the keep-it-simple rule. How many of us would look at this cluttered mess and say Home Sweet Home?

It takes very little to dress up outbuildings and bring them into harmony with the total property image. An attractive window and wooden presswork—both from a salvage yard—make this toolshed into an asset instead of a blight.

This corrugated fiberglass wall covering was a nice try at low cost, but how much better a high-quality professionally installed wall covering would look.

Laundry rooms are extremely popular features in houses today. It is worth the relatively little expense to transform your laundry area from a depressing hole into an attractive "garment-renewal center."

Opposite: A deck is another popular feature that can complete your property. The very sight of even a simple wooden deck implies a leisurely life of enjoyment and contentment.

Extra features such as these French doors, which lead to a dining room (formerly an unused porch), add elegance and value to your home at little cost.

HOWARD BLUME

HOWARD BLUME

3

Prime Surfaces
A HOUSE IS JUDGED BY
ITS COVER

Several years ago my wife bought a new house in another state while I remained behind to finish up some business. Nearly 100 years old, the house sat on 3 acres of land in the country. "A lot of potential," my wife wrote me, "but needs some work."

I had seen only a realtor's snapshot of the outside of the house before the day I arrived with the U-Haul truck and began moving boxes in. One look at that monstrosity—its "potential" notwithstanding—and I despaired on the spot.

Mary had spoken enthusiastically of the "wonderful oak stair rail and newel post," and indeed, this seemed the only redeeming feature of the house. There were four-by-eights holding up the plaster in both kitchen and living room, greasy Venetian blinds at all the windows, uneven plaster everywhere, except in the rooms where fifty-year-old wallpaper of ivy-and-swan vintage was peeling off. We spent our first Christmas Eve in the house stripping off the remaining dark-green rosebud wallpaper in the living room because the Christmas tree looked so awful against it.

In the kitchen the only cabinets were two huge portable metal structures with black linoleum tops. The entire room had been paint-ed with a grass-green enamel, including the ceiling, from which hung two 3-foot fluorescent lights—one over the kitchen table and one over the sink. Black mock-tile linoleum was glued halfway up the kitchen walls and showed decades of wear. The floors were the much-sought-after wide pine boards—some covered with several layers of paint, others decorated with old and worn linoleum.

Seven years later, we sold this monstrosity for twice what we paid for it. It wasn't the new pump, the new furnace, or the new wiring that did the selling for us. It was the old barn siding we hauled back from my mother-in-law's barn and placed over the cracked plaster in the living room. It was the period wallpaper Mary hung in the halls, and the stained "beams" with which we boxed in the four-by-eights. And it was the refinished pine-board floors, new Sheetrock, and re-surfaced countertops in the kitchen. What really changed this house from an eyesore into a profit-maker was replacing its worn and ugly surfaces with surfaces that were clean, solid, and visually space en-hancing. And of course any of the house's original charm you can re-veal with a little sanding and polyurethane is all to the good.

Through my experience over the years as a builder, owner, and seller of homes, I've learned the remarkable contribution surface ren-ovation can make to the salability of a house. Figure it this way: Most people would rather move into a house that's already clean, comfort-able, and attractive. Moving is quite enough work; who needs to antic-ipate months of repainting, spackling, sanding, and hammering? By spending a minimal amount of money and putting in a little labor to get your house in tiptop shape, you can raise its sale price a good 5 to 10 percent over what you might have gotten otherwise. And 10 per-cent of a $70,000 house is $7,000—a *fast* $7,000 in your pocket if all you have to provide is a week's worth of work. It's important for you to know *where* to put your money and work, however, for the greatest return.

Attention should be paid to both the exterior and the interior sur-faces of a house you plan on selling. A buyer is interested not only in the total effect of a house and its property but also in the details—the condition of the tile in the bathroom, for example, and how clean the wall-to-wall carpet in the living room is.

To ensure the best possible profit on your house, imagine that *you* are the buyer. Start at the roadside and look carefully at the house and grounds. (Landscaping is discussed in detail in chapter 5.)

The Road to Profit

The driveway is a surface worth considering. Evenness, consistency (no bumps or potholes), and a good definition between lawn and driveway indicate a well-maintained access to your home. Buyers become discouraged by potholes and large cracks in the asphalt even before they get out of the car. Spend a little time restoring a badly worn and weathered entrance road. It's part of the all-important setting for your investment gem.

A rake may be the only tool you'll need. If you have a gravel driveway—one composed of local bank-run gravel, shale, crushed bluestone, even seashells (loose fill that moves with use and weathering)—chances are that a lot of stones have found their way onto the lawn, leaving the traffic lanes noticeably bare. A careful job of raking will return the fill to its intended place.

If you find you need to repair large holes with additional fill, call a local sand-and-gravel company and ask to buy a small amount. While ordinarily they sell by the yard or by the ton (a truckload is 17 to 20 tons, or about 15 to 16 cubic yards), many companies will allow the purchase of smaller amounts, provided the customer is willing to do the shoveling and hauling. A few cardboard boxes in the trunk of your car and you're all set for a small hauling job.

An asphalt driveway requires more in the way of maintenance. Unless your driveway is in poor condition, however, you can save a lot of money by repairing it yourself. To ensure a smooth, even surface, three steps should be taken: caulking, patching, and sealing.

Caulking—the process of filling the cracks with a plastic waterproof material—takes time, but is made easy by a special gun you can buy at a hardware store and fill with either latex or oil-base caulk sold in tubes. Messy but equally effective is hot tar; just pour it into the cracks.

Patching mixes are available for fixing larger cracks and potholes. Simply add water and shovel the mix in. (Sakrete and Red-E-Crete are good asphalt patch mixes. An 80-pound sack costs under $5.)

Sealing the surface of your driveway, once it has been caulked and patched, serves the same function as painting your house. The seal makes the surface look better while protecting it against wear and weather damage. Both water- and oil-base sealers are available. The advantages of the first are that it can be applied to a slightly damp surface and the cleanup is easier. Spreading capacity will vary largely, depending on the condition of your driveway. The rougher the surface, the thicker the sealer should be. Prices for a 5-gallon can of sealer range from $6 to over $12. Unless you want to be out there resealing your driveway every spring, use one of the more expensive brands. Your local building-supply yard or home center no doubt carries several lines.

SIDEWALKS AND PATIOS

You can repair broken areas in concrete sidewalks, patios, and steps by using premixed polymer-reinforced masonry products, such as Watta Bond and Top and Bond (under $8 for a 20-pound bag).

If the damaged area is very large, say half a sidewalk section, either remove the entire section or cut out the bad spot with a chisel, leaving a clean edge. Then set up the "frames" (boards that have been oiled to prevent the cement from sticking). These will hold the concrete until it dries. If the drainage is good, you can pour the concrete directly onto the ground. Otherwise, construct a 4- to 6- inch bed of gravel. Use a gravel-mix cement. (Sand-mix is sometimes recommended because it's stronger and finer, but it can be expensive on a project that's over 2 inches thick.) Again, your local building-supply center or hardware store will have all the materials you need.

THE WRAPPING PAPER

Some authorities say you should always repaint the outside of a house before attempting to sell it. This is an expensive proposition, however, and you will be unwise to invest the time and money unless you can significantly increase the price, or the speed, of the sale. Unless the old paint is so worn that the bare wood is showing through, don't bother painting. Instead, touch up spots where the paint has peeled or chipped away; prime the wood first with a quality primer to ensure good adhesion. The *trim* and *front door* are areas buyers pay special attention to, so be sure to include these in your touching up.

Repair any damaged siding or screening. Nothing makes a place look shabbier, in summer, than holes or tears in the screens.

Mildew damage can be a problem in houses with poor ventilation or in parts of the country that are prone to consistently high humidity. And a telltale mildew odor will assail the buyer's nostrils the moment he crosses your threshold. Treat mildew—and odor—by washing with a solution of trisodium phosphate cleaner, strong detergent, bleach, and warm water. (For a large area, pour 3 quarts of warm water into a pail and add 3 ounces of trisodium phosphate, 1 ounce of detergent, and 1 quart of bleach. If you can't get trisodium phosphate at the hardware store, Soilax will do as a substitute.)

If you have aluminum or vinyl siding, you are blissfully free of onerous repainting jobs (except for the trim, of course), but you might consider getting out the hose, a ladder, and a long brush (an auto brush works well) and sprucing things up.

Brick and masonry may require repair if large cracks are apparent (see Bibliography for suggested sources of help). If you're repainting brick, masonry, or asbestos siding with a latex paint, dampen first to get a good bond.

Although I don't recommend painting unless it's absolutely necessary, I *do* recommend restaining. If the old stain has become faded and spotty with weathering, a smart new coat of stain may well increase buyer interest, especially if your neighbor's siding has turned faded and dull. Remember the principle of Conventionality Plus: Don't look different from the market you're in, but *do* stand out in it.

FACING UP TO A BIG JOB

Suppose the siding on your house is in very poor condition, and you're pretty certain no one is going to pay the fair market value for your house in the state it's in. What are your options? You can pay to have the house resided in aluminum, vinyl, or steel (or in thicker re-siding products such as composite hardboard, various natural woods, or Texture III plywood). Or you can buy several gallons of paint or stain and start scraping. In order to make the decision, ask yourself first: What are the comparable costs of my options and their respec-tive advantages and disadvantages? Second, ask: Am I likely to recov-er the cost when I sell?

Consider Table 1 carefully and compare the cost of residing with the cost of repainting given in item 4 of Table 8 (p. 190). Remember that the energy crunch is on people's mind these days and that pro-spective buyers are impressed with any surface improvement that will contribute to fuel savings. Most people are also attracted by exteriors that need little maintenance and will pay extra for the convenience.

Once you've decided which method to use, buck up and get this rotten job done. If you don't, you may never get rid of that asset of yours without taking a loss.

BRUSHING UP ON PAINT

If you decide on paint, the all-important question is, Who will do the painting, a professional or I?

More than any other factor, the answer to that question has to do with time. Let's suppose that, like most of us, you work nine to five. You're considering painting your two-story house yourself. That means you'll have to paint during the evenings and on weekends. This could make a big job drag on interminably—a distinct disadvan-tage if you're trying to sell your house fast. Figure that each time you paint it will take about an hour to set up: ladder in place, paint

TABLE 1

HOW PREFINISHED LOW-MAINTENANCE RE-SIDING MATERIALS COMPARE

	VINYL	ALUMINUM	STEEL
Description	Formed or extruded solid polyvinyl-chloride	Formed or coated aluminum sheet	Formed or coated steel sheet
Approx. cost per 100 sq. ft. for material (dollars)*	60–80	60–90	70–90
Approx. cost per 100 sq. ft. for material and labor (dollars)*	140–200	140–200	155–210
Textures	Smooth, wood grain, other textures	Smooth, wood grain, other textures	Wood grain, other textures
Usual warranty (years)	20–30	20–40	20–30
Corrosion	No	Possibly	Possibly
Moisture resistance	Excellent	Excellent	Excellent
Trim and accessories available	Yes	Yes	Yes
Repaint if necessary or desired	Not recommended	Yes	Yes

*Prices vary with shipping costs, local labor costs, job complexity, and trim materials required.

stirred, bushes covered, brushes cleaned, surface scraped, bee bomb in back pocket (*very* advisable—a painter friend of mine had one of his helpers break his nose on a ladder as he turned to avoid an angry hornet). Allowing half an hour to clean up, this gives you maybe one-and-a-half or two hours each evening to paint, assuming it doesn't get dark until around nine o'clock.

It's easy to see that painting an entire house in your spare time will take quite a while, and if you need to sell your house next week, you'd better quit your job or hire someone to do the painting for you. Generally, it takes a crew of four men working from nine to five two

HARDBOARD	CLAD PARTICLE BOARD	MINERAL FIBER
Coated compressed wood fiber	Wood particle board with bonded wood fiber overlay, coated	Coated compressed Portland cement and mineral fiber
35–80	40	30–50
100–125	80–125	100–125
Smooth, wood grain, stucco	Smooth, wood grain, textured	Wood grain, shake
5–15	Finish: 5 Material: 20	20
No	No	No
Good	Good	Excellent
Yes	Yes	Yes
Yes	Yes	Yes

or three days to complete a two-story house. The average labor cost is from $8 to $12 an hour per man.

Once you've decided to paint, consider carefully the type and quality of the paint you buy as well as the color. Red over white or white over gray may require two coats. Generally one coat will be sufficient if the old paint is a similar color.

Paints vary in quality, and this is not always reflected in the price you pay. To make an economical decision on paint, check *Buying Guide* or *Consumer Reports*. *CR* evaluates different brands for such properties as ease of brushing, sagging and leveling, hiding power, uniformity of appearance, resistance to color change and mildew, and adhesion quality. It's worth doing a little research here; overpriced paint can quickly run up the cost of the job and eat into your sales profits. I know a fellow who actually paid more to paint his own house than his neighbor spent hiring a teenager to do it. They had identical houses and used the same quantity of paint. The first fellow went out in a rush and bought top-of-the-line paint, fearing anything cheaper wouldn't do the job in one coat. The second fellow bought a gallon of Sears, Roebuck paint on sale and tested it. When he found it covered, he bought the amount he needed. (Note: When hiring teenagers you may pay less than minimum wage if such a practice is accepted locally; be sure, however, that whoever you hire is experienced at painting. Check references.)

Here are some tips that will help you save on your painting investment. Be sure all the cans you get are from the same factory batch (check the number on the top or bottom of each can) to avoid color differences. Before applying, look for such defects in the paint as lumps of pigment or resin (such paint is called "seedy"). Take the time to open one can and paint a piece of glass or metal for inspection the next day. If you find specks or pockmarks, return the paint—*all of it*—and ask for paint with another batch number.

Prime bare or new wood and badly chalked surfaces before applying paint. "Chalking" is the white residue left on your hands after you run them over the surface of an exterior paint. Some paints— particularly the whites—are formulated to chalk since that allows consistent shedding of dirt with rain. To get a good bond between old and new paint, you need to wash off old chalking first.

Rain can be a problem. It will wash a fresh coat of latex paint right off, and it will put little goose bumps in oil paint. With latex, rain is less of a problem; as soon as the weather clears you can repaint those six or eight boards that didn't dry before the rain hit. Oil paint is another story entirely. You'll have to wait a week for oil paint that's been rained on to dry. Then you have to hand sand the goose bumps off before repainting.

If you see a storm approaching and you're painting with an oil-base paint, get down from the ladder pronto and turn on the hose (after first removing the nozzle). Your objective is to speed-set your last six or eight boards. This is accomplished, strange as it may seem, by allowing the water to pour like a waterfall over the fresh paint. Get back up the ladder and hold the hose so that the cold water flows down over the fresh paint. This speeds the setting time, takes out the tackiness, and encourages a skin to form over the "green" paint so it will not be affected by the oncoming shower. (Most paint, whether oil or latex, will "set up" in about an hour, after which it will not wash off or blister in the event of rain.)

One more tip on exterior paint. If you're painting a hard surface, such as asbestos shingles or Masonite, it's a good idea to add 1 pint of bonderizer per gallon to any type of paint. The bonderizer penetrates the shingles or siding and gives a good base. You can even use it straight on surfaces that get a lot of abuse, such as those near the front door, where new paint may not adhere.

COLOR YOUR HOUSE BIG

My friend Willy has a house painted avocado green. Down the road there's another house the same color and about the same size and style as Willy's. My friend's house looks considerably bigger, however, although its square footage is no greater. The reason? The trim on Willy's house is the same color as the siding. The house down the road has a combination of white-and-black trim around the windows and doors. Contrasting trim will almost always make a house appear smaller. If your house is large and gracefully proportioned, but somewhat bland in its architectural detailing, contrasting trim may add character. On the other hand, when you're trying to create a larger look, stick with a single color.

The actual color you choose will also affect the illusion of size. Picture a light-brown, one-story house in Phoenix, Arizona. There's little vegetation surrounding the structure—just a palm tree or two and some scrub brush. The ground is flat and mostly sand, similar in color to the house. Now, let's paint that house blue and see what happens to the visual effect. The house stands out from its surroundings like a sore thumb; it also looks considerably smaller. A potential buyer might pass it up, thinking it's too small for his family. Or he might think the house looks out of place.

Here is a rule I can give you without ambivalence. *The brighter the exterior colors, the more limited will be the range of potential buyers.* Remember the concept of Conventionality Plus. Most people are conventional. They prefer bland—wood tones or white or tan—over strong or unusual colors. It's a fact worth considering when you repaint to increase your chances of a sale. This is *not* the time to get wild and expressive.

The Roof over Your Head

While we're on the subject of color and its effects, take a good hard look at your roof. A buyer is going to be concerned with two things: the condition of the roof and its color. You should (1) fix any leaks before unseen moisture can rot roof boards and damage rafters; (2) replace any loose, curled-up, broken, or missing shingles; (3) replace cracked shingles in the ridges and deteriorated shingles in the valleys; and (4) reseal around antennas and chimneys where vibration and temperature differences have caused cracking.

If you need a new roof and have decided to invest in one because you're sure no one will buy your house unless you do, there are a number of options. Wood shingles look great, but they're expensive and can warp, rot, and split, necessitating periodic repairs. They are also more combustible than other types of roofing.

Slate and tile lend elegance to a home, but they're among the most expensive roofing materials. It's unlikely that you will recover the cost of installing either of these at the time of sale. On the other hand, you can't beat slate and tile for durability, and both are fireproof.

Asphalt shingles may be your best bet. Four out of five houses have asphalt roofs, and most potential buyers will be acquainted with their advantages. They're economical and easy to apply; come in a variety of colors, textures, and patterns; and ordinarily last from fifteen to twenty-five years. They're also fire resistant, something the buyer may appreciate.

If you decide on asphalt, bear in mind that the lighter weight the shingle, the lower the cost, but the heavier the shingle, the better the roof. Standard-grade shingles usually carry a fifteen-year limited guarantee. The heavier, more expensive grades are warranted for twenty-five years, and the guarantee is transferable. The life expectancy of your new roofing may not be of much concern to you, but you can be sure it will be of concern to anyone interested in buying your house.

Roof color can greatly affect the impression a house makes. A light roof adds height to a one-story home, while a dark roof can reduce the impression of height. A contrasting roof color will usually divide the roof from the rest of the house. Earth tones, which are the most popular, tend to blend with any surrounding wooded areas.

When trying to decide what color scheme will have the greatest buyer appeal, remember this rule: Never use more than three colors for roof, siding, and trim. More than three colors gives an unpleasantly "busy" look. Remember, again, that *conventionality pays*.

THE WALLS WITHIN

The surface revealed to the buyer when you open your front door should be clean, in good condition, and bright. Water damage, cracks in walls, droopy ceilings, and dirty floors will immediately turn a buyer off. The operative question is this: How can you spruce the place up without spending a fortune? Let's consider some of the tactics that are likely to improve the salability of your home.

Vacuuming the walls and ceiling is sometimes all that's necessary to render them clean and attractive. Smudges and stains, particularly near doorways and light switches, come off quickly with a wet sponge and some nonabrasive cleaner such as Soilax. (Avoid the "instant" spray-type cleaners; they'll wear down the paint before long.)

Ordinarily, houses that have been lived in for a while require a little spackling. Some people need to make five holes in the wall before they're satisfied with the placement of their fondest artifacts. That's fine, as long as the objects remain there to cover the other four holes. But when you're moving out of your house and the paintings go with you, the walls can look like victims of a buckshot spree. Some time ago, Mary saved the day when we found ourselves in this predicament in a rented house. The landlady was on her way over to return our deposit; the moving van was packed. We didn't have time to search the boxes for Spackle or run to a hardware store and buy some. Mary plugged the holes with toothpaste. It worked like magic, even matching the wall's color. Toothpaste hardens overnight, doesn't shrink, smooths out easily, and can be painted.

I'm not suggesting you keep extra tubes of toothpaste on hand for emergency repairs. A can of Spackle is cheaper and the consistency is more appropriate. The point is that you must do whatever's necessary to fill holes, cracks, and scrapes to ensure a good-looking, finished wall. You can touch up interior walls with spot applications of flat paint from the leftovers you should always keep on hand; a careful job will leave no noticeable color or texture difference. If you don't have the right color and don't want to invest the time and money in repainting the entire room, try adding a little food coloring to water-base Spackle. (Acrylic paint can be used to tint plastic-base Spackle.) Blue and yellow make green; red and green make gray; a touch of yellow and red can produce a nice off-white. First, experiment on one spot; let it dry (it will dry lighter) to make sure the color is right; then touch up all the holes and cracks in the room.

Sometimes more is needed than cleaning and filling some holes with Spackle. A leaky toilet seal or a defective roof has caused water damage to Sheetrock or plaster, or the wallpaper has loosened and become worn, or a doorknob has knocked a hole in the plaster, and more extensive repairs are needed. The idea is to restore a smooth surface as effectively as possible. The more inexpensively you can make these repairs, the better and more confident you will feel when negotiating price with a buyer, since you won't be anxious about compensation for a large outlay of cash prior to a sale. In some cases you won't be able to avoid spending a substantial amount, but money spent wisely is sure to come back to you when your house is sold.

Armed with a little knowledge and some free time, you can often make the more substantial changes and repairs yourself, thus saving the cost of a carpenter, which will run you between $12 and $25 an hour. Most Sheetrock and plaster repairs—popped nails, tape marks, small gashes and holes, and even large sections of damaged wallboard or deteriorated plaster—can be repaired inexpensively by you.

If the walls are in very poor condition, it may be worth your while to cover them over. Here are a few cost-saving suggestions for coverings that appeal to buyers.

- Inexpensive paneling (which can be painted) is cheaper and often just as attractive as Sheetrock, which would cost you $100 in labor to have installed.

- Printed bedsheets stapled to the top and bottom of a wall will cost you less than a similar print in vinyl wall covering, and you don't have to do anything to prepare the surface.

- Instead of buying pure vinyl wall coverings for kitchen, bathrooms, and other areas that are subject to wear and moisture, consider the less expensive, vinyl-coated paper. You can apply a coating or two of low-gloss or matte-finish polyurethane over it. This will provide additional protection for the paper, making it completely water and stain resistant and scrubbable, and will not appreciably alter the wallpaper's color. (Note: Wallpaper that's been treated this way will have to be sanded to break the seal before it can be removed.)

- Glue and nail old barn siding over a badly cracked wall. If you're able to find an old barn and secure permission to remove its boards, your only expense will be transportation costs, nails, glue, and furring.

- Add sand to paint and "texture" a wall or ceiling to cover unevenness and create an appealing effect. Joint compound—available in 5-gallon cans at paint and hardware stores—can be used to create a stucco effect that will cover a multitude of surface imperfections.

- Don't avoid a clever cosmetic scheme when it can make a really big difference in visual effect. A handyman friend of mine recently made a $250 investment in his small, two-bedroom tract house. He covered one wall of his living room with mirror tile. I thought he was acting pretty foolishly, but it turned out I was wrong. When the appraiser arrived he commented on the wall, saying that the feeling of space was so much greater than in the other houses in the development, he thought my friend could raise his asking price by $1,000.

THE RICHES-UNDER-YOUR-ROOF COLOR PRIMER

Often it's the wall treatment in a house that creates excitement in the buyers. They fall in love with the paneling, the wallpaper, or the color of the paint.

Unfortunately buyers can also reject a perfectly suitable house because of the wallpaper or paint. Smart realtors advise their clients to look beyond the frills, but emotionally most of us find this difficult to do. If we walk into a bright-yellow living room we wonder how our newly purchased green curtains will look or how we're ever going to cover that awful yellow paint.

The general rule on color, both interior and exterior, is that it will appeal to a lot more buyers when it's neutral: white, tan, beige, a light pastel. I don't mean you have to rip off that plaid wallpaper just because you're going to put your house on the market. But if you're considering repainting the dining room and bedroom before advertising your house anyway, why not try to please the majority of potential buyers with antique white rather than eye-popping yellow or Williamsburg blue.

Rooms that adjoin should be planned to harmonize in both color and design. It is disturbing to find that each room in a house creates a radically different environment from the next. The buyer wants to feel that the new house he moves into will envelop him with serene authority, almost as if *it*, the house, were going to take over his life during this period of adjustment. If you're smart, you'll give the buyer what he or she is looking for: cleanliness, order, space, muted harmony.

Ultimately your objective is to make the rooms in your house appear as large as possible. The more space that seems available, the more the buyer is likely to pay. Color plays a significant role here. Let's consider some of the ways in which the use of color affects an environment visually.

• Dark colors can make a room seem smaller, particularly if the dark colors are warm, such as deep orange, gold, brown, or red. Go with this principle if you want to create a dark, cozy room such as a den or library, or even a Victorian kitchen. Dark colors will make them seem even mellower and more intimate.

• Cool colors, such as light blues and greens, tend to recede. Visually, they move away from you, making a room seem larger.

• Pale colors reflect light and can be used to make a room appear larger than it is.

• Busy prints—wall coverings that have a lot of lines or contrasting colors—decrease the feeling of space in a room.

• Large prints—paper that has gigantic poppies on it, say—can make a room appear smaller.

• Small prints with little contrast can make a room appear larger.

• Small-scale geometrics, all-over florals, brightly colored plaids can be used to unify a room with broken-up wall areas. They can also be used to conceal a rough wall, exposed pipes, or other structural flaws.

• Vertical stripes and prints visually heighten a room—something to remember when you're dealing with low ceilings. Paneling has that effect also.

• Dark-colored ceilings appear lower; light-colored ceilings appear higher.

Looking Up: The All-Important Ceiling

Uneven ceilings can drastically undermine the overall effect of an otherwise spiffy house. The natural shifting and settling that occurs as a house grows older can cause cracks and sags. Sometimes the weight of a bathtub or a heavy piece of furniture in an upstairs room is enough to distress a ceiling. A leaky toilet seal is often the cause of water damage to Sheetrock and plaster.

If loose and hanging plaster covers a large area, it's better to tear out the old ceiling and replace it with new Sheetrock. If the plaster is tight but cracked and uneven, it can be evened up and new Sheetrock can be placed right over it. Sheetrock work is better done by a professional, unless it's simply a patching-and-painting job. Many zealous homeowners have despaired when they found themselves in the midst of falling plaster and broken Sheetrock. A professional, experienced in handling large pieces of wallboard, works quickly and efficiently, confining the mess to as small an area as possible for as short a time as possible.

If the ceiling has to be torn down or evened up, ask for free bids from several reputable tradesmen (I will give some hints on choosing someone later on). A 12-by-16-foot ceiling, finished and painted, will cost between $225 and $300. (This doesn't include the additional labor charge for removal of the old ceiling.) If you decide to attempt the job yourself, and you don't have to level the old ceiling, your material cost will run about $50, including furring strips.

A lot of people are converting old, low ceilings to cathedral ceilings by removing the plaster or Sheetrock, exposing the beams, and finishing off the roof boards with new insulation and Sheetrock. This can be an extremely effective way to make a room appear larger, but it can also add dollars to the fuel bill. Consider the advantages and disadvantages carefully, and remember that providing air vents or fans to promote circulation of rising warm air will be essential for comfort in hot weather. (A skylight facing south adds considerable light and solar heat in the winter.) The cathedral ceiling is a job for the professional; removing extra beams without interfering with the structural soundness of the house demands educated calculations.

A suspended ceiling can be used to solve a range of problems, from ceiling unevenness to cracks to water damage (providing the leak's source has been found and repaired). The tiles or panels are simply suspended from the old ceiling on a metal or vinyl grid (available at hardware stores or home-improvement centers) or are glued or stapled to furring strips. Following the manufacturer's directions, most homeowners will be able to install a suspended ceiling quickly and easily. It's really much easier than one might think, like putting linoleum tiles on a floor.

If your old ceiling is level, a new ceiling can be installed only $1\frac{1}{4}$ inches away; often, though, it's necessary to lower the new ceiling several inches to level it. Lowering the ceiling actually decreases the room size very little, but the visual effect can be disproportionate and the feeling of lost space can be disturbing. This is more likely to happen if the room is small or cramped to begin with.

I have mentioned previously the use of sand in paint and also joint compound or special acrylics in texturing an uneven surface. These options have many advantages: They're cheap, they're easy, and they're appealing. On a previously painted ceiling, it may be necessary to add the sand to a calcium paint, such as Calso or Calcoat, for proper adhesion. Conventional paint (latex or oil to which sand has been added) will not adhere to a ceiling that chalks unless the ceiling has been washed and a bonderizer, such as Wilbond, has been applied.

Sand paint and textured joint compound are nearly impossible to clean, but they can be renewed easily by repainting with a nontextured paint applied with a deep-pile roller or a brush. To prevent water stains from old leaks from showing through, cover the area with two coats of pigmented shellac as a sealer/primer before painting.

Most ceiling materials today fall into three categories: wet applications (plaster, paint, and wallpaper); dry applications (drywall and gypsum board); and manufactured ceilings (12-by-12-inch tiles or 2-by-4-foot panels made of mineral or wood fibers). All wood- and mineral-fiber tile and panels offer essentially the same advantages: They're easy to install; they absorb sound; they resist rot, mildew, and mold; and most carry a five-year no-warp guarantee. They are fire resistant, and the vinyl-coated, more expensive ones can be vacuumed or washed. An additional big advantage is that they require little maintenance compared with a drywall ceiling, which has to be painted. And fiberglass panels add insulation value.

Suspended ceilings are especially practical in extra rooms such as family rooms, utility rooms, and converted cellars. Some people object to them for aesthetic reasons, suggesting that they give a "waiting-room" appearance (just add five-month-old magazines, a No Smoking sign, and a receptionist).

With Table 2 you'll be able to do a pretty accurate job of figuring how much it will cost you to install different types of ceiling material. Tiles and panels cost more than Sheetrock, but the labor cost is less.

TABLE 2

COST OF INSTALLING VARIOUS CEILING MATERIALS

PRODUCT	AVERAGE UNIT PRICE (DOLLARS)	COST TO COVER 12-by-16-Ft. CEILING (DOLLARS)
ACOUSTICAL TILE	0.51/sq. ft.	97.92
Furring	0.08/ft.	15.36
Construction adhesive	1.89/tube	11.34
Staple gun	15.00	15.00
Staples	0.97/7 oz.	3.44
Total		143.06
FIBERGLASS PANELS	0.44/sq. ft.	84.48
Grid		
Main runners	3.45/10 ft.	27.60
Crosspieces	0.52/2 ft.	12.48
Wall angles	1.71/10 ft.	10.26
Tie wire	2.59/roll	2.59
Total		137.41
SHEETROCK (½ IN.)	0.29/sq. ft.	55.68
Nails	0.65/lb.	0.65
Tape	1.50/roll	1.50
Furring	0.08/ft.	15.36
Joint compound	3.50/gal.	9.00
Labor	10.00/hr.	90.00
Total		172.19

Floors:
The First Thing You Notice

Many people have told me that the very first thing they see when they enter a house for the first time is flooring: its type, condition, and aesthetic appeal or lack thereof. I can't overemphasize the importance of flooring in creating the first—and lasting—impression on anyone who's thinking of buying your house. Its solidarity, its color, its sheen all contribute to a sense of security as well as to visual pleasure.

Most floors have a hard finish, whether they be masonry, vinyl, ceramic, linoleum, or wood. Restoring these surfaces to a clean, smooth, and bright condition is absolutely imperative before a sale. (Elbow grease can do wonders, so be sure to try it before resorting to a replacement scheme.)

Fixing up most floors is not that big a deal. Here are some ideas and techniques for fast, cheap floor improvement.

Wood

Builders say floors of oak, maple, and other hardwoods carry a lot of buyer appeal. Most people whose houses I build prefer a finished wood floor to plywood and carpet, even if they plan to cover it eventually. If your carpet covers a hardwood floor and is showing signs of wear, consider removing the carpet and spiffing up the floor. Badly distressed carpet is definitely a deterrent to the sale of a house. People know they're going to have to remove it all and either replace it or have all the floors refinished—at what untold cost and inconvenience. Don't make your buyer worry over the future untold cost. It will *always* affect the offer that's made.

Old wax yellows a floor and makes it appear dirty when it isn't. If your floor is in this condition, the buyer will be convinced either that you're a lousy housekeeper (which suggests the more serious possibility of poor maintenance) or that the floor actually needs to be replaced—at *his* expense.

It's best to remove old wax. I haven't found any product on the market that will obviate the chore of scouring the old buildup with number 2 steel wool. Wax removers soften layers of acrylic and wax and make the scrubbing easier. Also effective is a mixture of 2 cups Soilax and 2 cups of ammonia in 1 gallon of cool water. This works on all floors where several layers of wax or acrylic have been applied. Let the floor dry at least two hours, particularly if it is a wooden floor, before applying a sealer or rewaxing the surface.

Mel Jones, a man in the business of refinishing floors for twenty-five years, gave me his ideas on the best treatment for hardwood floors. "I don't recommend any wax," he said. "Instead, put polyurethane on the floor once the old wax has been removed." A well-sealed floor, as Mel points out, is virtually maintenance-free. A damp sponge can remove accumulated dirt and immediately restore the floor to its original luster. For spots where a polyurethane finish has worn off, Mel suggests sanding lightly by hand with medium and then fine sandpaper, and applying a touchup of sealer. If the entire floor needs resanding, an electric sander can be rented, but such a machine is cumbersome to operate and can easily gouge your precious floor if you're not experienced in using it. When refinishing or touching up an already polyurethaned floor, use a small hand sander; you're not going down to the raw wood, only scarifying for a new bond.

Today, polyurethane sealers are generally used on wood floors because of their extreme durability and appeal, but it's possible that the wood floors in your home were finished before the advent of these marvelous plastic finishing products.

Lacquered floors should be scrubbed gently with mild lukewarm suds and rinsed with cool water to clean and restore gloss. They do not need wax. Worn areas should be sanded and lacquer reapplied.

Varnished floors can be washed if the varnish is waterproof. If it isn't (do a small patch first, as a test), use a cloth tightly wrung out in a solution of mild soap or detergent and clean a small area at a time, rinsing carefully with another cloth wrung as dry as possible in clear water. Use a thick pad of newspaper under your pail to protect the floor from spills and be sure not to let the water stand or splash on the floor.

Shellacked floors must be kept waxed or spilled liquids—even water—will leave white spots and blotches. To clean a shellacked floor, use a cloth moistened with denatured alcohol. Rub lightly or the shellac may begin to come off.

Oiled floors should be dusted with an oil-treated cloth or floor mop. Be sure to remove all the excess oil before polishing. You'll find that too much oil is as unsatisfactory as too much wax. It leaves a dust-catching, slippery surface. Polishes with a paraffin or linseed-oil base are best.

Painted floors look better and are easier to keep in good condition if they are waxed. To clean, wash with warm water and mild soap. Then use fine steel wool dipped in liquid or paste wax (or a mild scouring powder) to remove spots and marks.

Resilient flooring

Vinyl (both the sheet and tile variety), vinyl-asbestos, composition tile, and linoleum are known as "resilient" flooring. These types of floors need different kinds of treatment. Whichever you have, the idea is to make the surface bright and shiny.

Inlaid vinyl is by far the most popular type of floor in use today. It may have a factory-applied wax or sealer, which eventually will wear off, or it may be of the no-wax variety, which manufacturers claim never needs waxing. The type with factory-applied wax should *not* be coated with varnish, lacquer, or shellac. Special sealers, obtained from the manufacturer, will restore the finish. A "coated" floor, on the other hand, can be waxed with any self-polishing product once it becomes dull.

Composition tile (made from resinous binders and fibers) is found in many older homes. It is nonabsorbent and resistant to moisture and stains. Like the vinyls, composition tile should *not* be coated with varnish, lacquer, or shellac. Once the old wax has been removed, a thin layer of any self-polishing wax can be applied. (Don't use an oil polish, liquid polishing wax, paste wax, strong soap, or chemicals.)

Vinyl-asbestos tile was widely used some years ago, and many older houses have this floor covering in heavily trafficked areas, such as kitchens, bathrooms, family rooms, and workshops. Vinyl-asbestos is resistant to abrasion and to grease, bleaches, acids, and alkalies. Waxing is optional.

Linoleum should be protected from too much water and against harsh alkaline soaps and detergents that can damage it. Avoid scouring powders, which will break linoleum's sealed surface. Water-base self-polishing wax is recommended. If the floor has become worn and discolored, linoleum can be finished with a good deck or floor enamel. Lacquers and varnishes damage linoleum and should never be applied.

MASONRY AND STONE

Masonry floors—including slate, marble, tile, and terrazzo—are usually found in areas such as foyer, bath, kitchen, and hearth. *Make a point of telling the buyer that these floors will last longer than the house and are virtually maintenance-free.*

It's a good idea to put a sealer (water-soluble acrylic finish) on a masonry floor. Otherwise, the grout will stain and discolor unattractively with normal use. If the floor has not been sealed, use bleach to clean stained grout. Don't use an acid cleaner or you'll etch the stone, leaving pitted areas where dirt will collect.

For a masonry floor, a cleaning wax like Jubilee is best because soap cleaners tend to combine with the cement in the joints, leaving an unsightly scum. If the floor has been sealed, polishing or self-polishing wax can be used to protect it further.

An *unpainted cement floor* can be cleaned of dirt and grime with a mixture of 2 to 4 tablespoons of washing soda or trisodium phosphate in 1 gallon of water. If that doesn't work, try a strong solution of muriatic acid and water (following directions on the label). Muriatic acid is an effective solvent, but should be used with care. It is highly toxic and must be kept off skin and out of reach of children. Good ventilation is important, as even the fumes are highly toxic.

A cement floor can be painted with good deck or epoxy paint.

CARPETING: THE SOFT TOUCH

Carpeting must always be vacuumed before a potential house buyer arrives. Often, however, only washing will remove accumulated dirt and stains. A professional rug-cleaning outfit will come in and clean your carpet at a cost of between $0.20 and $0.25 per square foot, depending on the size of the room (the price per square foot is higher on smaller jobs). Or you can rent a steam cleaner at a cost of about $10 for half a day, plus the cost of chemical cleaners.

You can also find your scrub brush, buy a bottle of rug shampoo, and take out your pent-up frustration by having a go at the carpet yourself! Sprays such as Spot Shot are good for badly stained areas, but first, try club soda or a solution of equal parts water and white vinegar. It's far cheaper and often just as effective.

You can always try hiding traffic-worn spots with area rugs, but a careful buyer may look underneath. If your wall-to-wall is really tacky, the best solution may be to rip it up and buff the floor, or replace the carpet with one of the floor-covering materials available.

Cost considerations of floor coverings

There is a wide variation in replacement costs for both resilient flooring and carpeting. Basically, you want to install the material that will carry the most buyer appeal. A tan carpet is a smarter investment than a red carpet (remember, neutral tones are better); a tweed in earth colors is better than a white pile; no-wax sheet vinyl is better than asbestos tile. Unless the old floor is very loose and uneven, these products can be installed right over existing flooring.

Is installing a quality floor worthwhile? The extra cost for the more expensive product may make the difference between getting your asking price and being bargained down by an aggressive buyer. Be sure to tell buyers about the special qualities of whatever floor covering you choose (stain-repellent treatments, mildew resistance, antistatic capabilities of carpeting; easy-maintenance qualities of other types of floor covering). See Table 3 on pp. 58–59.

Kitchen and Bathroom Surfaces

Probably no other rooms are scrutinized as carefully by house buyers as are kitchens and bathrooms. If the kitchen surfaces are dirty, you can be sure this will be privately noted and will act as a deterrent to sale. Abrasive powders, bleaches, and nonabrasive chemical cleaners are all inexpensive considering the remarkable results they can provide when the time comes to remove stains and grease from kitchen and bathroom surfaces.

TABLE 3

INSTALLATION COST AND SPECIAL QUALITIES OF VARIOUS FLOOR COVERINGS

FLOOR COVERING	MATERIALS COST (DOLLARS)	INSTALLATION COST (DOLLARS)	SPECIAL QUALITIES
Inlaid vinyl (no-wax finish)	17.50/sq. yd.	4.00/sq. yd.	Low maintenance, permanent, brittle and tough to work with, comes only in 6-ft. width, must be professionally installed
Inlaid vinyl (without no-wax finish)	8.00–15.50/sq. yd.	4.00/sq. yd.	Semiporous, must be maintained
Vinyl-asbestos tile (dryback or peel-and-stick)	14.00–19.00/box (0.35–0.43/sq. ft. or 3.15–3.87/sq. yd.)	0.30–0.50/sq. ft.	Economical, long lasting, difficult to maintain, porous finish, can be installed by homeowner
Solid vinyl (regular or custom design)	0.27–0.45/sq. ft. (3.00–5.00/sq. yd.)	Up to 1.00/sq. ft.	Inexpensive, very low maintenance, durable, hard finish, can be installed by homeowner
No-wax vinyl-asbestos tile (dryback or peel-and-stick)	1.10–1.25/sq. ft. (9.90–11.25/sq. yd.)	0.30–0.50/sq. ft.	Low maintenance, good for cut-up kitchen, easily installed by homeowner

COUNTERTOPS

Countertops are probably the single most immediately noticeable feature in a kitchen. They can be clean, spacious, well lit, and inviting—suggesting a kitchen that's pleasant and easy to work in; or they can be cluttered, marred by ugly cuts and stains, poorly lit—and a major deterrent to the sale of a house. In the mind of the buyer, kitchen countertops are as important as walls and flooring.

TABLE 3 Cont'd

FLOOR COVERING	MATERIALS COST (DOLLARS)	INSTALLATION COST (DOLLARS)	SPECIAL QUALITIES
Wool carpet (not including pad)	35.00–100.00/ sq. yd.	2.00/sq. yd.	Best looking, longer lasting than other carpets, best cleanability, high static
Nylon carpet (not including pad)	6.00–30.00/sq. yd.	2.00/sq. yd.	Maximum wearability, strong, best dollar value, cleanability good, stain and mildew resistant, nonallergenic, low static
Polyester carpet (not including pad)	8.00–13.00/sq. yd.	2.00/sq. yd.	Not quite as strong as nylon, prone to matting, cleanability good, stain and mildew resistant, nonallergenic, low static
Acrylic carpet (not including pad)	10.00–15.00/sq. yd.	2.00/sq. yd.	Wool look-alike, holds soil, high static
Herculon-Olefin carpet	5.00–9.00/sq. yd.	2.00/sq. yd.	Stain resistant, nonporous, minimum wearability, can be used indoors and outdoors (good for basements), totally antistatic

Most counters—whether made of old linoleum, wood, plastic laminates, or quarry tiles—can be renewed simply by wiping with a damp sponge and a mild detergent. *Mild* scouring powder can be used on porcelain, Monel metal, stainless steel, and plastic laminate. A good paste wax protects and enhances these surfaces.

Composition surfaces of various types (vinyls and plastics) are not sensitive to dampness and can also be waxed. Wood makes a durable work surface; in fact, butcher block is a good replacement for a damaged section of the counter. It's easily renewed by scrubbing with steel wool, rinsing, and rubbing with vegetable oil after it's thoroughly dried (boiled linseed oil, which is sometimes recommended, is toxic for a period of time after its application). At $56 per 2-foot section, butcher block is more expensive than a plastic laminate (a 3-by-6-foot piece is around $22), but has a lot more buyer appeal.

Another way to restore a damaged section of countertop is with something called Counter Saver. This is a piece of ceramic, glass, or porcelain with a chrome edge that can be recessed into the existing counter and provides a heatproof surface. It costs only $20 or so, but must be installed by a professional since installation necessitates cutting out part of the countertop.

Quarry tile and domestic ceramic tile are popular materials for kitchen and bathroom work surfaces. These come in a variety of colors, sizes, and textures; the prices range from very expensive to reasonable. (Plastic laminates are much cheaper.) Tile has a lot of eye appeal; it looks attractive, solid, and durable. It is brittle, however, and will crack if a heavy object is dropped on it.

Glazed ceramic tile can be cleaned with a damp sponge and a mild solution of trisodium phosphate, borax, or some other water softener. For heavily soiled areas, sprinkle some softener on a damp sponge and rub the tiles clean. Mild abrasives and commercial tile cleaners can be used on glazed tile, but be sure to rinse carefully. Harsh scouring powders and acids should not be used.

Plastic tiles should *never* be cleaned with abrasives. Use warm water with soap and a detergent. These tiles are usually made of polystyrene or vinyl plastic and are not damaged by water, oil, alcohol, vinegar, or the usual household acids. They are damaged by cleaning fluid, gasoline, nail polish or polish remover, and oil from lemon or orange peels. (Don't try your grandmother's cleaning recipe if it has any of these ingredients in it.)

Tiles become loose, especially around leaky shower faucets and places where water consistently hits the surface. Replacing or repairing those missing or loosened tiles takes a little time, but is not difficult. Loose tiles are defects that buyers pay particular attention to—

probably because they don't want to be bothered with the repair. Clean, unstained grout is important too; scrub with an old toothbrush and some bleach (or toothpaste!).

CABINETS

Painted surfaces in your kitchen and bath should be cleaned with a grease-cutting detergent and rinsed. If you wax them when they're clean and dry, they'll resist stains and dust. When repainting cabinets—and I recommend it if they're nicked and worn—use a semi-gloss or gloss paint. Flat paint doesn't resist wear and washing to the extent that harder-finish paints do.

Stripping off the old paint from wooden cupboards and refinishing with a stain and varnish can add richness and warmth that is appealing to buyers. I have found the best way to strip cabinets is to remove the doors (be sure to mark the location of each hinge on the door and on the cabinet it was removed from, otherwise you may have to fill in the old screwholes and make new ones) and lay them out on a picnic table or on horses. This facilitates the removal of the old paint, reduces the mess and odor in the kitchen, and makes refinishing easier and less time consuming. Sometimes you can sand off the old finish or paint if there are only one or two layers, but usually a commercial, water-soluble stripper like Zip Strip or TM-3 works best.

PORCELAIN

Most stains can be easily removed with bleach, either straight or in a solution with warm water. Scouring powders, such as Ajax or Comet, should *not* be used on a porcelain surface. They etch it with tiny scratches that can become more and more difficult to clean.

Old, discolored tubs and sinks will look better if you scrub them thoroughly with a paste made from cream of tartar moistened with hydrogen peroxide.

To remove light iron-rust stains from the sink and tub, rub them with a cut lemon. More stubborn stains can be removed by using a 5 percent solution of oxalic acid or a 10 percent solution of hydrochloric acid. (You can get both in a drugstore. These are poisonous substances and should be handled and stored carefully.) Apply the acid with a piece of soft cloth and rinse away after several seconds. If you wait too long, it will scratch the porcelain.

Blue stains caused by copper rust can sometimes be lifted with a solution of ammonia and soap. If this doesn't work, rub them with a little of the 5 percent oxalic acid solution and rinse immediately.

Some products on the market, such as Soft Scrub, are mild abrasives and will not scratch porcelain surfaces. They can be used for stainless steel, countertops, fiberglass, shower doors, chrome, tile, and stove tops. Once the tub or sink has been thoroughly cleaned, you can apply a paste wax such as the kind you use on a car. Buffed, this serves as a good protection against staining.

Unsightly chips can be painted with an epoxy or porcelain paint. Both come in a variety of popular colors. The trick is to build up thin layers in successive applications, sanding in between. The results are not perfect, but this method *will* conceal dark spots and prevent further chipping. New porcelain sinks, and even stainless-steel sinks, aren't particularly expensive. Porcelain costs about $35 for a single and $50 for a double; stainless steel runs about $55 for a single and $70 for a double. It may be worth your while to invest in a replacement sink if your old sink is in really revolting condition.

Through a Glass Darkly

Windows and mirrors that are dirty have the unfortunate effect of making your entire house look dirty. I've found that the best cleaning solution is a little no-suds ammonia in water; wipe the glass dry with newspaper (the acid in the ink cuts grease and grime). Paint left on the windows after a paint job should be neatly scraped off with a tool consisting of a razor blade that can be retracted into the handle. If you don't want to scrape, there's a commercial product called Latex Paint and Stain Off Cleaner (about $3.95 for 22 ounces), but oil-base paint still has to be scraped.

Any broken or cracked glass ought to be replaced before the realtor rings the doorbell. Wood framing that shows weather damage can be repainted after it has been primed with a good wood preservative such as Cupinol.

The Finished Product

Whenever I am asked to make suggestions about how much to spend and what to do with prime surfaces, I recommend thinking about the problem for two days. Many times seeing what's needed is just a matter of sharpening our awareness level. When we live with a stain on the rug or a loose tile in the bathroom or a scratch in the kitchen countertop, we fail to see the defect after a while. Our lives are busy, and home is a place to relax and forget the anxiety of unfinished business. In the house where I now live, the balcony is unfinished and the wood molding still needs to be stained. It's been that way for a year. I know that when the time comes to sell the house I will have to finish the job (if I don't get to it before then) to have the best possible chance of getting my asking price.

Buyers are initially attracted to a house because of its size, price, and location. But right after those comes the *condition* the house is in. What a buyer sees on his first tour of your humble abode will determine the likelihood of his returning for a second look. Prime surfaces that are in good condition, that sparkle and shine, invite a second look which ultimately may lead to a sale. Remember two things: (1) *money invested wisely in surface renovation will increase buyer interest*; and (2) *the more interested buyers you can attract, the greater your profit potential will be!*

This charming farmhouse is seriously flawed by its rutted driveway. The shade trees and plantings are a big plus, however.

This horrible cellar entrance gives an impression of neglect that will affect the buyer's response to the entire house. A new cellar door, costing only $100 to $200, will keep rain and snow out of the cellar and will certainly look better. The cinder-block chimney is tacky. It should be covered with cement and planted with ivy or faced with Z-brick.

This house in New Jersey gives us dramatic proof of the power of a decorative feature like shutters to change the entire look of a house from nondescript to impressive. The feeling of substantiality imparted by the shutters would make anyone—neighbor, appraiser, banker, buyer—think of this house as worth far more than the improvement cost of the shutters. Like many great improvements, the shutters don't seem "added on"—they seem to have always been there. Note also the contribution of foliage, a few new plants, and white-painted trim.

A clever way to have two different floors meet. Joining this good-looking linoleum floor to the nicely finished wood floor with an angle is a touch that adds a feeling of space and style and costs no more than an abrupt and conventional straight line.

PENNY LOEB

A stainless-steel sink appeals to nearly everyone and never shows age. A double sink is best, and any sink should be well lit, with good counterspace near it.

HOWARD BLUME

Opposite: People often overlook the dramatic effects of well-finished stairs. Vertical-patterned wallpaper gives a feeling of majesty and height. Good-quality wallpaper also hides chipped or cracked plasterwork. Note the beauty of the refinished wood.

HOWARD BLUME

PENNY LOEB

What a difference a prime
surface makes is evidenced by
this kitchen transformation.
In the redone room, note the
orderly and beautiful cabinets,
the extensive counterspace,
the excellent light, the
gourmet stove, and the high-
quality linoleum floor. It pays
to spend a little more on
kitchen floors, for both looks
and durability.

HOWARD BLUME

HOWARD BLUME

4

How To Find Out If Your House Is Structurally Sound
(AND WHAT TO DO IF IT ISN'T)

I remember a song I used to sing in Sunday School, about the wise man who built his house upon a rock and the foolish man who built his house on sand. "The rains came down and the floods came up," I'd bang my fists together and sing, ". . . and the wise man's house stood firm." The foolish man's house, as you may recall, got the big squish of total destruction.

The message in this song speaks to the issue of structural soundness. Wise men don't buy and good builders don't build houses on sand (not, at least, without compensating for the weakness of the terrain).

The best way to ensure the continued value of your house is to maintain its structural and functional integrity.

Structural soundness is basic to worth. A poorly built house, or one that has a major flaw in one of its systems, isn't worth anywhere near as much as a house that's sound.

If you're planning to market your house or to live in it a long time,

doing whatever needs to be done to correct its structural flaws is probably going to be worth the cost—and more. An antiquated plumbing
system could cost you $2,000 to replace, but it could cost you a whop-
ping $5,000 later on if you don't. A buyer determining the value of
your poorly plumbed house is sure to bargain you down that much.
The way the buyer figures it, repair and replacement could cost him a
mint. To be on the safe side, he will want to swack a goodly chunk off
your asking price.

Evaluating your home for structural soundness is a job for a professional home-inspection engineer—one who really knows where to
look and what to look for. To find such a person, consult the Yellow
Pages, under "Home-Inspection Services" or "Building-Inspection
Firms," or ask your local bank for recommendations. Builders and
architects sometimes offer inspection services. A professional consultation will cost you $75 to $150, but it could be worth every penny.
These people make it their business to evaluate accurately the
strength of a house's structure as well as the functionality of the systems, and their knowledge can definitely save you money in the long
run.

Don't, however, underestimate your own ability to look critically.
There's a lot you can find out about the condition of the plumbing,
the wiring, the foundation, and the other structural underpinnings of
your home investment.

An ice pick, a flashlight, a level, and a magnet can take you a long
way in unearthing the structural defects discussed in this chapter.

INSECT INFESTATION

Have you ever noticed a house that is under construction before the
insulation and siding have been applied? It looks like a big toothpick
sculpture. Termites get very excited about all that wood—and so
should you. This is especially true if you live in a hot and humid area,
such as a southern or Pacific Coast state.

Insects considerably weaken the wooden supports of a house, and unless their eating and burrowing are halted, they will eventually cause the house to collapse. Termites are the most dangerous offending insects because they eat rather quickly and very heartily. If they are caught in the early stages of infestation, however, they can be stopped for a mere $200 or $300, compared with thousands later on.

This is where good eyesight and your flashlight and ice pick come in handy. Head for the cellar or crawlspace and poke at those large supporting beams with the ice pick. Then pluck up your courage and check Table 4 (pp. 72–75) for evidence of the most common types of insect infestation and what to do about them.

In areas where termite hazard is high, homeowners often purchase contracts with pest-control companies for regular inspection and treatment of their houses. (Better firms are listed with the National Pest Control Association, Vienna, Virginia, or with the Better Business Bureau in your area.) Such a termite-control contract can help dispel your fears about insects silently destroying your house while you sleep.

You can also research past contracts on your house to find out if any infestation occurred while the house was under contract and what particular treatments and repairs were instituted at that time. Don't be shy about asking for this information.

Termite proofing on a new house can be expected to last about five years. Ultimately, the best safeguard against insect infestation is a dry house and one that has a poured concrete foundation (no cracks for bugs to enter).

MOISTURE DAMAGE

A good house ought to stand solid for hundreds of years. Wood in a house that's been properly constructed and maintained will endure because its moisture content is hardly ever above 15 percent. *Wood that has been kept dry is strong wood.*

On the other hand, wood that has *not* been kept dry has definitely been jeopardized. Wood loves water, soaks it up, and retains it for

TABLE **4**

EVIDENCE OF AND MEASURES TO CONTROL INSECTS THAT DESTROY HOUSES

INSECT	PRIMARY AREA OF INFESTATION	CHARACTERISTICS
Subterranean termites	Southern and Pacific Coast states	Spend entire lives either underground or in completely enclosed galleries in wood
		Must avoid contact with dry air
		Need source of moisture to survive
		Speed of destruction increased with temperature and moisture elevation
		Usually enter house from surrounding soil, either by tubing over foundation walls or by attacking wood in contact with soil
Drywood termites	Deep South, southern Texas, New Mexico, Arizona, and along Pacific Coast in California	Most likely to occur in old buildings
		Damage wood more slowly than subterranean termites
		Do not have ground connections
		Entrance holes difficult to detect because sealed with brownish-black, paper-thin secretions that contain many pellets
Wood-destroying beetles	Anywhere in U.S., but most common in warm, humid climates	Damage done by larvae
		Must have bare wood on which to lay eggs
		Can infest kiln-dried lumber during storage
		Usually reinfest wood after emergence

EVIDENCE OF ACTIVITY	FEATURES THAT INVITE INFESTATION	SOLUTIONS
Winged termites *inside* house (yellow, brown, or black bodies and two pairs of long, whitish translucent wings of equal size)	Spaces in bricks or blocks Earth–wood contacts Wood debris near house or under crawlspace	Fill voids in foundation Remove soil from wood near house and under crawlspace
Discarded wings beneath doors or windows and around light fixtures.	Untreated planting soil against exterior walls	Treat soil underneath and around foundation with insecticide
Honeycomb appearance of wood not usually visible on exterior (try probing with ice pick)	Untreated soil beneath carport or slab additions	Treat soil underneath and around foundation with insecticide
Termite tubes from soil to wood ($\frac{1}{4}$–$\frac{1}{2}$ in. wide)	Termite shields less than 12 in. above and less than 2 in. outward and 2 in. downward at 45° angle	Hire a professional pest-control operator
	Cracks in metal termite shields	Hire a professional pest-control operator
Piles of pellets below damaged wood Large, clean cavities cut across grain of dry wood	Dry firewood stored in house or basement Untreated, bare, old wood	Apply insecticide to galleries in wood under attack (involves boring holes in infected wood and sealing) Fumigate if infestation is severe
Very fine sawdust on or beneath damaged wood	Wet crawlspaces	Spray or brush structural members with insecticide
Small, round or oval holes in wood surface	Absence of moisture barrier in wall	Fumigate if insects in wall

TABLE 4 Cont'd

INSECT	PRIMARY AREA OF INFESTATION	CHARACTERISTICS
Lyctus or powder-post beetles	Anywhere in U.S., but most common in warm, humid climates	Attack recently seasoned hardwood sapwood
Anobiids	Anywhere in U.S., but most common in warm, humid climates	Attack both hardwood and softwood Usually found in buildings older than 10 years
Old-house borers	Anywhere in U.S., but most common in warm, humid climates	Attack softwood, primarily framing lumber Prefer recently seasoned wood most often in houses less than 10 years old
Carpenter ants	Anywhere in U.S.	Do not eat wood, but rather nest in it Cause considerable damage in nesting
Bees	Mostly in South and West	Damage usually slight unless uncontrolled for long period

long periods. Moisture in the wrong places will eventually damage important wood supports in your house.

Here are the ways in which water can damage your real estate investment. A leaky roof will allow the supporting roof members to get wet with each rain. The longer such a situation goes unattended, the weaker the roof structure becomes. Wood that's in direct contact with the soil will soak up moisture from the ground, endangering the foundation. Condensation will occur within walls when there's a significant temperature difference between the outside and the inside and

EVIDENCE OF ACTIVITY	FEATURES THAT INVITE INFESTATION	SOLUTIONS
Very fine sawdust on or beneath damaged wood	Wet crawlspaces	Spray or brush structural members with insecticide
Small, round or oval holes in wood surface	Absence of moisture barrier in wall	Fumigate if insects in wall
Very fine sawdust on or beneath damaged wood	Wet crawlspaces	Spray or brush structural members with insecticide
Small, round or oval holes in wood surface	Absence of moisture barrier in wall	Fumigate if insects in wall
Very fine sawdust on or beneath damaged wood	Wet crawlspaces	Spray or brush structural members with insecticide
Small, round or oval holes in wood surface	Absence of moisture barrier in wall	Fumigate if insects in wall
Presence of large ants around house (reddish brown to black, ¼–½ in. long) Scratching sound in beams, supports, etc. Piles of evacuated sawdust	Damp wood (porch pillars and supporting timbers, sills, girders, joists, studs, and window and door trim)	Keep wood coated with paint or stain Spray insecticides frequently in areas where ants are seen Locate nest and spray with insecticide
Presence of bees (look like bumblebees but have bare abdomens) Entrance holes (⅝ in. in diameter across grain)	Old, soft, unpainted, weathered wood Somewhat sheltered porch ceilings, windowsills, siding, doorframes, and headers	Apply insecticide to nest galleries

the insulation doesn't allow moisture to pass through. Other causes of unwanted condensation are an unvented clothes dryer or a frequently used shower stall located in a small bathroom without window or vent fan. The absence of air vents at attics and eaves will prevent moist air from circulating. The results are woefully predictable: The wood will rot!

The two commonest causes of wood rot are *clogged roof drains* and *poor water drainage* away from the house.

A sure way to test the condition of the wood is to examine it carefully. But don't lose sight of the forest for one tree; concentrate on the overall construction of your house and how it has been designed to keep the moisture out. The ideal time to inspect your house is right after a heavy rain. If you suspect moisture problems, check the wood for rot by poking it with your trusty ice pick.

If you have one or more of the following conditions, it's probably a sign that you should consult a builder or home inspector for further evaluation of your moisture problem.

- Earth sloping toward house.

- Earth-filled porch or other structure attached to the house.

- Unvented crawlspace beneath house.

- Damp soil underneath house.

- No insulation under ground floor or around inside walls of closed-off wallspace.

- No moisture barrier under concrete floors. (The only way you can be sure of this is to have known the builder, but if mildew exists, you can certainly suspect it.)

- Wood elements of house located less than 10 inches above ground level.

- Damp- or mildew-smelling basement.

- Discoloration of floor tile, stained paneling at floor level, dark stains on cinder block.

- Roof overhang narrower than 18 inches.

- Missing roof shingles or other waterproof material, especially around edges of roof.

- Sagging roof (a sign of possible rafter decay due to moisture).

- Missing or misaligned gutters and downspouts.

- Attic insulation moist to touch.

- Inadequately ventilated attic (large air-vent louvers are superior to small ones).

- Peeling or blistering paint.

- Leaky plumbing.

- Presence of mildew or mold on exterior or interior wall and ceiling surfaces. (Replastering of one section of ceiling or wall is a good indication that moisture damage has occurred in the past. Stains are another. Check to be sure the situation that created the water damage has been corrected.)

- Sticking doors and windows.

- Cracked or absent caulk around tubs and showers.

- Unlevel floors, and floors that feel spongy when walked on.

In dollars and cents

Proper evaluation of moisture damage and repair/replacement cost is key to both the current and future value of your house. You can recaulk around the bathtub, replace a rotted piece of molding, and clean out the stopped-up drain without spending much time and money; *but* watch out for that soggy-feeling floor or an inadequate roof overhang. These are signs that you could end up having to spend a small fortune. (In my area, a backhoe and operator run at least $25 an hour. If the land around your house is improperly graded, bringing water into your cellar every time it rains, you may have to spend at least $1,000 to get the earth moved and have a contractor lay an outside drain system before the cellar dries out and you can stop using your sump pump.)

Remember, *the only remedy for rotted wood is replacement with new wood.* Replacement is expensive, both in materials and in labor. Therefore, prevention is your best guarantee of maintaining the worth of your house.

MATERIAL FAILURE AND FAULTY CONSTRUCTION

Sagging may be the result of insect infestation or decayed wood, but it may also be the result of low-grade materials used in the initial construction or an improper application of high-grade materials. A house that's weak because of either of these defects is a lemon in the world of real estate—the costs of correcting the defects too often exceed any realistic return. Of course, the extent of the defect has everything to do with the economics of repair and return. Careful calculations are absolutely essential to financial as well as structural soundness.

All houses settle some, but severe settling ought to be evaluated carefully by a professional. You can be suspicious if your house is significantly out of plumb. Stand about 2 feet away from each exterior corner of the house and visually check for straightness. For more accuracy, hold a level against each wall. A big bulge with broken or bent siding probably indicates that some major renovation work has been done. Find out *why* and what precisely needs to be done to correct the condition.

Check whether doors and windows are level and notice if the doors line up squarely in their frames. Have they been resawn at the bottom to allow freedom of movement? If so, this is another sign that the house itself may be seriously out of plumb.

Put a marble on the floor and observe its movement. If it stays put, the floor is level. If it rolls to one side of the room or the other, and rolls quickly, something major may well be wrong. (Usually that something major involves the foundation itself or the floor joists.)

Look for cracks in walls, particularly cracks that run at angles from the upper corners of windows and doors. Cracks between chimney and foundation are especially significant, since both the chimney and the foundation have their own footings and a separation suggests settling of one or both of these, which will eventually be reflected in other areas of the house. (Masonry chimney walls should *always* be separated from combustible construction.)

As you have probably deduced from the above discussion, there are two critical areas of construction strength: *the foundation* and *the roof*. One professional home inspector I know says, "Even most real estate people don't know the significance of a crumbling foundation wall or a sagging roof. They don't seem to realize that either the house will fall down eventually or the homeowner will have to pay thousands of dollars to make his home safe."

CORNERSTONE STRENGTH

Watch out for cracks in the foundation wall. Little horizontal cracks often occur at the frost line, where dirt freezes against the foundation. Extremes of heat and cold cause expansion and contraction of the ground against the cinderblock, stone, or concrete, producing the cracks. They are relatively insignificant *if* they are small. Joints can be "pointed up," which means the old mortar can be removed and new mortar applied.

Vertical cracks and cracks that are large, however, spell trouble, even if the house is still standing pretty true. Repair usually involves excavating outside to remove the dirt against the foundation wall, releasing the anchor bolts, jacking the house up about an inch, taking out the old masonry, pouring new footings if the footings are bad, and then laying the block. It's all professional work, and it's all highly costly.

It's possible, of course, that the addition of a few supporting columns will correct sagging. Screw-jack columns are often used to shore up a house, but they tend to make potential buyers nervous, indicating understrength and overstress as well as failed floor framing. Lally columns (although they can possibly rake the roof or bulge the floor) are used for the same purpose and don't seem to cause as much buyer suspicion as the screw-jack columns do.

Shoring up sagging beams with additional supports runs about $350 to $400. If the foundation is so bad that the structure needs to be raised so that the wall (or walls) can be replated, the project can cost between $4,000 and $5,000.

ROOF PROBLEMS

I did a job for a family last winter that ended up costing them over $2,000. They called me because their kitchen cabinets had begun to separate from the kitchen walls. The house was a summer cottage that had been renovated into a year-round home. The house had been expanded on all four sides of the original cottage, and the old roof had been removed. A new roof had been put over the expanded structure, but the home renovator failed to install the proper supporting joists—two-by-six or two-by-eight heavy-duty boards that hold the sides of the house together. Heavy snow that winter had caused the roof to drop and the wall on one side of the house to move out. I reinforced the roof with collar beams on the rafters. This will hold the spreading in check, but the walls will never be straight again without an additional outlay of about $5,000—the cost of jacking up the roof, pulling in the walls at the same time with steel cables and pulleys (these must go right through the walls, necessitating a lot of subsequent Sheetrock repair), and then adding the collar beams.

That $7,000 is a lot of money to spend as a result of someone else's shortsightedness. (See how to steer clear of an incompetent contractor in chapter 10.)

The roof must be constructed in such a way that it will support its own weight, keep the sides of the house together, withstand loads of snow and gusts of wind, and provide a good base for roofing materials.

The common systems of roof construction are trusses (usually these result in limited attic space), joists and rafters, planks and beams, joists alone, or panelized construction. Your home inspector or contractor can tell you if the lumber used is of adequate size and strength for the span covered and the type of construction used, if the supports are spaced properly, and if the wood used is of the right species (strength varies with type of wood).

The condition of the *roofing*, on the other hand, is something you can usually ascertain from visual inspection, particularly after a heavy rain. A good roof looks even and uniform; a bad one contains broken, warped, or bent shingles (and probably leaks!). Check a metal roof for rust; a tile roof for cracking on sides; a slate roof for rusty nails and tar coming off the ridge; and a built-up roof (gravel) for bubbles and spongy spaces.

Usually an asphalt-shingled or built-up roof will last about fifteen years. Replacing the roof with medium-weight asphalt shingles costs about $60 a square foot, and the shingle comes in quantities of 100 square feet. (Roof replacement considerations are discussed further in chapter 9.)

INADEQUATE WIRING

Overloaded wiring is the defect most frequently found in houses fifteen or more years old. Unfortunately, it's a hidden defect that can go unnoticed until your lights go off or your house fills with smoke.

Did you know that houses that were wired with aluminum wiring between 1966 and 1973 have a higher-than-average fire potential due to overheating of the outlets? Do you know whether you have aluminum wiring in your house? Have you looked to see how many wires are coming in from the main electric pole to your fuse box, or how many circuit breakers there are? Problems are easy to spot once you know what to look for and where to look.

EIGHT SIGNS OF AN INADEQUATE ELECTRICAL SYSTEM

1. Only two main wires coming from the pole to the house (there should be three).

2. Fewer than ten circuits in the main switch box.

3. Absence of branch circuits to various appliances and rooms.

4. Minimum supply of 240 volts and 100 amperes (150 to 200 amperes is better; look for ampere ratings on board or on the inside cover of the fuse box).

5. Fuses being used are of a higher ampere rating than is specified (for example, a 20-ampere fuse in a 15-ampere plug).

6. Many extension cords or monkey plugs in use about the house.

7. Lights that are dim and appliances that do not work at peak efficiency (particularly those that produce heat, such as irons).

8. Hot wires, especially the cables leading from the main electric box (these are usually found next to the meter).

The approximate cost of rewiring an average three-bedroom house is between $1,000 and $2,500, depending on the number of stories the house has and estimated electrical usage. (A large family that uses heavy appliances such as clothes dryers, ranges, and dishwashers, or a house whose heating and cooling systems run on electricity, may require more circuits and increased amperage.)

Faulty wiring is the major cause of house fires. Living with an antiquated electrical system is dangerous, inconvenient, and impractical. Moreover, *all* these factors will affect the future resale value of your home. If your house is otherwise sound, it is worth your while to pay for rewiring. Your comfort and safety will be assured, as well as the potential for profit on your home investment.

TIPS ON REWIRING

It is wise to draw a rough diagram of the areas that need new or additional outlets, as well as any changes in switches. You should also note additions you might like on the outside of your house, such as outside recepticles and spotlights. In your diagram be sure to include any and all appliances and their locations. This will enable an electrician to comprehend the scope of the work quickly and give you an accurate cost estimate. (A diagram is particularly useful if you're considering the purchase of a home that's still occupied and you don't want to bother the present occupants by trooping electricians through their abode.)

Be sure to get estimates from three reputable electricians, showing each the same diagram of work to be done. After you've made your choice of electricians, try to get the work done at a time when plaster dust and strange workmen milling around will be the least inconvenient.

FAULTY PLUMBING

Carl Hagel owns a golf course way up in the mountains of North Carolina. Four years ago he built a lovely house overlooking the course. The house is well constructed in every way, but the plumbing system has turned out to be a disaster. Here is the note that appears in the downstairs guest bathroom.

An Ode To Our Dear Guests

We must warn you this house hath
A most mysterious shower bath;
When you shower at your ease
Suddenly you'll start to freeze.
Of course, the reason soon will dawn,
Someone turned the hot water on . . .

Or you're soaped and wet and caught,
As water turns from warm to hot.
Here again, the light will dawn,
Someone else has flushed the john.

We will try to think of this
When we hear your shower hiss,
Or should you hear ours running too,
The Golden Rule applies to you!

The Management (Pearl Hagel)

The Hagels know (now) what the problem is, and unfortunately there's nothing they can do short of spending a couple of thousand dollars for repairs. The contractor installed the wrong size pipe, $\frac{1}{2}$-inch diameter instead of $\frac{3}{4}$-inch so that the more-than-adequate flow of water from their well is reduced drastically in its travels to the various faucets throughout the house. They paid good money for a high-quality house, but it has a major flaw which will affect the resale value, reducing the worth by *more* than the $2,000 that replacing the pipe would cost.

As long as the water in your house continues to erupt with the same reasonable force and speed as usual, don't worry. But if the water pressure drops in the bathroom faucets when the toilet is flushed, or the shower spray dwindles to a trickle when the washing machine fills, you should be concerned. *As the water pressure drops, so does market value.*

THREE WAYS TO SPOT TROUBLE

1. *Take the flush test.* Turn on all the faucets in the highest bathroom and then flush the toilet. If the water pressure drops substantially or the flow of water is noticeably inconsistent, the plumbing system is failing or inadequate.

2. *Do the magnet test.* To determine the quality of the pipes, hold a magnet near them—behind the toilet, in an accessible area behind the shower or bathtub, under the sink. The magnet will be drawn to iron or steel. Steel and iron pipes are prone to corrosion; the newer (later than the 1940s) nonferrous copper and bronze and the even newer plastic pipes are not. If you have iron or steel pipes, check for corrosion everywhere you can, and have your water tested by your county water department.

3. *Do the optic-and-proboscis test.* Find the location of the septic tank and leach field (the area where waste water is absorbed into the soil). Notice if the grass growing over the area is unusually green and abundant (a bad sign) and if the pungent odor of sewage is noticeable downwind (also a bad sign). If, in addition to these, you sink into soggy soil while performing the test, you can consider a faulty disposal system a virtual certainty.

WHAT CONSTITUTES A QUALITY PLUMBING SYSTEM

The value of your plumbing system depends on two basic facts: the *abundance* of available water and the *quality* of that water.

If the source of your water supply is a well, it should be located outside the house at a minimum depth of 20 feet. It should be at least 100 feet away from the absorption field or seepage pit and 50 feet away from the septic tank. A properly functioning well is capable of delivering a sustained flow of at least *5 gallons of water per minute*. If you have a bored well, it should be lined to prevent sediment from entering the water and ultimately closing off the flow of water to your house. To provide such a smooth flow of water from your well, you should have a storage tank with a minimum capacity of 42 gallons.

If you are plugged into a municipal system, the abundance of water is generally assumed to be adequate, though this isn't always the case. (In one small town near me, the pressure is so poor that when one resident flushes his toilet, the flow of water is noticeably decreased for a few minutes in houses down the line.) Sometimes whole communities are threatened with shortages in water supply. Adequacy of the municipal water supply can affect the overall value of houses in the area.

Homeowners often make the mistake of thinking that as long as there's an abundant source of water, the *quality* is of little importance to the overall value of their home. Be advised that many lending agencies require that the water on a given property be tested before a mortgage is granted. A poor report can blow the loan.

Foul-smelling, heavily chlorinated, murky-colored, debris-filled, or contaminated water will cause the scrutinizing buyer to reconsider his initial enthusiasm for your house. All water—particularly well water—should be tested occasionally for bacteria and mineral content. A well that is shallow or lies near a swamp or lake or is newly dug and has not been flushed out with chlorine, is apt to become contaminated. The local health department will test your water for bacteria cheaply or free of charge, and an independent laboratory will perform a mineral analysis for around $10 to $20.

Water of poor quality can cause a substantial reduction in the market value of your home; an insufficient amount of water is *sure* to. Abundant, superior-quality water will add two more advantages to the list of selling points that will eventually bring you a good return on your home investment. If you have a water problem, spend some time finding a reliable plumber. *This work is beyond the capabilities of most homeowners.*

THE PIPES

Pipes should carry water throughout the house without making a lot of noise, leaking, reducing the pressure, or adding any color or taste to the water. Different kinds of pipes pose different kinds of problems, but the commonest cause of concern is the old iron or steel pipe that was used in most homes prior to the early 1940s. Iron and steel corrode and the pipes become clogged like hardened arteries. The only way to rid yourself of the pressure problem corroded pipes create is to move from the house in question or replace the pipes. The average cost of new pipes for a three-bedroom house runs between $1,000 and $2,500—more if the house is large. Copper, bronze, and plastic pipes are superior to those of steel and iron.

The pipe, or main, which brings the water in from the street in a municipal system should have a diameter of at least ¾ inch if it's copper and 1 to 1¼ inches if it is galvanized iron (which it often is). Too small a main can be the source of pressure problems. Replacement costs run a few hundred dollars depending upon the distance from the street to the house.

THE FITTINGS

You can expect to replace fittings such as faucets, shower heads, and so forth many times in the life of your house. Cheap fittings wear out quickly; quality fittings look better, last longer, and add value to your home.

FAUCETS. You can tell a cheap faucet by the cross-shaped handle and tarnished look. These faucets are made of lightweight zinc or aluminum. Better-quality faucets are made of solid brass with a coat of chrome, nickel, or brushed or polished brass. You can recognize these by the solid handle with grooves in it for finger grip. Superdeluxe models, which are fancier-looking and in some cases designed to control the temperature of the water reaching the fixture, don't last any longer than the better-quality type.

SHOWER HEADS. A cheap shower head has no spray-direction control. A shower head of better quality is self-cleaning and has a flexible ball joint for direction and spray control. An automatic diverter is a quality feature in a shower/tub setup. This mechanism diverts the water back into the tub faucet after a shower so the next person who wants to take a bath isn't scalded or shocked by hot or cold water.

CUT-OFF VALVES. Each fixture should have a cut-off valve (behind toilet, sink, washer, and so on) so the water supply to that individual fixture can be turned off when repairs need to be made. There should also be a shut-off valve at the street and at the point where the pipe enters the house. Outside faucets (called "sill cocks") should be frost-proof and have individual shut-off valves inside the house so they can be drained and turned off in the winter.

THE WATER HEATERS

Have you ever waited at the bathroom sink late at night, in your bare feet, yearning for the water to get warm enough so you could wash your face? Or felt the hot water turn cold while you were in the middle of washing your hair?

Many houses have undersized or low-quality water heaters. The average expectancy of a good-quality water heater is about ten years; heaters of poorer quality last only three to four years.

Inadequately sized hot-water tanks are the commonest cause of too little hot water. Old tanks are often too small. They simply don't hold enough water to accommodate today's showers, washing machines, and dishwashers. You can determine the gallon capacity of your water heater by reading the nameplate located on the tank.

Remember that the replacement cost of a new water heater is relatively low ($200 to $400) when compared with other potential costs in a house that is structurally deficient in other ways. The improvement in quality and quantity of available hot water adds to the value of your house, as does the ten-year guarantee that usually accompanies a good heater. See Table 5 on p. 88.

If you don't want to incur the expense of a new tank, consider leasing one. Utility companies often lease hot-water tanks for a minimal monthly charge. They also take care of installation and maintenance.

TABLE **5**

COST EFFICIENCY OF VARIOUS TYPES OF WATER HEATERS

TYPE OF WATER HEATER	SIZE OF FAMILY	MINIMUM CAPACITY (GALLONS)	PURCHASE COST (DOLLARS)	COMPARATIVE OPERATIONAL COST
Solar	4–7	80	1,500–2,500*	Most efficient
Oil	1–3	30	700–900	Moderately to highly efficient
	4–7	40		
	7+	50		
Gas	1–2	40	250–400	Moderately efficient[†]
	3–4	50		
	4–5	75		
	5+	100		
Electric	1–3	50	200–350	Least efficient
	4–7	80		
	7+	100		

*Less federal tax credit.

†Exceptions are "fast-recovery," "high-speed," and "high-watt" models, in which 30-gal. capacity is usually adequate for a family of 4 to 7 persons, provided heater is run by gas or oil. A fast-recovery electric heater should have 80-gal. capacity. As price of oil and gas continues to rise, electricity may become most cost-efficient method of heating water (next to solar).

THE SEPTIC SYSTEM

In a private residence the septic system consists of a large concrete tank buried in the ground. The waste from the house enters the tank via a drain line. Bacteria in the tank decompose the grease and solids so that a relatively clear liquid flows out from the opposite end of the tank and into a series of buried perforated pipes (called a leaching field) or into a seepage pit. This liquid remains underground and is absorbed into the soil.

My experience over the years has shown me that nearly half of the

TABLE 6

CAUSE, SOLUTION, AND COMPARATIVE COST OF REPAIR FOR COMMON PLUMBING PROBLEMS

PROBLEM	PROBABLE CAUSE	SOLUTION	COMPARATIVE COST*
Low water pressure	Failing pump Shallow well	Replace pump Dig new well	Moderate Very high
Spongy area around toilet	Leaky toilet seal	Replace seal; repair floor	Minimum Moderate to high
High-pitched whistling sound when toilet is flushed	Valve in toilet closing too slowly	Adjust valve	Minimum
Sucking sound when toilet is flushed	Improper venting of waste stack	Unclog vent; change vent system	Moderate High
Leak in toilet flush tank	Defective ball in toilet tank	Replace ball	Minimum
Leaks under sink	Loose washer Cracked fixture	Replace washer Replace fixture	Minimum Moderate
Leaky faucets	Corroded or worn washers	Replace washers	Minimum
Hammering noise in water pipes†	Built-up pressure in pipes	Install air chambers	High
Sound of running water	Undersized pipes or pipes that are not insulated against sound	Install larger pipes or wrap pipes with insulation	High
Sulfurous or earthy taste or smell in water	Minerals in well or pipes	Add water softener	Moderate
Sewage backed up in basement	Clogged septic tank or outside drain	Pump out or add caustic in septic tank Snake drain Replace system	Moderate Moderate Very high

*Minimum cost, less than $10; moderate cost, less than $150; high cost, $150–$1,000; very high cost, over $1,000.

†A serious problem that may eventually cause the pipes to leak.

HOWARD BLUME

Excellent exterior construction ensures that this is a house that will last. The gutters and downspouts (a) are top quality and properly installed. The siding (b) is vinyl and looks just as good as wood (but won't need periodic repainting). The skylight (c) is properly installed to avoid leakage. The box cut out from the eaves (d) is a neat trick to give more light to the window below it.

houses that have their own waste-disposal systems have faulty ones. (Refer to page 84 and the optic-and-proboscis test for information about malfunctioning septic systems.)

A backed-up septic system can sometimes be corrected by having the tank pumped out and the cycle of bacterial action begun anew. This costs $50 or $60. Sometimes, however, both a new tank and a new leaching field are necessary; then the total cost can run as high as $5,000. If the water table is high and the soil's absorption rate poor (this can be determined by a percolation test, which is carried out by the local health department for a small fee), the problem of a faulty septic system is likely to remain unsolved, unfortunately decreasing the value of your home. Buyers are very aware of the importance of a septic system to value. If yours is updated and functioning well, by all means maintain it to ensure the highest market value possible.

5

LANDSCAPING
THE PROPER SETTING FOR YOUR INVESTMENT GEM

If your home is not graced with mature landscaping, you're missing an important opportunity to increase its value significantly. Even the most barbarous real estate developer has learned that if a property is going to lure prospective buyers out of their cars, it has to look good from the curb. And nothing contributes more to the "curb appeal" of a house than landscaping. Fifteen years ago developers bulldozed the tracts of housing developments to expedite construction work; now they're willing to pay landscape architects to map existing plant features so that construction will not interfere with these valuable resources. Trees located as near as 12 feet to the foundation of a house are left standing. Today developers know their increased construction costs will be more than repaid by the higher prices they'll get for houses with well-developed landscaping.

The actual value landscaping can add to your house may surprise you. F. J. Micha, a landscape appraiser and consulting arborist in Rochester, New York, says: "Well-landscaped homes with trees that are well kept bring an average of 15 percent more on resale." This jibes with the findings of a U.S. Forest Service study which established that trees alone can contribute up to 15 percent of the value of a home property.

No matter how modest your house, take the advice of Mormon leader Brigham Young, who preached real estate principles to his followers on their barren settlement on the Great Salt Lake. "Ignore," he said, "those who say that it is not worthwhile to plant around a log cabin. I say that it is worthwhile. Plant vines over the door, plant fruits and trees and flowers so that everyone who passes will say, 'What a lovely little cottage.' "

By transforming your log cabin into a lovely little cottage you accomplish the two main objectives of *Riches Under Your Roof*. You create an image that increases the *perceived value* of your home and you add *real value* that will appreciate every year those plantings grow.

The Lawn That Launched a Lucrative House Sale

From the curb, your lawn is one of your property's most important prime surfaces. A well-kept, healthy-looking lawn is a good index of how the entire property has been maintained and establishes that vital first impression. This is what we call "perceived value," this impression your house makes on others. Because of its perceived value, a rich, vigorous-looking lawn also contributes to the *real* value of your home. A survey commissioned by the Scott lawn-care company established $1,421 as the mean value "that would be added to a $45,000–$50,000 suburban home after improvement of lawn."

Improving your lawn can add 3 percent to the total value of your property. Figure out what 3 percent of your property is. You can add that amount—thousands of dollars, perhaps—to the value of your home for the price of a few bags of grass seed and some fertilizer. If you want a clear profit, however, be prepared to do the labor yourself. Professional lawn services will charge about a dollar a square foot to seed lawn and almost half that for the labor involved in laying sod. If you own a typical half-acre plot, having a lawn service do the work for you will eat up all your potential profit.

If you've bought a house with no lawn at all, your seed expense will be twice what it would take to reseed an existing lawn. Still, you can make a tidy profit and have the advantage of creating exactly the kind of lawn you want. Go buy some grass seed. You may also want to rent a Rototiller from your local hardware store to dig up some of the most ragged patches of your potential lawn. And don't forget the fertilizer. You are about to plant a crop of grass. Think of it as a crop and you won't be tempted to slight its cultivation. Think of it as a *cash* crop and you may even enjoy yourself.

As with all investments, timing is important. All crops have ideal planting seasons, including grass crops. For grass, the season is early fall. In spring plant a tree, dig a vegetable garden, find some other way to use up your excess physical energy; but leave your lawn alone. It's not that you'll do irreparable damage if you sow grass seed in the spring. You'll just be wasting your time and money. The seed will sprout; some of it may even last through June. But most of it won't last through July, unless you can be out there with your hose watering the stuff several times a day. The heat and drought of midsummer are too much for most tender grass seedlings. Give the seedlings the growing conditions they need to produce strong roots: long, cool nights and plenty of moisture. The payoff will be a lawn that can hold its own with winter and be ready to take off next spring. If you feel you *must* seed early, do it before April 15. If you've got a really terrible lawn and are planning to sell your house this spring or summer, for instance, it's worth taking a chance on spring seeding. But if you have a choice, always opt for seeding in early fall.

BUYING SEED

Something else you have to resist besides the urge to seed too early is the urge to grab a satchel of grass seed in a supermarket. Sold in the produce department alongside the bananas, grass seed becomes an impulse purchase rather than a carefully considered addition to a major investment.

The grass seed you finally choose for your lawn should be determined by several factors. Most important is climate. Seed catalogues have maps showing climate zones; these tell you what will grow where you live—and what won't. Advertisements in magazines and on the back pages of Sunday supplements are not always so scrupulous, however. Widely advertised zoysia grass, for instance, does not do well north of Washington, D.C.; yet in some advertisements it is said to be "guaranteed" to grow in any soil, in any area.

Mixtures (of species) or blends (of cultivars) keep a lawn from being wiped out by a single disease or rampant pest, at the same time allowing the lawn to establish itself through natural selection. Such a lawn will be less finicky, but also less elegant, than a lawn of a single seed variety. Whenever you envy one of those thick, soft, velvety lawns, be assured that it's been grown from high-quality, single-variety seed—and hovered over, endlessly.

Don't skimp on seed quality. The premise behind spending any money on a lawn is to create a lush, rich-looking surface. At the same time, if you spring for good-quality seed, don't waste money throwing down an extra *quantity* of seed. More seed will not necessarily translate into more grass.

FEED WHAT YOU SEED

You have bought quality grass seed. You have cultivated your lawn surface to create a receptive growing medium. You have invested your time and money, in other words. Now, with proper fertilization, cash in your chips. The lush lawn you're after won't happen unless you fertilize it.

In a northern lawn, autumn is the planting season for grass; it is also the fertilizing season. Bluegrass, which spreads by underground rhizomes, will thicken; its root system will be strengthened and enlarged. Leaf color will green up, and food for future growth will be stored in the roots for springtime action. And with autumn fertilizing, you won't be feeding weeds.

If your lawn is recovering from long neglect, spring fertilizing may be needed as well. But once you build up the nutrients in your lawn, autumn fertilizing should be all that's necessary.

If you're unsure about the condition of your soil, have your county agricultural agent analyze a small sample (the cost is about $5 in New York State). The analysis will let you know, among other things, what fertilizer formula is best suited to your lawn's needs.

The important thing to remember is that lawns need *nitrogen* for healthy growth—at least 1 pound of nitrogen for each 1,000 square feet of lawn per year. The new slow-release fertilizers are best—they avoid nitrogen burn, that browning that can occur if you put too much fertilizer in one place.

If your lawn has responded to all your attentions, it should be thick enough to discourage weed growth. Healthy, thick grass doesn't give weeds much of an opening. Assuming that you will have a few spoil-sports, however, get them out with careful application of chemical weed killer; or, if you're antichemicals, dig them out. The herbicides available for weed control are dangerous toxins that should be used minimally and only after carefully reading the directions on each package. Different kinds of weeds require different herbicides, so don't think you can kill your poison ivy, wild onions, and dandelions with the same weed killer. If your lawn is weed infested, start from scratch instead of applying large amounts of herbicide. Till the weeds under and make a new lawn. Do the same for large patches infested with weeds. Not only will you end up with a good-looking lawn, you will have avoided adding troublesome amounts of chemical toxins to your soil. Some weed killers (poison-ivy killer is one) are capable of severely damaging or killing trees and shrubs. It's a sad homeowner who has killed a maple tree while attacking some bothersome weeds.

PLANTINGS THAT LEAD TO RICHES

Trees and shrubs have the visual effect of anchoring your home to its site. They create a feeling of substance and well-being that others will be only too willing to pay for when the time comes. Evaluate your landscaping to see if it's doing its job.

Landscaping reaches its prime value ten to fifteen years after planting, according to landscape appraiser F. J. Micha. To capitalize on this principle, you should invest in landscaping immediately if your property lacks it or if the landscaping you have has grown scrawny and unattractive.

If you're quite sure you're not going to be moving for several years, you can afford to buy less expensive, less mature plants and let their annual growth accumulate profit for you like interest in the bank. However, since most shrubs take twenty years to reach maturity—and shade trees take more than thirty years—you will probably want to buy the biggest plants you can afford. This is especially true for anything that's going to go near the house.

Five-year-old shrubs are about half their mature size. This is an economical size for you to buy. The plants will be large enough not to look skimpy and will be manageable enough to plant yourself. When you don't do your own planting you'll have to pay about 50 percent of the price of the plant to have it put in for you. Most professional installations include a guarantee on the plant; still, if you buckle down and dig your own holes, you'll save enough to cover the cost of another third as many plants.

Shade trees

With shade trees you may not be able to save on installation charges. Shade trees need to be bought large if they're going to provide any shade. For the short- and midterm, any tree that gives reasonable shade will be at least 8-inch caliper. ("Caliper," the measure plant professionals use to describe shade trees, is the diameter of a tree's trunk.) Such a tree will weigh a couple of tons and require a hole 10 to 12 feet across and almost as deep.

Installed, an 8-inch-caliper shade tree will cost around $1,000, but if your property has no well-positioned shade tree, you can easily justify its expense given the value mature landscaping adds to your property.

Even for $1,000, however, you won't be buying instant maturity. An 8-inch-caliper tree is an adolescent—underdeveloped, but growing at a good clip. The geometrical progression of branches growing branches growing branches on a tree this size makes a discernible difference in the amount of shade created from year to year.

The largest tree that's safely transplantable is 15-inch caliper. This is a 40-foot tree weighing between 18 and 20 tons. A tree this size is delivered by tractor trailer and off-loaded by derrick. Installed, it costs from $2,500 up, depending on how far it has been hauled and the site conditions the planting crew has to deal with. If you have built yourself a lavish home in a cornfield and named it Twin Oaks, you are in the market for 15-inch-caliper trees. Otherwise, go for something smaller.

Except for the long term, never buy trees under 6-inch caliper. Consumer research has found that house shoppers don't even notice trees smaller than 6-inch caliper. Trees this small seem to "disappear," thus adding no value whatsoever to a property.

A final word on the great tree investment. Driving through a rather barren development of ranch-type houses recently, I was struck by the visual presence of one particular house. It differed greatly from the rest, not in size or architectural style, but in the fact that it was shaded by a 25-foot maple. I later found out this was not an accident of good fortune for the owners, but the result of a $1,600 investment in a 10-inch-caliper tree. Even though they don't plan on selling right away, they have the pleasure of the tree and the shade it throws on their house. The shade lowers their indoor temperature in the summer as much as 8 degrees, or the difference between running or not running an air conditioner on an 85-degree day.

FOUR PRINCIPLES OF LANDSCAPING

Since you should buy the biggest landscaping plants you can afford, you may not be able to afford many. That doesn't matter. It is far more important to make sure that what you *do* plant counts. And that you plant it *where* it counts. Here are some landscaping rules that will help you decide how to apportion your plant money if you can't do everything at once.

1. *Be sure your entry is focused and welcoming.* The mistake most often made with entry landscaping is having too much rather than too little. Your entry should be focused with the help of landscaping, but don't feel you must have an elaborate horticultural show to greet everyone who graces your doorstep. Most of-

ten used around entrances are evergreens, which are by their nature heavy and formal—psychologically somewhat distancing. You may want to add some deciduous plants. And don't let them become overgrown. *Entry planting should never be taller than the door.* It should never encroach on the entry space itself. You want to give people a little psychological support when they approach your house or wait at your door. You don't want them to feel threatened by brushing limbs and low-life insects. By planting taller trees at the corners of your house, modest-sized shrubs near the front door, and taller shrubs between these two areas, you can create an inviting U-effect that draws the eye in toward the entrance.

2. *Use foundation planting to hide unsightly exposed foundation.* Foundation planting often suffers the same potential problems as entry planting: too much evergreen or too much everything. Don't consider foundation planting an essential. Not every house needs it or should have it, because not every house has an ugly or high foundation. If you have Victorian gingerbread or a fieldstone random wall, it is foolish to hide it behind shrubbery. If you have features best left exposed, let your lawn sweep up to meet the house with only minimal accent planting. If you do have a foundation that needs hiding, try a combination of ivy and shrubbery. Don't ring the house with plants, but group them strategically. The eye will focus on clumps of green and ignore spaces between them. Spot planting will cost you a lot less and will be more attractive. *Foundation planting does not return its cost if it was unnecessary in the first place or if it is used in large, visually cumbersome quantities.*

3. *Screen eyesores on your property or a neighboring property.* If you need to screen out some unsightly building or view, you'll probably need a *lot* of landscaping. Vines are the quickest and cheapest way to create large areas of greenery. Growth rate varies with climate. (In Texas, for instance, evergreen ivy can be trained to completely cover a chain-link fence or cinder-block wall in two summers.) Putting in a lot of screening won't save a

classic Colonial house that is located next to a gas station, however. Never assume that copious screening can make up for serious location problems.

When choosing larger plants for screening purposes, you can't get better advice than from the people who plant the roadsides in your state. Plants that line important state roads are chosen for such qualities as *quick growth*, *low cost*, *hardiness*, and *visual interest*. Drive along a nearby parkway or freeway and see what's been planted. For more detailed information, call your state highway department.

4. *Use landscaping to create privacy*. Landscaping that provides a private outdoor area for family relaxation helps sell property. Real estate ads for properties selling for more than $100,000 rarely fail to mention *privacy* as one of the important features of the property.

Creating privacy may be as simple as planting a tree where it will interrupt a neighboring window's sightline into your backyard. Or it may mean planting a hedge to block a view from the street. You may want to combine trellis and vines to enclose one or two sides of a patio area. Whatever steps you take to create a private outdoor area will repay you in the ease with which you are able to sell your property. Your cash outlay need not be great. You can use fast-growing, inexpensive deciduous shrubs rather than slower-growing, more expensive evergreens. The leaves on deciduous plants will be out at the same time of year you are.

FLOWERS AND FINAL TOUCHES

While you're getting your landscaping to perform certain functions for you, bear in mind as well its overall aesthetic appeal—the total visual image you'll be creating. Let a utilitarian fence become a showcase for rambler roses. Plant a lilac by the kitchen door so the smell drifts into the house. Combine dogwood with evergreens for a woodsy feeling. Transform a dull side porch into a pleasing bower by draping it with wisteria. Think about landscaping effects that have charmed you and consider them for your own property. Which ones will work for you? Can they be achieved as part of your functional landscaping plan and thus at no extra cost?

The cost of flowers can't always be justified in terms of adding real value to a property, but flowers frequently help to sell a property. When a prospective buyer drives up to your house on a spring afternoon, who's to say $25 spent on a flurry of daffodils and tulips won't have been worth the expense? The $6 worth of petunias flowing out of your windowbox won't be there next summer, but maybe you won't be either if they've helped you sell your house. *The key to spending money for flowers is to buy enough of one kind to make an effect*—and then plant them where they will thrive and be seen.

A friend of mine confesses that some beautiful deep-blue irises lining a stone path almost led her to buy a slightly overpriced house. While trying to weigh and put values on the qualities she liked and disliked about the house, my friend admits the picture created by the irises kept deviling her normally clear-thinking mind. Those irises became one of her overriding images of the property, completely outweighing their $30 value.

To protect your investment in landscaping, proper culture and maintenance are essential. Don't spend any money for plants you aren't willing or able to take care of. In fact, plants can actually *detract* value from your property if they look neglected or unhealthy.

Keep that added 15 percent for mature landscaping in mind and you will not forget to feed your hedge or water your rhododendron or prune your crabapple. You may even want to hire a professional landscape gardener to take you through one season with your landscaping so you can learn the best way to care for it.

PENNY LOEB

Above: How much better this house would look with its foundation plantings trimmed and its driveway spruced up with a few gallons of blacktop sealer. Rather than inviting the visitor in, the plantings are barriers to the front door that seem to say Go Away. Potential buyers might. *Below*: Most homeowners prefer the carefully pruned shrubbery and well-maintained driveway of this house to the overgrown landscaping of its neighbor.

PENNY LOEB

PENNY LOEB

These two houses show the value of attention to the entrance area. Plantings and paint are two of the most cost-effective improvements you can make. The brick walks of the house above are expensive, but what do they do for the overall look? The foundation planting of the house below is less expensive and much more attractive.

PENNY LOEB

PENNY LOEB

PENNY LOEB

Opposite: You don't have to spend much money to achieve a lovely, tranquil, ethereal look. Here we see the effect of simple white stones and ivy. A brick patio, laid in dry sand in an afternoon, provides an attractive feature for very little expense.

Below: We all want to have privacy and to block ugly views, but this expensive eyesore is hardly the answer. For the same amount of money, this homeowner could have installed handsome pine trees.

HOWARD BLUME

6

CREATING NEW LIVING SPACE

Knocking down, building up, concealing, and rearranging; exposing and covering, raising and lowering, subtracting and adding—there are as many different ways of expanding your living space as there are people who feel cramped in their homes. The question is this: Is the improvement you're considering going to be *worthwhile*, not only in terms of immediate comfort, but also in terms of the profits it can add when the time comes to sell?

As we already know, improvements that increase space generally give the highest return, provided they're in keeping with the neighborhood and aren't extravagant. But there are some important criteria that must be considered if you want to maintain a balance between present convenience and future stability. Ask yourself the following questions.

Is it possible to improve living space simply by changing the function of existing rooms? Can you, for example, convert the little-used guest bedroom into a private den or workshop, or enlarge the living room to include the dining area and let the family eat in the kitchen?

Is what you plan to do within the law? Are there zoning ordinances that may limit your expansion or building permits that are difficult to get?

Is the improvement you're considering practical? Consider such things as cost, storage, air circulation, convenient traffic patterns, decor you'll be able to live with.

Will the improvement look good? Will it constitute a visual asset—or, put another way, will it visually detract from either the interior or exterior of your home?

There are three basic types of space-creating improvements you can make. We'll look at each in turn in the rest of this chapter.

Stage I: Minor Renovation

Features of a house that detract from a feeling of space are often overlooked after we've lived with them for a while. Take, for instance, a door that opens the wrong way. If you've got one, you may have made a mental note some time ago to rehang it so that it swings in the proper direction. As time passed, you let the job go, developing a tolerance to inconvenience. But such a minor renovation can make a big difference in how the room looks and feels.

It wasn't until I purchased an old oak wardrobe from a friend that I discovered the improvement an altered door can make. I feared I had no place to put such a big piece until it occurred to me that the wardrobe would fit nicely in the space where the opened door had stood for three years. Now we have both extra storage *and* a new focal point for the room instead of dead space and an uninteresting corner.

Traffic Patterns

The apparent size of a room can be increased or decreased, depending on the kind of access people have to it. By blocking off an extra living-room entrance, for example, and rerouting all the traffic through the adjacent hall into the kitchen, you will create a living-room space that's more conducive to privacy and good conversation. (People are no longer charging through to get a sandwich or answer the kitchen phone.) An added dividend is that the blocked-off entrance will increase the wallspace in the kitchen and may serve as an area for a counter or a piece of furniture.

It's easy to get used to inconvenience. Cast a cold eye at the arrangement of your "public" rooms: kitchen, living room, dining room, and den or library. Plot them on graph paper, if that helps you visualize their arrangement. See if there isn't a more effective way to get from one room to another. Consider removing a wall entirely or creating a passthrough—between kitchen and dining room, say.

Just as removing a door can create more space, so can adding one—if you add it in the right spot. A new door that opens from the hall into the dining room, for example, will invite people to avoid the living room instead of tramping through it. A second entrance from the family room into the bathroom eliminates congestion in the kitchen, where the only entrance to the bathroom was originally located.

Consider installing space-saving doors in areas where there is limited space, such as between dining room and kitchen. Folding doors hung from tracks are often advisable for wide openings, such as between dining room and living room. A split-door arrangement, in which half the door rests against each side of the frame when opened, is another possibility. (Hinging a split door in the middle allows only one side of the frame to receive the halved door when it is open.) Track-hung sliding doors are yet another possibility. If there's a clear space to one side of an opening, the door can be hung on a track and slid along the empty wall. In new construction, doors can be made to slide right *into* the wall.

The removal secret

A cheap and surprisingly effective means of increasing the apparent space in a room is to remove some of the furniture and rearrange what remains so that different areas of function (eating, lounging, sleeping, and so on) are well defined. Nothing detracts from a feeling of spaciousness as much as a disorganized clutter of objects, whether furniture or accessories. Miraculous transformations can be achieved simply by removing excess furniture and paraphernalia—or at least rearranging them in a more effective manner.

Storage space

Nooks and crannies you never thought to use can be adapted to store clutter and make a house look bigger. Space under a stairway can be inexpensively converted into a utility storage area. Narrow bookcases can line a hall, surround windows, frame a fireplace. Doors of pantry and kitchen cabinets can be lined with narrow shelves to accommodate extra cans and utensils. Even the toe space under the kitchen counters can be used to store cans and bottles (a magnetic board can be installed to hide them from sight). These are little extras buyers fall in love with. The challenge is to store items as inconspicuously as possible so that storage plans *enhance* the feeling of space rather than detract from it. Remember that space used well is space made.

Here are ten additional space-utilizing ideas.

1. Sliding rack above the refrigerator or stove to store pots.

2. Built-in vanity, wall storage units, and multiple towel bars in the bathroom.

3. Sports locker, spice rack, phone holder, bathroom organizer, three-way mirror—any of these can be built into a wall between the studs.

4. Multipurpose storage modules that double as room dividers.

5. Rolling carts and center work island for the kitchen.

6. Overhead shelves for open display around the perimeter of any room.

7. Built-in drawers and storage areas under platform beds.

8. Circular clothes rack and/or double rods in high-ceilinged closets for hanging off-season clothes high up.

9. Window seats with storage underneath.

10. Fold-out storage units, especially useful in the kitchen. (They can be created in a former doorway that has been closed off to reroute traffic.)

DECORATING FOR DIMENSION

How a room is decorated affects the feeling of space in that room. The lighter and paler its wall color, the larger the room appears. The fewer changes in pattern, color, and texture, the larger the room looks. A border on a plain wall or a strongly contrasting wainscoting visually draws the room in and makes it appear smaller.

One of the quickest and cheapest ways to create an illusion of more space is with color. For more information on the effects of color and patterns on room size, consult chapter 3.

LIGHTING AND ILLUSIONS OF GRANDEUR

Installing larger windows and skylights can greatly increase the feeling of spaciousness in a house. If need be, sills can be positioned higher than usual to accommodate a sink or a large piece of furniture, giving an interesting horizontal expanse of light. Windows can be cut into inside walls to lighten dark parts of a house. Fixed windows—windows that let in light but don't open—are far less costly than windows that open. Not all windows in a house need to open. One of the most exciting houses I've ever seen (in Woodstock, New York) had a single wall of fixed windows of differently sized and shaped pieces of colored glass. When the afternoon sun shone on this west wall, the streams of light created all colors of space-enhancing rays.

The positioning of windows has surprising effects on the layout of the room. An ill-placed window can easily interfere with a comfortable and pleasing bed placement or some other convenient furniture arrangement. For an outlay of $200 or $300 you may be able simply to reposition a window. Raising a window, for example, could add just the amount of space you need.

Mirrors can work wonders, since their effect is to visually double existing space. If you have a dark, unused area in your house, you may be able to turn it into a light, functional space simply by adding mirrors. Consider using 4-, 6-, or even 8-inch mirror squares, which are easy to put up yourself and are much less expensive than big sheets of mirror.

As a cost-effective investment, light-creating improvements yield among the highest immediate and long-term returns.

TIPS ON CEILING HEIGHT

If you compare two living rooms with the same floor measurement and wall color, one of which has a 12-foot ceiling and the other an 8-

foot ceiling, the room with the higher ceiling will look larger by far. Unfortunately, raising a low ceiling usually isn't possible since the rafters which support the ceiling can't be raised. (An exception is the creation of a cathedral ceiling; in this case the old plaster or Sheet-rock is removed, the rafters exposed, and the under-the-roof-ceiling finished off.) Here are a few tricks of the trade, however, which can help to create the *illusion* of a higher ceiling.

- *Paint the ceiling a light color.* White is best. A matte finish is more in keeping with convention than a glossy one, and subtly reflects light in such a way that the room "opens up" from above.

- *Install indirect lighting.* Ceiling fixtures that line the perimeter of the room reflect light off the walls. The old central overhead light doesn't accomplish the same thing. Besides being harsh, it casts shadows that make a room look smaller.

  Lighting that seems to raise a ceiling can be accomplished with floor lamps, pole lamps, track lights, and even table lamps that are carefully arranged along the outside walls and shaded in such a way as to reflect light off the ceiling.

  Shoji screens laid on a gridwork with soft light behind them also help illuminate a ceiling. Not only can this give an unusual, spacious feeling to an entire room, but the screens can be used to hide unsightly pipes or a flawed ceiling.

- *Round off the ceiling corners.* Although time consuming and fairly costly, this trick is highly effective because "blurring" the edges causes the eye to drift, making the room seem larger. Insert sections of metal curves over the joints, where ceiling and walls meet, and plaster to blend.

Stage II: Structural Renovation

Existing spaces can be made more useful in one of three ways: *combining* small rooms to create a larger space; *dividing* a large room to make small rooms that function differently; *converting* a room so that it can be used for something else.

Common combinations are hallway with living room, kitchen with dining room, pantry with kitchen. Rooms that are often divided in two are a large bedroom to form two smaller ones; a living room to form a foyer; and a combined living and dining room to form an eat-in kitchen and a separate living room.

The most common conversions in houses today are garage to family room, screened-in porch to den, carport to kitchen, and deck to breakfast room.

Even though structural renovations are expensive, they nevertheless provide a substantial hedge against inflation. Converting into usable space any structure that already has a roof, a wall, and a floor is going to cost less money than would be required to create living space from scratch. And in addition to your inflation hedge, you'll have more space to live in.

FIRST STEPS IN PLANNING A STRUCTURAL RENOVATION

Visualizing how your improvement will look and how much extra space it will provide is the first step to successful and potentially profitable renovation. Analyzing your family's needs is the second step. This order of priority may seem wrong—but consider. Isn't assigning priority to the profit potential of the family's biggest investment really putting family first?

Before proceeding with a major renovation project you may want to build a model to scale, using lightweight strips of balsa wood and fast-drying glue. Make sure to review furniture requirements and think carefully about window and door placement. The position of electrical outlets should be measured, bearing in mind their intended use. (This is the time to reevaluate insulation needs. You'll want sound insulation in room dividers, for instance, and heat insulation in external walls.)

When planning your Stage II renovation, don't forget to consider how the outside of the house will be affected. If you're going to convert your garage into a family room, try to keep the windows similar in type, size, and height to those in the house—maintaining aesthetic consistency.

Walls: SUBTRACTIONS AND ADDITIONS

Visualizing the effect of knocking out a wall can be quite exciting when you get a sense of the space that will be created by its removal. However, these fantasies are worthless expenditures of creative energy if the wall you're considering can't be torn down because it happens to be holding up the house. Weight-bearing walls must remain in place, or nearby areas must be reinforced to allow for their removal.

Several easy-to-remember rules apply here. *All outside walls are weight bearing.* Internal walls that run parallel to the floor joists are weight bearing; nonbearing walls run perpendicular to the floor joists. A simple way to check is to look at the way the floorboards are nailed to the floor joists. If they're perpendicular to the wall, the floor is probably load bearing. If they run parallel to the wall, the floor is probably not load bearing.

Before attempting any wall removal, consult a professional. There are exceptions to these rules. For example, in very old houses *all* the walls bear some weight because of years of settling. A contractor will be able to advise you not only in identifying structurally important walls, but also in methods of reinforcement that will allow you to remove what you want to remove.

Another important consideration in the removal of walls has to do with what's inside them. It's imperative that you consider the location of wires, heating ducts, and water pipes when planning any wall-removal project, both to save costly repair and adjustment later and to assure adequate function of the new space.

HEATING. Can pipes, radiators, and/or ducts be removed without a major overhaul of the entire heating system? If you're adding a wall, can the present heating system be adapted to accommodate the room division?

ELECTRICITY. Now is a good time to check the condition of the wiring. If the house is old, are the cables worn or the electrical supply inadequate? A qualified electrician is a must for safe rerouting of cables and fittings, as well as for the installation of new outlets, if you're planning a new wall.

PLUMBING. If the drain from an upstairs bathroom runs through the wall you're hoping to remove, a major renovation of the waste-line system may be required. By the same token, if you're planning to wall off a corner of the bedroom to create a new half-bathroom, consider carefully the cost of bringing water to and from the site. In either of these cases you'll want to consult a plumber and ask for estimates before proceeding with a project that could cost more than it's worth.

CREATING AN ATTIC NEST

My wife and I have a housetop suite, a 26-by-35-foot room of our own, complete with beautifully refinished wide pine floor, a huge sliding glass window that allows light and sun to illuminate and enhance the natural wood walls, white sheetrocked ceiling, and a variegated wood canopy in the gable over our bed. This dramatic renovation of previously unused space cost us $1,500 seven years ago (about half of what it would have cost if I hadn't done the work myself). But figure the returns. If the average price of new construction was $20 a square foot seven years ago (it's now about $40 a square foot), to have created that much living space from scratch would have cost over $18,000 then and would today cost over $35,000.

While remarkably economical as a space provider, attic renovation takes careful planning. Below are some special considerations.

MAKE SURE THE FLOOR IS STRONG ENOUGH. Building codes will apprise you of the minimum size of floor joist required to adequately support your new attic living space. If you have two-by-six joists (which many houses do), they may well be adequate for supporting additional weight. If the span between joists is unusually large, however, two-by-eights will be needed. Some homes are built with two-by-four beams, and when attic conversion is desired the floor has to be reinforced by a professional to provide the required support.

CHECK FOR SUFFICIENT HEADROOM. A minimum of 8 feet is considered adequate headroom unless the room is to be used as a playroom for small children. Headroom can be increased by raising the entire roof (this can be prohibitively expensive), building a shed dormer, or installing a conventional dormer. Make sure there's at least an 18-inch extension from the exterior wall to ensure the most headroom for the price. Shed roofs provide more space than dormers, but cost more to build.

If the headroom is adequate to begin with, large windows installed at the gable ends provide space-enhancing light and ventilation. Large areas of fixed glass, as noted, are cheaper to purchase than windows that can be opened, and ventilation can be provided with either vents or a small, strategically located conventional window.

MEETING INCREASED INSULATION NEEDS. Because of the close proximity of the roof to the outside elements it's essential to have plenty of insulation in your attic room. The ceiling should get at least 6 inches of batting and may require as much as 12 inches, depending on the area of the country in which you live (see map on page 163). Extra floor insulation isn't necessary if the attic space is to be heated and cooled in the same way as the rest of the house. But leave any previously installed floor insulation; it will provide a good barrier against sound from the rooms below.

HEATING AND COOLING A ROOFTOP HAVEN. For heating my attic suite, I use a small woodstove that is flued into an existing chimney. This has a few disadvantages, such as making it necessary for me to haul the wood up and the ashes down, but it's cheap.

Usually it costs less to install a gas heater or even electric baseboard heat than to extend the existing heating system into the attic. (Floor vents will encourage hot air to rise from below, but the disadvantage is that noise will rise from below as well.)

Sometimes attic rooms can be successfully incorporated into a central air-conditioning system. If not, an individual unit can be installed, provided the wiring is specifically for that purpose and overload on the electrical system isn't created.

GETTING UP THERE. Ultimately, the convenience of the stairs is paramount to the functionality of the attic room. The ideal stairway to an

attic is 3 feet wide and rises at a 30- to 35-degree angle. Safety becomes an issue with stairs that are steeper. Ideally, tread depth plus
riser height should together equal no fewer than 18 inches.

Pull-down stairs can be used if there's really a premium on space,
but they're inconvenient if you want to carry anything besides yourself upstairs (a basket of laundry or a peanut-butter sandwich and a
glass of milk).

ENHANCING SPACE WITH A CATHEDRAL CEILING

Many people these days remove a low ceiling and finish off the underside of the roof with insulation and Sheetrock. The result can be a
dramatic effect of spaciousness. However, care has to be taken to pre-
serve the structural integrity of the house in the floor joists. Sometimes it's possible to remove all but a few supporting beams, but often
all have to be retained. You can box them in or simply expose them
for an interesting horizontal contrast against the peak of the roof.

Cathedral ceilings have two disadvantages: (1) they aren't particularly energy efficient, since warm air rises into the unused space and
remains there; and (2) perhaps more important, the attic space is gone
forever.

LOFTS FOR INCREASED LIVING SPACE

A bed takes up valuable living space in a room. Creating a loft area
for the bed utilizes upper space, which previously just collected dust
and hot air, and frees the floor space for any number of functions.

With an 8-foot ceiling, a loft is out of the question unless the ceiling of the room below can be dropped. But a 10-foot or higher ceiling
can accommodate a loft with varying amounts of headroom above and
below.

Crucial to the functioning of a loft is a stairway that's easily
climbed. While conventional stairs take up considerable space, they'll
probably allow you to get the most use out of those lofty spaces. Too
often the loft that was created to increase space in the home proves
nearly impossible to utilize because access is via a toothpick ladder
only.

Also, consider an opening skylight and have plenty of windows to ensure good ventilation and cooling breezes in summer.

PLATFORMS: SINKING AND RISING

If the ceiling is too low to allow you to build a loft, consider a platform to increase the feeling of space. Raising a dining area 2 feet or so on a framed and carpeted plywood platform not only gives new definition to the eating area but creates new storage space as well. The platform—really just a big three-sided box—can likely be constructed for $500 or so.

Another trick is to sink your bathtub. Not only will the bathroom look bigger with the tub at floor level, but the effect on the underside (that is, the lowered ceiling in the area below the tub) can suggest, for example, a cozy dining room or a more intimate living-room conversation area, depending upon where the bathroom is located.

Building platforms for beds increases the available space for storage by providing convenient under-the-bed space to keep shoes, off-season clothes, and so forth.

GOING DOWN: BASEMENT REMODELING

Although *the demand for basement recreations has definitely decreased in the last ten years*, basement renovation can still be a smart move for the homeowner who has limited cash and a serious need for more functional living space. A laundry room for washing, drying, and folding clothes is a good way of making otherwise wasted basement space functional. So is a workroom or an exercise area. You might consider an away-from-it-all playroom for the children. But don't spend your money on a wet bar and expensive paneling. Today people want a *functional* below-grade space, not a pleasure pit.

There are three main problems the homeowner will encounter in basement remodeling: moisture, ventilation, and lighting. Dampness originates from one or more of three sources: moisture that rises from underneath the foundation; moisture that penetrates the walls as a result of deterioration or faulty construction; and moisture that collects on walls, floors, and ceilings from condensation. A dehumidifier and weather-sealing paint on the interior walls can help reduce some of the moisture, but the cause of the problem must be found and corrected before conversion is begun. (For detailed information on how to correct a waterlogged basement, see chapter 3.)

Problems of ventilation and light are usually solved simultaneously. Windows provide the ideal ventilation for a basement room. They let in light as well as air and help prevent the dungeon syndrome.

Sometimes it's feasible to enlarge small cellar windows by digging wells outside, which are reinforced to hold back ground-level dirt. It may also be possible to build shafts or ducts into the walls from above-ground windows; the shafts serve to provide light and ventilation for the basement. One particularly effective approach is the basement bubble greenhouse which, when built adjacent to a below-grade family room, serves as a source of light and air for the entire below-grade living space.

If there's no natural light available, artificial lights that give the illusion of daytime are best. Recessed ceiling lights and track lights that run around the perimeter of the room and reflect off the walls make the room appear larger and less like an underground cave. Mirrors and light-colored walls and ceiling add considerably to the feeling of light and space. You may want to consider some of these lighting techniques even if your basement is not refinished. A clean, bright, adequately lit basement is inviting to potential buyers. They imagine workshops and laundry rooms and fast games of Ping-Pong with the kids. Dark, damp, smelly basements, on the other hand, definitely *detract* from the overall appeal of your house. They summon forth images of mold, mildew, and slithery creatures—no way to pry that extra few thousand dollars from a buyer.

Basement rooms have excellent acoustical insulation from the rest of the house by virtue of their thick walls, solid doors, small or absent windows, and low ceilings. However, there's usually an increased resonance within the basement itself for these same reasons. For the best noise reduction, use sound-absorbing finishes on walls, ceilings, and floors (such as Homosote, curtains, moisture-repellent carpet, acoustical tile). If, as in some old houses, there is only the flooring for the ground floor and no actual basement ceiling, you may want to consider insulating under that flooring. It will provide a sound barrier and prevent any basement moisture from seeping upstairs through the floorboards.

To finish off basement walls, paneling is preferable to wallboard because of its greater resistance to moisture damage. Wallpaper and paint are likely to peel if there's a constant presence of even a tiny amount of moisture, so products that are moisture-proof or moisture-resistant (plastics and treated synthetic fibers) are the most appropriate for below-grade use.

Stage III: Building Out

Before you decide on the size and type of any major addition, ask yourself a lot of questions. If the addition is going to be a family room, it helps to know, for example, if teenagers are going to use it for a disco palace or if toddlers are going to use it for a playroom. If the former, you're going to want good sound insulation and as much distance as possible from the rest of the family's activities. If it's a playroom for toddlers, you want to situate it close to parents and the heart of the house.

Practical creation of new living space takes hours of careful evaluation if it's to be an economically sound and useful improvement. Here are some aspects you should consider.

Know exactly what the addition is to be used for. Plan storage space, entrances and exits, position in relation to the rest of the house, as well as the *minimum* amount of space required for optimum function in terms of light, ventilation, heating, cooling, and electrical supply.

Consider carefully the design of the addition as it relates to the rest of the house. Ordinarily it's best to extend the character of the main house to the addition. This includes such aspects of style as pitch of roof and roof finish, color of siding, type and placement of windows and doors, and floor and wall finishes.

If continuity of design isn't possible, strive for an artful but definite contrast rather than a middle-of-the-road compromise that will end up looking as if you don't know what you're doing. Be clear, be thoughtful, be decisive, and your house—addition and all—will have character and integrity.

Find out the requirements of the building codes in your area. It may be that you can't build what you'd like where you'd like or that the plan you were intending to follow doesn't incorporate the lawfully required structural support. We know people who had their 200-year-old house completely rewired. Six months later the whole job had to be done over again—including ripping holes in newly sheetrocked walls—because neither the owner nor the electrician had paid attention to local electrical codes. An ounce of prevention—*and* a licensed electrician, whom these people forebore to use, thinking they'd save money—would have prevented the loss of several thousand dollars.

Consider such factors as wind direction, sun position, and the location of neighboring houses in relation to the site of your proposed improvement. You won't want to block out morning sun or interfere with privacy—yours or your neighbors'.

One of the most incredible blunders I ever witnessed was the construction of a beautiful new "sun room" on the north side of a house in New Hampshire. The sun room made the house miserable in winter because the cold north winds blew right through the window frames, even with an additional heat source in the sun room and extra insulation. What's more, the room could be used only in late spring, summer, and very early fall. The rest of the time it became a storage bin. Had the sun room been located on the south or even the east side of the house, it could have been used comfortably year round.

Think beyond the room's immediate use. For example, if a new family room will eventually be used as an apartment for an elderly relative, it's far less costly to install the plumbing lines that will be used in a later bathroom than to add them at some future time.

Use initiative in the management phase of construction. The total cost of your new addition can be fairly equally divided among materials, labor, and management expense. If you plan well during the management phase, you'll be able to save considerably on both labor and materials. If, due to lack of adequate planning, you are forced to make changes during construction, the addition will cost two or three times what it would have had it been built right during the original construction.

A CHEAP BUT SOLID FOUNDATION

In building your addition you will not necessarily need a full cellar with crawlspace. Consider the slab-on-grade construction, which is far cheaper and perfectly functional. Moisture proofing and insulation are incorporated right into the slab construction, making it suitable as a foundation beneath an extension in most parts of the country. (Areas subject to extremes of cold may be exceptions.)

ROOFING THE ADDITION

A simple gable roof is the cheapest. Ridges or valleys, such as over a dormer window, increase the cost of a roof because extra construction is required. Flat and low-pitched roofs require heavier structural support to hold the roofing materials. Also, several layers of asphalt are needed to keep out moisture in a flat or low-pitched roof. The extra cost in labor and materials can add $1,000 to the cost of the roof.

WALLS AND WINDOWS

If you live in a warm climate you can save yourself a considerable amount of money if you use a single type of material for both exterior and interior walls. Stone is the most expensive of such possibilities. Then come split rock, brick, concrete block, and cinder block.

In northern climates it's necessary to treat exterior and interior walls differently to eliminate heat loss in winter. A masonry-veneer wall is slightly more expensive than a solid masonry wall but cuts heating and cooling costs considerably.

The size and number of windows also affect heating and cooling costs. In new construction, the cost of installing a sliding glass door is about equal to the cost of building a solid wall, but measured against the heat loss that occurs naturally through large sections of glass—even when double glazed—the glass is more expensive.

In northern climates, windows in the north wall of any addition should be kept to a minimum. Storm windows or double-glazed panes will reduce heat loss by half. Generally, wooden frames and sashes tend to insulate better than aluminum, which was traditionally used only in warm climates. New vinyl-and-aluminum frames, however, have built-in thermal breaks that stop the transfer of heat and cold from the outside to the inside and cost almost half of what wooden frames cost.

Doors

If sound insulation isn't a concern, hollow-core doors are the least expensive you can buy. Standard sizes are cheaper and easily installed into most existing frames.

It's often possible to buy good doors—sometimes beautiful solid and paneled ones—at used-furniture places, garage sales, and demolition companies. (When contemplating a hand-carved oak door complete with gargoyles, though, remember that you want to maintain continuity with the rest of your house.)

Electricity

The cost of wiring your addition depends on the condition of your present electrical system. Often a larger electrical service will be needed because your current system is either antiquated or large enough to accommodate only existing electrical needs.

Using modestly priced fixtures and adding just enough new wiring to meet codes and provide convenience can help keep costs down. If, however, you think you may one day want to install a spotlight or a washer and dryer in the new addition, it's better to do the wiring for that now. A return visit from the electrician, when his hourly rate will no doubt be higher and when he'll have to rip out and replace pieces of wall and floorboard, is bound to end up costing you more.

It's always wise to hire a *licensed* electrician whose work will meet code standards. Wiring is not the place to try to save a few bucks, as our friends with the 200-year-old house would be the first to tell you.

Plumbing

Sometimes the biggest headache in building an addition is caused by its distance from the water source or the waste-disposal site. If you add a master bedroom with bath, the bathroom hot-water faucet may be the farthest point in the house from the hot-water tank, and the toilet may be on the opposite end of the house from the main drain line to the septic tank.

While it's possible to run in new pipes for both purposes, the cost will be high and the efficiency of the system marginal. It may take as long as five minutes to get hot water to and waste away from the addition's bath. And if plastic piping is used, the sounds of both will be heard coursing through the rest of the house. Thoughtlessly rigged plumbing is no fun. It can take the edge off the pleasure from your new, hard-earned addition and can make potential buyers suspicious.

Concentrate the location of plumbing fixtures to reduce piping costs. When possible, create a new bathroom over an existing kitchen or bath so that the plumbing is stacked. This keeps costs at a minimum compared with running new lines in new directions. Consider a second water heater rather than a single larger one. The first might be installed close to the downstairs bathroom, where it would handle the hot-water needs of additional fixtures in the area. A second heater could be installed in another part of the house to handle the needs of, say, laundry room and master bath. (For maximum efficiency, a water heater should *never* be farther than 15 feet from the taps.)

Fixtures themselves vary widely in quality and price. Bathtubs made of iron with a porcelain-enamel finish are the most expensive *and* the most durable. The next most expensive tub is steel with porcelain finish; tubs of acrylic and fiberglass-reinforced polyester are the cheapest.

Lavatory and bathroom cabinet materials, from the most expensive to the cheapest, are vitreous china, enameled cast iron, stainless steel, and malamine plastic. Enameled cast-iron sinks are the most expensive, followed by enameled steel and stainless steel.

Colored fixtures are always more expensive than white ones. In general, good-looking fixtures that fit your space and maintain your total house image are what's important—the particular kind of construction matters much less.

If there could be a single rule to guide you in the wise—and financially sound—renovating of your house investment, it would be plan, plan, plan. If you use contractors and subcontractors, don't leave the work up to them. Be involved every step of the way so you can assure your-self that the project is going according to plan and can intervene be-fore some costly mistake is made. Even if you are hiring the most highly qualified workers you can find, don't leave things to chance. Consider the workers your collaborators and remain as actively and as thoughtfully involved in the whole process as if your most precious asset were at stake. It is!

HOWARD BLUME

Bifold doors hiding this laundry center give the bathroom in which it's located a space-saving double function.

This space-saving peninsula is made of plywood, nicely designed and painted to give it a quality look. A center island or peninsula with plenty of storage space is a highly attractive feature.

Open storage is a good, inexpensive way to increase your space if it's tastefully done.

This spice rack, hidden and hinged in the cabinet, saves space and gives a tidy look when the doors are closed.

126

Nothing enhances a house like the light from a skylight. And the effect on plants is an extra bonus.

HOWARD BLUME

PENNY LOEB

Handsome, large windows that bring the outside in are more attractive than walls. Note the overhead canister light—simple and effective.

There's no limit to what you can accomplish with glass. This small house is made infinitely more interesting by its unusual window treatment.

PENNY LOEB

PENNY LOEB

Sliding doors of glass are the most cost-effective way of gaining large areas of light. A large skylight is good for a semi–outdoor porch where you don't have to worry about energy loss.

Two ways to enhance space: visually, with light, and structurally, with a window seat. If you have a bay window, by all means add a window seat; it's almost like adding an extra room.

This spacious living room was originally two small parlors. The visible beam in the middle is hardly noticeable when you're actually in the room.

Every bit of space can be used: The eaves behind a refinished attic were converted into this little getaway space. Interest and coziness were added with stained-glass light.

A typical inexpensive attic refinishing, ideal for a children's room, TV room, guest room. Short walls at either side help make the room seem less like an attic, and storage space can be created behind them.

PENNY LOEB

A loft is an innovative way to gain extra space if you have a high ceiling or unused attic space. Here, a rolling ladder presents an unusual means of access that doesn't interfere with the main space.

PENNY LOEB

This dining room was formerly an unused porch. The solar window greenhouse keeps it warm during the day and provides a showcase for a cactus collection.

Below: Here is an outside view of the former porch, now enclosed to create the dining room (above) and a living room/study. The vinyl siding is good-looking and care-free.

HOWARD BLUME

HOWARD BLUME

7

THE SIX COSTLIEST MISTAKES MADE BY HOME IMPROVERS

Basically, there are two reasons for making home improvements: to be more comfortable and to earn a larger return on that major investment, your home. Unfortunately, the two don't always go hand in hand. If, for example, you were to build a 700-square-foot family room onto your house, the convenience and comfort your family would derive from it would only partly compensate for the $20,000 the addition could cost. When the time came to sell, you might well expect to receive more compensation money than the buyer would be willing to give you.

Your improvement will fail to increase the value of your house if (1) the neighboring houses do *not* have family rooms, (2) the workmanship in your house is shoddy, (3) the decor is eccentric or the style and design of "improvements" are not in keeping with the rest of the house, and (4) a buyer can build a new house of equal size for less money than you are asking for yours.

A 100 percent *immediate* payback on an improvement such as the $20,000 family room is rare simply because it's more expensive to build on than to start from scratch and plan your space from the bottom up. Existing houses, however, increase in demand as the price of new construction keeps climbing, and the greater the demand for existing homes, the greater your chances of realizing added value—especially when you make the right improvements.

Improvements that increase space usually offer the greatest compensation when it comes time for you to sell. Adding a family room in the basement, or putting a bathroom on the first floor, or extending your kitchen are improvements that usually pay back well. But before you pick up a hammer or hire a contractor, consider the *kinds of improvements that will be best*—their quality and appropriateness. Homeowners too often overimprove, which simply means that *they will never get their money back* because no one else is as interested as they are in the improvements they have made.* A rough guide to home-improvement payback looks like this:

IMPROVEMENT	EXPECTED IMMEDIATE RETURN ON COST (PERCENT)
Added space (plain, minimum cost)	75–100
Modernization (such as upgrading bathrooms or kitchen appliances)	50–75
Added luxury items (such as hot tub or tennis court)	0–50

A wise investor considers the improvement's potential to increase the value of his or her home as well as to meet the family's needs, and then figures out what he or she can reasonably expect to get back on the investment in the future. Balancing your family's personal needs against what would make the most financial sense isn't always easy, and chapter 8 will deal with just that dilemma. This chapter cautions you against the improvements most likely to make you *lose* money.

*Over time, say five to ten years, nearly all improvements will return their cost plus investment "interest" due to inflation and increased replacement costs. However, the improvements with the greatest *immediate* return through increased value will also give you the greatest *long-term* profits.

1. OVERIMPROVING FOR THE NEIGHBORHOOD (OR CASTLES IN THE SUBURBS)

Every time I travel to New Jersey to visit my relatives I pass a lovely house with a greenhouse, swimming pool, and Japanese garden and marvel at the absurdity of it. It belongs not among the conventional tract houses of the neighborhood, but on a nice wooded piece of property, away from the surrounding city. Though charming and well groomed, the house, because of its location, becomes ridiculous—almost an eyesore. The owner may be happy living in it, but he's sure to be disappointed if he ever puts his house on the market and expects it to draw $30,000 more than the house on his left is worth. Taking an educated guess I'd say he'll eventually sell that house for maybe $2,000 more than the houses are going for in his immediate neighborhood—hardly enough to compensate for the landscaping.

Before you consider any improvement, look realistically at the houses around you. If the home-improvement project you're thinking about will bring your house up to neighborhood standards (for example, creating a family room when most houses in the neighborhood have family rooms), then you can begin your addition confident that when you sell you will get a price that reflects cost plus return on the space you've added. If, on the other hand, all the houses in your vicinity are about the same size and offer approximately the same features, adding a fourth bedroom, say, may not raise the market value of your home very much—certainly not enough to make up what you'll pay for the addition. (A less ambitious improvement, such as adding shutters, will pay off very well, however.) So think again before adding that guest bedroom for your mother-in-law.

MARKET TRENDS AND LOCATION

A declining neighborhood is not the place to improve a house unless there are sure signs that a reverse trend has begun and that property values will increase with renovation. Such a reverse trend is occurring in many cities today. "Sweat equity," however, will never ensure cash equity when the location is poor and demand for houses in an area has dropped. *If it is to carry a potential for profit, any improvement must be measured against location, buyer demand, and marketing trends.*

2. Diminished Net Living Space (The Case of the Nonfunctional Living Room)

Tom Hacket and his family bought into a co-op in the late sixties. The co-op, which cost $90,000, was spacious and quite elegant, although it had only two bedrooms. Since the living room was unusually long, and the family's need for a third bedroom pressing (there were three kids in the family), Tom decided to create a new bedroom by installing a wall and door at one end of the living room. The work—done by professionals—was expert, and at first everyone was pleased.

It soon became evident, however, that while the new bedroom was functional and attractive, the new living room was anything but. Once elegant with its flood of light from several large windows, it had unintentionally been transformed into a small, rather dark foyer leading to a huge, well-lighted bedroom.

Tom suspected the worst: that if he wanted to receive top dollar for his co-op in the future, he would have to return the living room to its original size. Fortunately (when the time came for them to sell, four and a half years later), he was able to rip out the wall with a minimal amount of damage and expense, although he had to spend close to $5,000 on new carpet and wallpaper.

This is a ploy that can certainly be used by the home investor: Make the place right for your own purposes, but change it when the time comes to sell. Chances are, though, that you won't end up with much profit, materials and labor costing what they do today. Tom claims he didn't lose much money and the changing back and forth was personally valuable. "The convenience of that third bedroom was worth a lot to us," he maintains; "more than the cost of removing a wall and buying new carpet, which it needed anyway!" But Tom is the first to admit that he would have lost thousands of dollars more if he'd *left* the glorious bedroom and the dinky living room. He knows that buyers like large, open spaces and are repelled by living places that are chopped up into small, dark rooms.

Valuable Alternatives to Diminished Space

Sometimes, for our own personal convenience, we want to *reduce* actual living space. People have been known to cut into a living room to add space for a two-car garage or to extend a beloved garden. In the interest of wise investment, however, any change that would *diminish* net living space should be carefully considered. Installation of temporary dividers or walls that can be easily removed at some future date may be a better solution than hard-to-remove structural alterations. After all, one measure of the value of a house is square footage of usable space.

Additional adjacent rooms that route traffic through existing living space (even though they create more space) can be better accepted in the marketplace if they have independent entrances created by additional hallways and foyers.

Loft beds, which utilize empty or wasted spaces, can provide a good alternative to partitioning off a large bedroom into two small rooms with less light and ventilation.

3. Eccentric Decor

Color Coded for Loss

Bill and Mary O'Donnell paid a bargain price for their seventy-year-old house in Upstate New York, and it wasn't just luck. The house had been on the market for more than two years, and the asking price had been reduced from $49,500 to the $40,000 they paid. The house was in good shape structurally, and all things being equal, there was only one reason why it hadn't sold—color! Someone had gone crazy with paint and paper. The entrance hall was bright green; the living room bright blue; and the busy, poppy-orange wallpaper in the dining room was enough to ruin your digestion. Every room in the house shouted bright color and uncommon definition. Even the realtor, before putting the key in the lock, apologized for this eccentricity.

Because of flamboyant color choice, the seller took a $9,500 loss on his house. And the O'Donnells made good on their investment. Ten gallons of off-white paint and $800 in labor charges quickly neutralized the disturbing effect of all that color and increased the resale value of their home within the first two weeks of ownership. A local broker told them if they wanted to sell next day they could probably get $50,000—$10,000 more than they'd paid for the place.

TREES AND INITIALS

Eccentric decor may reflect individuality, but it is singular: No one else will appreciate it as you do or be willing to *pay* for it. Real estate, unlike fine art, functions optimally on sameness: *practical* sameness.

Sam Silversmith, a creative, sixties-generation fellow now in his late thirties, took a chance when he installed a huge, illuminated, plastic *S* from a defunct Esso sign on the back wall of his sunken shower. Friends gasped at the cleverness of it, but Sam had thrown caution to the winds, so far as resale value was concerned. Suppose a future buyer is named Alfred Alexander?

The *S* wasn't Sam's only indulgence. He installed a tree in his living room. Not a dainty little *Ficus* or mock orange, but a mature dogwood that one day will be the cause of either great emotional trauma when it has to be removed or extensive structural alterations if it is allowed to grow bigger. Everybody loves to visit Sam's. His house is a kind of museum of unrelated relics in unlikely order. But those far-out-of-the-ordinary "improvements" that he has built into his house may ultimately reduce its cash value.

By and large simplicity is best. If you want the most money for your house, your best bet is to leave the outside a fresh white or a muted green instead of painting it your favorite azure. Metallic wallpaper in dots and bold patterns, or red carpets, or strobe lights and ceiling mirrors in the bedroom should stay in magazines unless you are willing to take a chance that someone else will share your enthusiasm and compensate your cash outlay.

On the other hand, if strobe lights and ceiling mirrors can be removed easily, use these minor effects as a means of expressing your individuality. Then get rid of them at selling time. Potential buyers want no visual reminders of how other people have lived in the house they're considering; they want the home to become theirs.

4. The Bathroom/Kitchen Delusion

Kitchen improvements in general give the highest instant returns of any major job—anywhere from 70 to 100 percent. But there's an important qualifier! You can expect a top return only on those improvements that *increase space and function*; you may not recoup the cost of extravagant appliances such as trash compactors, garbage disposals, high-line refrigerator/freezers with ice makers and door spigots. (In general, watch out for appliances that require a lot of energy and maintenance. Many homeowners have become wary of these.) Rearrange kitchen appliances so they have a better working relationship to one another, but don't invest in a ceramic-tile floor. Put a double-sink vanity in the bathroom rather than $30-a-roll wallpaper. Above all, keep ease of living in mind. People want it. People work so hard these days just to make the mortgage payments that they want as much comfort and convenience as possible in their off-hours.

An official representative of the New York State Board of Realtors told me that *overimproving* kitchens is where home improvers tend to take their biggest losses. I know a young couple who bought a 200-year-old-house in a suburb of Boston. They got it for a song, and their aim was to restore it, enjoy it for five to ten years, and eventually resell it for a fantastic profit.

In the six years since they bought the house, they have sunk a whopping $30,000 into the place, as well as a tremendous amount of energy and labor. The kitchen became a focal point of their improvement efforts. In it lies a home-investment moral.

The original kitchen was small, with inadequate counterspace and open shelving. There was charm in the old hand-painted Delft tiles that lined the space over the sink and above the cabinets, but the room definitely needed some updating. Instead of preserving those features that would have created a continuity of design with the rest of the house, however, the owners gutted the entire kitchen—wide pine floors, Delft tile, the works. By the time they finished, they had spent $17,000—$10,000 on solid cherry cabinets and the rest on appliances, Formica countertops, vinyl floor, and labor. While they now have an ultramodern, functional kitchen with increased counterspace, they have actually effected a closed-in feeling with all the wall-hung cabinets. Worse, the room bears no visual relationship to the rest of the house and as a result undercuts the historic value.

Was the market value of this house raised by the $17,000 the couple spent on their kitchen alone? The answer emphatically is no! The modernized kitchen helped to sell the house for sure, but not at the price they would have liked. Had they known what they were doing this couple could have modernized *and* made a profit. As it was, they didn't recoup their full investment because (1) the style of the kitchen was not in keeping with the "image" of the rest of the house; (2) there was no room for a table or eat-at counter in the kitchen (a highly marketable feature); (3) the new appliances were energy gobblers and cost a lot to run and maintain; and (4) the high-quality cherry cabinets, however aesthetically appealing, housed the same amount of equipment—no more and no less—as the cheaper pine ones would have accommodated.

Last year, when they finally did sell their house, these people realized a payback of only $3,000 on their $17,000 kitchen improvement. Their comment to me? "I guess we overdid it."

Studies show that most people spend an average of between $4,000 and $6,000 on kitchen renovation. As a general rule, it's unwise to spend over 10 percent of the estimated selling price of your entire house on improving the kitchen or over 5 percent on bathrooms. If you can do the job for less, so much the better. A second bathroom can up the value of your house immediately by at least the cost of the materials and appliances, provided the construction is high quality, practical, and conventionally appealing. Bidets, fountains, and whirl-pools don't pay back.

5. SMALL BUT RUINOUS FLAWS

OVERLY ELABORATE LANDSCAPING

You say that you just spent $600 on Chinese gingko trees for your front yard and $2,000 on a carpet-smooth "installed" lawn? Surely you're not planning to recoup all that money, are you? Most people will pay extra for an easy-to-maintain, pleasantly attractive yard, but few will part with their hard-earned dollars for a botanical delight that will require tremendous energy and expense to maintain. It's simply too extravagant. Be aware of the difference between personal pride and smart money. Travelers may slow down to admire your exotic shrubbery and your goldfish pond, but few people will want to pay you back for your invested expense at selling time. Landscaping can pay well, but there's a limit. As chapter 5 makes clear, a nice lawn, tasteful foundation and entrance plantings, a few choice shade trees, and a few fruit trees are all appropriate investments. Keep it simple and keep it conventional.

THE BASEMENT REC ROOM

There was a time back in the fifties when a basement rec room was considered an addition to the value of a house. Refinishing your base-ment was an easy way to gain valuable space at a minimal expense. But studies show that buyers are no longer impressed with below-grade family rooms. Unlike moles and woodchucks, human beings are more comfortable on a higher level. We prefer to spend our time above ground. The day of the basement rec room is long gone, and any immediate return on one will be 40 percent at best. Creating *func-tional* space in the basement, though, such as a workshop, laundry, exercise area, or well-organized storage space, is extremely attractive to homeowners and buyers today.

THE GARAGE CONVERSION

Converting a garage into a family room may seem a practical idea, but financially it's disastrous. Surprisingly, most people prefer a garage to a made-over fourth bedroom or even a conveniently located family room. (I have a theory that it's because they want the storage space for all the extra stuff we haul around from garage to garage and can't possibly live without.) In any event, having a garage will enhance the value of your house by probably the cost of the garage, while recouping the expense of converting your existing garage will take a long, long time.

6. LUXURY FEATURES: INVESTMENTS YOU WON'T RECOUP IN A MILLION YEARS

SWIMMING POOLS AND MADONNAS

A swimming pool in Florida carries more buyer appeal than a swimming pool in Vermont, but neither will pay for itself—at least not through the buyer's pocketbook. The same is true for tennis courts, gazebos, shooting ranges, tree houses, dog kennels, shuffleboard courts, cabanas, lawn statuary, and grottoes with plaster saints.

Probably the most excessive luxury I ever encountered in a private residence was a miniature golf course, complete with movable windmills and running streams. While it provided hours of entertainment for the owners and their friends, once the kids were grown and gone it soon fell into disrepair. I remember the disgruntled owner's complaints when she called me to remove it because the interested buyers would sign the binder only if the entire antiquated structure was dismantled and carted away. Generally speaking, the feature you consider an utter luxury is probably going to be as interesting to the next buyer as a pig in mud. You could almost say the law of averages is against you. Because most people do not think of themselves as being able to afford luxury items, they don't yearn for them, don't go looking for them, and won't pay extra if they stumble over them in your backyard.

GREENHOUSES

Traditionally greenhouses have fallen squarely into the no-recoup, luxury category, but that rule has been modified now that a green-house, if properly located and constructed, can be made solar and provide a supplemental source of hot water and heat to your home.

If you have a greenhouse next to your house, you should rush right out and consult a solar-energy specialist. The cost of utilizing the stored heat may well come back to you, and then some, not only in fuel savings but in increased value to your home because of energy efficiency, which has great appeal these days. (See chapter 9 for a breakdown of how different energy-saving features affect the value of your home.)

Any scheme for installing a new greenhouse (always on the *south* side) should be carefully evaluated ahead of time, since in most cases the cost of such a feature runs into the thousands. Again, practicality will determine investment return. Remember, an independent green-house—one not attached to the house—*never recoups cost*. The same goes for an attached greenhouse that faces east, north, or west. It just *adds* to the fuel bill.

COOLING CREDIT

Central air-conditioning is thought to be a luxury item by most of us, though in hot, humid areas it's considered a necessity. In these warm parts of the country, the cost you invest in cooling equipment can come back to you in increased home value by almost 100 percent. The key is buyer demand. Most buyers expect air-conditioning in Florida and Texas, for example, and are prepared to pay for it. On the other hand, central air-conditioning in a home in Ann Arbor, Michigan, doesn't carry the same potential for return since most buyers consider it a luxury item and one they can ill afford. So in Ann Arbor (and other areas where people don't suffer without air-conditioning) you can expect your payback percentages to drop to less than 50.

THE EXCEPTIONAL HEAT PUMP

A heat pump is the one big exception to the location criteria for return on central air-conditioning. The heat pump not only offers an economical means of providing heat for your home in the winter, but also provides an economical means of cooling your house in the summer. Because of the efficiency savings inherent in the system, as compared with other, more conventional systems of heating and cooling, the heat pump is considered a value-adding improvement. Returns can run as high as 80 to 90 percent, depending on the degree of dependence on the heat pump (it is most often used as a supplement to an existing system) and the length of time you will be maintaining ownership of the house once the heat pump has been installed. (Note that a heat pump works efficiently above 30 degrees Fahrenheit and requires a supplementary heater when outside temperature is lower.)

8

FOURTEEN SMALL IMPROVEMENTS THAT PAY

It is a quirk of home improvement that small changes can reap big dividends—if they are the right sorts of changes. Many of the small changes mentioned in this chapter help create illusions: illusions of more space, more air, more light; illusions of greater privacy, warmth, security. In short, they are insubstantial changes so far as labor and materials go, but they do a great deal to produce wanted emotional responses in the buyer.

For example, by treating a small but image-wrecking flaw, such as the chipped porcelain in a kitchen sink, you can hide a defect a buyer may notice almost subconsciously. The buyer doesn't actually *register* the chip in the sink; what *is* registered is a feeling that things aren't maintained quite properly. Subliminal perceptions are every bit as important as impressions of which the buyer is fully aware.

The homeowner with a really restricted budget for improvements might do well to concentrate on making small changes and ignoring the larger ones.

1. Two Rooms for the Price (Almost) of One

All but the tiniest rooms can easily be made to do double duty, thereby creating the effect of two rooms where there is only one. What you need to accomplish this is a modular storage unit. So long as it's appropriate for the room, the unit can be almost any size and shape. It can be a "wall" that rises to within 1 foot of the ceiling, or it can be a set of waist-high shelves big enough for storage and to serve as a divider in a bedroom. Both wall unit and waist-high unit can turn that ordinary bedroom into a bed/sitting room or a bedroom/office. The wall unit can create a dining room or library out of one end of the living room, for example, or a guest room out of a television room. These units can be built in or free standing.

When creating one of these divisions, the important thing is to design a unit whose proportion best creates two separate spaces while retaining as much light and feeling of spaciousness as possible. Materials can be cheap, so long as you construct the unit out of something that holds straight and true under the weight of things stored. Painting (to match walls), laminating (Formica is the ultimate care-free surface), or wallpapering is then in order.

2. The Dressed Bedroom

Here's a really small improvement that can work wonders in boosting the salability of your house. *Dress* your bedrooms so they delight the eye. A buyer will do little more than register the number of your bedrooms if they're colorless, *dull* spaces. Be sure they aren't. The idea is to invite buyers to imagine themselves living in your house.

Begin with a dressed bed as a focal point for each bedroom. Use a charming antique quilt, a provincial-patterned ensemble (coverlet, pillow sham, dust ruffle), a handsome Navajo-style blanket. Dressers and chests, to be appealing, should be clean of line and free of clutter. If they're dingy and old, apply two fresh coats of enamel; or strip off

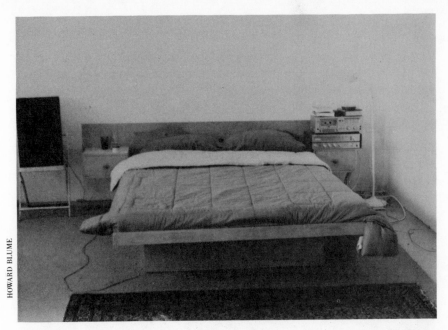

Sometimes we get accustomed to a bare and univiting bedroom, and after a while we don't even *see* how spartan it really is. Yet it takes so little to turn your bedroom into a pleasing space. You needn't add a picture window or sundeck (though that would be nice). Some curtains, a wall sconce, an antique mirror, a hooked rug can vastly improve the appearance of the room—and your enjoyment of it—as well as the salability of your home.

the old finish with water-soluble paint remover, then stain and seal with low-gloss polyurethane.

Add softly spectacular plants: a huge Boston fern on top of a blanket chest or pedestal; lovely, light-diffusing asparagus ferns hung in pots before the windows. Make those bedrooms look irresistible. Don't be afraid to buy new bedclothes and comforters for the frank reason of showing off your home. Once these purchases have done their selling job, you take them with you.

3. FAKE CLOSETS

Some houses (indeed, many houses) just don't have enough closets—not for us and not for the folks who eventually will be interested in buying from us. What to do? Make more.

But what if the room that needs the closet is too small. The answer is to fake it. Across a corner of the room, run two parallel rods for hanging clothes; slightly farther into the room run a single rod catty-corner on which to hang a clothes-hiding screen. You can hang *any* kind of screening material: fabric to match the bedding, curtains, or wallpaper; split bamboo or matchstick blinds; rice-paper-and-bamboo shading (comes in different widths and is available by the yard at shops that sell Asian imports).

4. THE INSTANT EAT-IN KITCHEN

Surveys have shown that an eat-in kitchen is considered a prime feature by couples and families across the country. No matter how small your kitchen may be, use your ingenuity to give it eat-in capacity. All you need is a couple of stools to assure potential buyers that the dining room needn't be messed up every time someone has a yen for a peanut-butter sandwich. Buy two unpainted wooden stools at $15 to $20 apiece. Then paint them with enamel, or stain and polyurethane.

Once you've bought the stools, you'll be motivated to find a place to use them. You need only a 4-foot sweep of counterspace to accom-

HOWARD BLUME

Instead of letting space go to waste in your kitchen, convert it to a breakfast nook with handsome table and chairs.

modate two stools—only 2 feet of counterspace if it's free standing and a stool can be pulled up on either side. If the counter isn't free standing, you'll need to attach a narrow leaf with hinges so there's room to hitch up the stools comfortably when it's lunchtime. The stools themselves can be stored just about anywhere, even hung on the wall from a chair rail, Shaker style.

5. Only a Pint of Porcelain Paint

There's no need to turn buyers off with chipped or stained tubs, sinks, and appliances. And this is just the sort of neglect that makes buyers feel they'd be getting less than the best for their money if they bought your place. Neglect of maintenance, in varying degrees, is something we're all guilty of. Sale time (at the very latest) is the time to make amends.

Porcelain—that beautiful, hard, bright material that lines bathtubs and kitchen sinks—can easily be patched with porcelain-repair material available at the hardware store. Follow directions carefully and you'll make an almost perfect patch.

If the tub, sink, or appliance you're repairing isn't white, it may be easier to follow up by repainting the entire piece with epoxy or porcelain paint (also at hardware stores) than to try to make the repair material match perfectly the color of the old surface. (This may be true even with white, which can yellow with age or discolor as a result of repeated scouring.)

Examine every porcelain surface in your house, from laundry equipment to guest bath. Then set aside a Saturday to take care of it all. Shining, pristine-surfaced appliances will definitely boost the sale price you can ultimately command for your house.

6. Entry Impact

Builders refer to "entry impact" when describing an entryway, vestibule, or front hall they hope will captivate potential buyers. Don't ignore the very first impression buyers will receive upon entering your house. A small effort can pay big dividends, especially if the rest of the house is up to snuff. A pretty wallpaper may be the answer, or a large, impressive poster (attractively mounted, please, not stuck on the wall with tape), or a handsomely framed mirror. The point is to do something to spark up that entryway. Search basement and attic for a large, handsome jug or bottle to fill with pussy willows or eucalyptus leaves. Or borrow the small but lively oriental rug from some less conspicuous part of the house and let it look smashing in the hall. Or shine up that old copper umbrella stand your grandfather left you.

Make sure the entry lighting is warm and inviting—not harsh—especially if you're showing your house at night. Wall sconces can be very effective. (Check a lighting store for the largest possible variety of lighting fixtures.)

7. MOLDINGS FOR CHARACTER

Decorative molding can give both architectural character and traditional charm to the most nondescript rooms. A heritage of the seventeenth century, when rich colonists began using it to give their homes distinction, molding today can be bought cheap and unfinished—in many shapes, from simple to intricate—at lumberyards. Stock molding can create a focal point in a plain living room when it's used to flank doorways and windows or to create large framed panels on bare walls. It can be used to make chair rails in a dining room or old-fashioned kitchen, or to visually enlarge a less-than-impressive fireplace.

Moldings can be stained, lacquered, or painted to contrast with surrounding walls. Applying molding is hardly more difficult than putting up wood paneling; it can be glued or nailed to walls. (See Bibliography for sources on how to use wood molding.)

8. THE COSMETIZED BATH

Say you have a standard, no-frills bathroom in your house. It could be the main bath or an extra bath or a powder room you never got around to fixing up. Get around to it. This is one of those quick and

PENNY LOEB

Dressing up the bathroom wall with pretty towels is cheap enough. Note the curved counter—a useful idea for, as here, turning a corner. A prefabricated counter can be cut out to fit the corner.

easy decorating jobs it's just plain stupid *not* to do, because an attractive bathroom makes such a big difference to buyers.

Keep it simple, as with all other RUYR decorating schemes—nothing gaudy or jarring. Simple but attractive wallpaper will do wonders, all by itself, to perk up a boring bath. Add one large mirror—as large as you can make it—preferably from the top of the vanity backsplash to the ceiling. Put a large, beautiful plant on the counter in front of the mirror (double the greenery and double the impact). Frame and hang some simple prints. Then fix up the bath as you would in preparation for guests: everything spotlessly clean; pretty, matching towels; a china plate or bowl filled with soaps. This, and nothing less attractive, is what should greet the potential buyer. (And remember: no chipped porcelain or dirty grout between the tiles—*spotless*. For more, see chapter 3.)

9. Blinding a Bum View

Elegance can be added to a room simply by obliterating a view that's offensive, distracting, or dull. Appropriate blinding lets in wanted light, diffuses or blocks out entirely the obnoxious scene outside, and at the same time can enhance the attractiveness of the room's decor.

What you use for blinding depends almost entirely on the overall look you're trying to achieve and the amount of money you want to spend. The new vertical metal blinds are starkly luxurious in a modern room; they are also one of the most expensive window treatments you can select. Thin, horizontal metal blinds are cheaper but still elegant. Cheapest of all are the varieties of wooden blinds: burnt bamboo (or tortoise), split bamboo (or matchstick), rice paper backed with widely spaced bamboo strips, and several varieties made of painted or stained wooden strips. The plain matchstick blinds take paint easily and look nice when painted the same color as the walls. All these blinds have the advantage of letting in light and yet providing some privacy, though the rice-paper shades don't provide complete privacy at night.

Even if you have become inured to a less-than-pleasant view or too-close neighbors, it's wise to install blinds to minimize this defect when you're ready to show your home to a potential buyer.

10. The $10 Kitchen-Cabinet Upgrade

You're all too aware that dingy cabinets downgrade the overall impression made by your kitchen, but you've spent your money fixing up the rest of the house and have hardly a cent left. What to do? There are several options, depending on the main decorating scheme you've chosen for your kitchen. The simplest and often the most effective solution is *paint*. Do what is necessary to smooth the surface of the cabinets, be they metal or wood. Then get the best quality of enamel you can afford ($10 should do it), remove hardware, and carefully give each cabinet two coats. If you wish, use a good grade of spray paint (after masking contingent areas with newspaper and masking tape). Be sure to shake well and spray in short, even strokes, *always* keeping your hand in motion so as not to produce drips. Give two or three *very light* coats for a perfect job. New handles—white china knobs, say—can make a tremendous difference.

Sometimes, removing cabinet doors entirely (including hinge hardware) creates attractive open shelving. This is more likely to work with old-fashioned wooden cabinets in a kitchen whose look is homey and functional, rather than elegant and spare.

11. THE MAGICAL MIRROR

Probably no material can create more fabulous illusions of space and light than mirror. The trick is to place the mirror where it will produce the greatest optical advantage. If you're clever, it's possible to use quite a bit of mirror without turning your home into a hall of mirrors.

This inexpensive mirror doubles the light and space of the bathroom and reflects the interesting window that makes the bathroom special.

PENNY LOEB

The window that brings in light and view will bring in *more* light and view if the wall it's in is fitted along its side with mirror, from windowsill to windowtop. This works wonders for small rooms (bathrooms, kitchens, dens) that have a closed-in feeling.

The tiny powder room (one that's carved out from beneath a stairwell, say) becomes fascinatingly magnified if you cover two opposite walls with mirror. (One-foot squares of mirror are far cheaper than solid slabs and easier to work with if you're doing the job yourself.)

Studies have shown mirrored closet doors to be a favorite among women across the country. Mirroring the sliding doors of a large closet can add impressive dimension to a room; but even an ordinary closet door, fitted with as large a piece of mirror as possible, will add a touch of luxury and convenience to the master bedroom.

12. BEAUTIFYING THE BARE WALL

You'd be surprised how many people are nervous about putting "art" on their walls. Many leave their walls blank and uninteresting rather than risk doing something "wrong." Should you fall into this category, be assured that a bit of study and experimentation will soon give you the confidence you need to brighten those boring walls. (Remember, those boring walls will look boring to a buyer, too.)

Study books (see Bibliography) and magazines on decorating for a sense of how things are put together on walls to create harmony and proportion. Whatever you do should please the eye as well as promote a feeling of harmonious warmth and security. Experiment with things you already have around the house (possibly in basement and attic). Look for old prints, mirrors, photographs. If you have little to experiment with, buy posters, which are cheap, colorful, and replaceable. Beautifully reproduced art posters can be purchased for between $10 and $20 at museum gift shops and shops specializing in poster art. Get the posters matted but not framed—not, at least, until you're sure you're in love with them and want to look at them every day. In the meantime, try them in the kitchen, the dining room, the living room, the halls. Move things around frequently, until you begin to get a strong sense of what looks good where. Experiment, as well, with groups of small, cheaply framed reproductions. See how you feel about color, and how pictures of different sizes and shapes work together. If you or someone you know does macrame, try wall mounting a macrame or other soft-fiber piece. Before long your walls will be neither bare nor boring.

13. ONE FANTASTIC TREE

Indoor trees have become quite the rage. Usually just one—large, healthy, and bountifully green—does the trick. Even if your home is low ceilinged, you can use a graceful *Ficus* (fig) tree. It will probably cost you over $100, but if you get it from a reliable nursery and give it proper food and light, it will be with you for years to come. The idea is that with a tree, be it *Ficus* or palm (another attractive, easy-care tree), you are making a strong, dramatic statement—one that is likely to intrigue the potential buyer. One fantastic tree, boldly positioned in the living room or master suite or even kitchen, will do more than a $1,500 couch to create a feeling of elegant luxury in your home.

14. RENEWING A WAXED FLOOR

I cannot leave the subject of small improvements without passing on my thoughts about old, dingy floors that may once have been beautiful but have not been revitalized (except for waxing) in many years. Whatever it costs you in energy, bring these floors back. It will cost next to nothing in materials and could add thousands of dollars to the purchase price of your house. If you do the work by hand—"By hand?" you shriek; yes, by hand—you can do as big an area as you want, night by night, until you have a whole room (or half a large room) completely stripped of old wax and ready for a finish so glorious it will stagger you. Use a solution of 1 gallon cool water, 2 cups of ammonia, and 1 cup of Soilax. Sponge liberally on an area 3 feet by 3 feet. Wait several minutes and begin scrubbing up the old wax and dirt with coarse steel wool (purchase the steel wool by the pound at the hardware store). You may have to repeat this process once or twice more before cleaning thoroughly with fresh water on a sponge. When the floor is completely and utterly clean of old wax and has dried for several hours, it is ready for a coat of good-quality polyurethane, which will seal the floor and provide a tough, bright, glowing surface that need never be waxed (indeed, *shouldn't* be waxed). Polyurethane almost floats on, brushmark-free, with a sponge rubber "poly brush" that you throw out when you're finished working. The wood floor will absorb this first coat of polyurethane and require a second coat for a lasting finish that will require hardly any upkeep.

Doing this job by hand will upset your family routine far less than hiring someone to come in, move furniture, and do the work for you. Even more important, if the floor is old, a floor-restoring specialist may want to sandpaper it—a job that's unnecessarily expensive and disruptive, and will probably ruin the old patina on the floor. For renewing floors, I heartily recommend do-it-yourself. A woman I know did practically nothing else to her home before putting it on the market, and the broker said he was sure they got $5,000 more than they would have had she left the floors the way they were.

9

THE HIDDEN VALUE OF ENERGY-SAVING IMPROVEMENTS

As I've discussed in earlier chapters, there are many factors that traditionally have determined the value of a home—factors such as its size, its location, its floor plan, the condition of the interior and exterior. Today, there's a brand-new factor: energy efficiency. Well, if not an entirely *new* factor, one whose importance in determining home value has climbed to the top of the list. These days, *energy efficiency is probably the single most important factor affecting the worth of your house.* This statement will be truer yet in the months and years to come, as we begin to rely more and more on alternate energy sources and new technology. By the time you finish this chapter you will have discovered an investment technique that promises returns greater than those from gold, diamonds, or the hottest of hot stocks.

Large, drafty houses and houses that are underinsulated and heated by an expensive fuel will become increasingly hard to market, as buyers seek improved heating methods and cheaper alternatives for energy. Not only will an energy-inefficient house become harder to sell, but as long as you continue to live there you will be spending more and more to maintain it.

Look at the economic situation. Energy prices are expected to rise as much as 10 percent faster than the general rate of inflation. (*Remember this*, because, as you will see later, it's a trend the homeowner-investor can actually use to advantage.) Although no one can predict the future prices of energy, it seems clear that production of oil and natural gas will continue to decline in the United States as the resource base becomes depleted. A house that is heated with either of these fuels alone will decline in value as the source of energy declines.

Not only will you save money *now* by making energy-saving improvements, but each improvement will contribute increased value to your home in the future market. *When properly planned and installed, efficiency measures such as a solar collector for hot water, a heat pump (alone or added to an existing furnace), new and better insulation, an airtight coal or woodstove, and energy-saving appliances can ultimately cut domestic energy consumption in half.* A wise home investor will therefore take stock of important energy trends and apply new technology to his or her home, aware that doing so will not only secure but enhance this major investment.

Payback and Tax Credit: Keys to Wise Energy Investing

There are currently many ways to save on energy consumption without making major changes or incurring tremendous costs. The question to be answered by the house investor is, Which of these methods will bring the best returns if and when the time comes to sell?

Insulation currently has one of the best payback rates. For example, $300 worth of 6-inch ceiling insulation can save you about $100 a year in fuel costs, so that in three years your savings will have covered the purchase price of the insulation. (Payback periods vary, but inevitably the cost of your energy-saving improvement comes back to you. *Then* you save that $100, and more as energy prices go up, year after year.)

Additional savings come from the tax break you get from the federal government. You can claim 15 percent of your total insulation purchases until you reach a new *maximum allowable credit* of $300 for each primary residence built before April 20, 1977. This federal tax credit not only applies to the cost of insulation, but it can also be taken on weatherstripping, caulking, storm doors and windows, devices to improve the efficiency of your furnace and air conditioner, clock thermostats, and meters to measure the energy usage in your home. (Note: To get the credit, you must file both Form 1040 and Form 5695. Don't forget to save your receipts.)

Financing made easy

Both federal and state governments recognize the need for energy-conserving measures in the residential sector and have established programs to aid the homeowner financially. Appendix 1 lists federal agencies and commercial institutions that offer financial assistance. Appendix 2 lists state agencies that supply information. In addition, you should ascertain whether you're eligible for a low-interest loan from your local gas or electric utility (see page 249).

Energy Efficiency and Market Value: The New Designation

Private, investor-owned utility companies nationwide have established a program for energy conservation called the National Energy Watch (NEW). The purpose of NEW is to establish *a system of points for energy-saving features which, when added up to a certain fixed number, will qualify a house for NEW certification.* A NEW-certified house will be recognized by real estate people, appraisers, mortgage lenders, and homeowners as a house that's highly energy efficient and therefore highly marketable. It will definitely pay you to do what's necessary to get your house NEW-certified—and be able to advertise it as such when you're ready to sell. Buyer demand for NEW-certified homes is going to increase, and as we've already seen, the more *demand* the greater the *value.*

Because of different climates, and hence different energy requirements, NEW points vary regionally. Features such as good insulation and ventilation, house construction and design, thermal-efficient windows and doors, and energy-saving appliances are assigned specific point values for each region. Certification is made through private utility companies across the country. Talk to your local utility company about the point system for your area.

This program is in the embryonic stage, but its eventual establishment will give homeowners, brokers, and bankers an important tool in assessing real estate value. It's not too soon to find out what you should do to get your home investment NEW-certified.

An Eye-Opening New Service: The Home Energy Audit

Utility companies in many states are now offering energy audits to their patrons. An energy audit is a computer workup of the energy efficiency of your house as it stands now and an assessment of how much money you can save annually by adding various energy-saving improvements. The audit also tells you the estimated number of years it will take for the suggested energy-saving measures to pay for themselves.

An audit costs only $10 or so (sometimes it's free). An energy expert hired by the utility company will come to your house and check it over thoroughly (see sample energy audit in Appendix 3). Many companies will waive the fee for low-income families or will put their auditing computers to work for nothing if you provide all the information on such things as caulking, weatherstripping, annual fuel-cost figures. (To find out if your state offers energy audits, call your state department of energy or your local utility company; a low-cost energy audit for homeowners may be available.)

If you supply yourself with statistical data relevant to your location, you can act as your own computer. In my state (New York) the department of energy has issued a homeowner's energy workbook that includes formulas you can use to find out how much you're saving—or

ENERGY-CONSERVING MEASURES BUYERS LOOK FOR IN HOMES NOW

1. Insulation in ceilings, walls
2. Water heater of cost-efficient age, size, condition, and fuel type
3. Storm windows and doors
4. Caulking in window and door frames
5. Weatherstripping in windows and doors
6. Furnace of cost-efficient age, size, condition, and fuel type
7. Ventilation
8. Efficient fireplace or stove

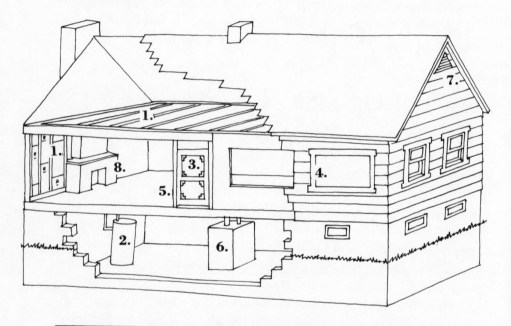

MAP OF R-VALUES

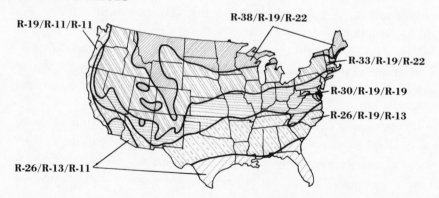

R-19/R-11/R-11

R-38/R-19/R-22

R-33/R-19/R-22

R-30/R-19/R-19

R-26/R-19/R-13

R-26/R-13/R-11

Energy-Conserving Measures Buyers Will Demand in Homes Tomorrow

1. Shade trees
2. R-value standards in insulation for climate in ceilings, walls, floors, foundation (see Map of R-Values)
3. Heat-convection fireplaces with glass doors, air-tight wood or coal stoves
4. Two or more zone controls; clock thermostats
5. Enlarged air vents; continuous ridge/eave vents
6. Windows of insulated glass with storm windows, insulated; reflective shades; panels
7. Furnace modified, convertible to cheaper fuel; heat pump piggybacked to or in place of furnace; supplemental heat source
8. Relative humidity 30–40%
9. Caulking around fans and air conditioners, water faucets, electrical outlets, chimneys; between porches and living areas where foundation meets siding; where pipes and wires penetrate ceiling
10. Heating outlets at outside perimeter where heat loss is greatest; heat ducts insulated in unheated spaces
11. Water-heater insulation; solar collectors

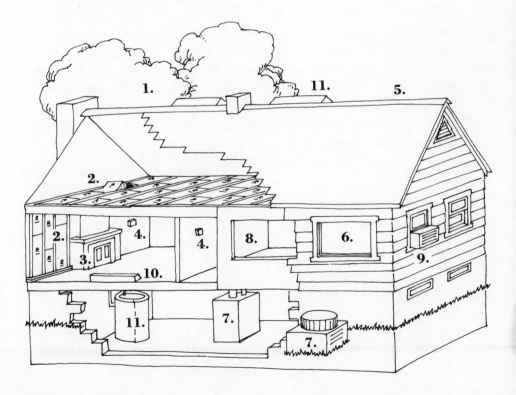

losing—on your own home right now. Find out from your state's department of energy or department of housing whether a similar workbook is available for your state.

Audits such as the one shown in Appendix 3 are most accurate if you own a 1,500-square-foot ranch house that's about ten years old. The computer is programmed to the "average" house and is regionally specific. That is, a typical house in Florida will return one set of figures while the same house in Oregon will return another. If your house is *atypical*—a turn-of-the-century Victorian, say—an audit is still useful because an energy expert will carefully consider your house, from stem to stern, and make recommendations that will tighten your house and increase its value.

While either a utility audit or a state energy department workbook will help you understand your house's energy usage and what you can do to reduce it, the most accurate and sophisticated method is a customized audit from an energy consultant. Such a study will measure your exact house and its construction details. It will provide a complete heat-loss study which shows you where, when, and how virtually every BTU escapes from your home. Only this kind of precise detail—every fact about your house is run through a computer—can tell you exactly how much a given improvement will save you in direct energy costs. Check your Yellow Pages or call local architects or builders to find an energy consultant with the proper computer capability. The cost for this "state-of-the-art" study is $150–$250, but you will easily pay for the cost of the service in energy savings the first year.

ESTIMATING HOW ENERGY SAVINGS WILL INCREASE THE MARKET VALUE OF YOUR HOUSE

While it's impossible to formulate a precise translation of the amount of money to be saved by a particular energy-conserving measure (an insulated water heater, for example), it *is* possible to make a rough dollars-and-cents estimate of the *value* such a measure will add to your house. For instance, if you spent $440 last year for hot water and have recently installed insulation around your oil-fired hot-water tank, you can expect to lower your oil consumption in the year ahead by 60 gallons. Currently, 60 gallons of oil costs about $60. Assuming that heating water accounts for one quarter of your energy consumption, the increased value to your home is $130. Here is the formula you use for making such estimates of value increase.*

$$
\begin{array}{c}
\text{Fuel savings} \\
\text{per year in} \\
\text{dollars}
\end{array}
\times
\begin{array}{c}
\text{Percent of} \\
\text{total energy} \\
\text{used per year}
\end{array}
\times 10 +
\begin{array}{c}
\text{Cost} \\
\text{of} \\
\text{unit}
\end{array}
=
\begin{array}{c}
\text{Increased} \\
\text{market value} \\
\text{of your house}
\end{array}
$$

As far as the market value of your house is concerned, remember that energy savings are provable. You can make the improvements and then show those before-and-after bills to potential buyers. Be assured that the less energy your home requires, the easier it will be to get your asking price. You virtually can't lose! Whatever you estimate as the dollar amount added to your home will only *increase* as energy prices increase. Take my word for it. Energy-efficient homes—particularly those which carry NEW certification—are absolutely going to soar in value.

THE MAGIC CASE OF THE SOLAR WATER HEATER

Solar water heating is a marvelous example of how *payback, tax credits, fuel savings*, and *increased home value* all mesh together in a financially savvy home improvement. All you need to pull this one off yourself is a little southern roof exposure. If you've got it, then figure solar hot water as an investment must. Following is an analysis of how this nifty device breaks down as an investment.

*Note: While essential to accurate calculation of *your* energy-improvement costs, payback periods are not given here since the buyer—who sets the market value—will not be concerned with affording the initial cost of the energy-efficient feature.

Approximate cost of unit	$4,000
Tax credit (40%) deducted from tax due	<u>1,600</u>
Actual cost of unit	$2,400

Fuel savings per year

At $1/gal. oil	$ 450
At $2/gal. oil	$ 900

Straight payback period

At $1/gal. oil	5 yrs.
At $2/gal. oil	2.6 yrs.

Profit per year after payback:	$450–900
Return on initial investment after tax credit:	18–40%

Immediate increase in home value (energy value + cost of unit = total)

$1/gal. oil: 450 × 25% × 10 = $1,120 + $2,400 = $3,520

$2/gal. oil: 900 × 25% × 10 = $2,240 + $2,400 = $4,640

As you can see, your real cost, including increased home value, is zero. In fact, you show a profit the moment you install. Amazing! Add to this "capital gain" a "dividend" of $450 to $900 in reduced costs each year and you've got the best investment since $35 gold.

SOLAR SPACE HEATING

Recently, we've discovered that solar space heating shows much the same kind of investment results as the solar water heater. Be careful now. We're talking only about space heating using solar collectors that are directly connected to the area of the house they're heating. No liquid passing through the collectors, no interior plumbing, no heat storage systems. Just collectors that feed hot air into a given space when the sun is shining.

Solar space heating costs from $1,250 on up, depending on the size of your house and the kind of equipment you buy. Since most collectors are of approximately equal efficiency, I'd advise using a lower-priced unit rather that a deluxe model. Most people think solar heat is still a few years away. In the case of solar air space heating, it's here, and working, right now.

MOVABLE WINDOW INSULATION

There's one more energy improvement you should think seriously about. New research shows this to be one of the most valuable things you can do to save energy, at very modest cost. Movable window insulation is terrific. It is actually much more cost effective than storm windows. In Boston, for example, a typical 2,000-square-foot house with 300 square feet of window area (15 percent) will lose 180,000 BTU per day, at a dollar cost of about $3.25 per day. Windows, you should know, account for some 40 to 60 percent of all heat loss, even though they only take up 15 percent of total wall area. If you have a movable insulation to put over the windows at night or when the sun isn't shining, *you can prevent up to 90 percent of window heat loss*. An inch of urethane foam board, for example (at $0.42 per square foot), will give you an insulation value of R-10, stopping 90 percent of heat loss if you always put the insulation up when the sun isn't shining (a bit much to ask, I realize, but at least you can see what's possible). You could save $3 per day using the foam board. There are lots of commercial products such as Window Quilt that are much more aesthetically appealing and convenient, though their insulation values are not as high as foam board. If you want to try this idea cheaply, take a thickness or two of plain box cardboard (it has air pockets and is a good insulator) and cover it with fabric. For a few pennies you can save real dollars and increase your comfort amazingly.

A FINANCIALLY LIBERATING EXERCISE IN NUMBERS

The RUYR philosophy is clear in the area of energy saving. Saving energy, you save costs in carrying your investment. Like anything else, when your cost is lower your ultimate profit is larger. And, in a double whammy, by creating an asset whose carrying cost is lower, you *raise* the value—the price a buyer will pay.

Let's say you keep your house for ten years, and you've been able to cut your energy usage in half this year by spending $5,000 on improvements. Assuming a 10 percent rate of *energy inflation* and a $4,000 energy cost if no improvements were made, your ten-year saving looks like this:

YEAR	UNIMPROVED	50% LESS COST WHEN IMPROVED FOR ENERGY SAVINGS
1	$4,000	$ 2,000
2	4,400	2,200
3	4,840	2,420
4	5,244	2,622
5	5,768	2,884
6	6,347	3,173
7	6,982	3,491
8	7,670	3,835
9	8,437	4,218
10	8,980	4,490
Total savings		$31,333

In addition to the savings of $31,333, you need to add the return on the theoretical investment of those savings, which, compounded, would add up to over $10,000 more. *Further*, you need to add the in-

TABLE 7

ENERGY-SAVING DEVICES THAT SAVE MONEY AND ADD PROVABLE VALUE TO A HOUSE

DEVICE	COST UNINSTALLED (DOLLARS)*	FUEL SAVINGS ON EACH ITEM (PERCENT)
Heat pump (not including ducts)	2,500–3,000	30–60
Solar collector for hot water	4,000	60
Solar air space heat	1,250 and up	30–60
Insulation for water heater	10/kit	12
Movable window insulation	25 and up	40–60
Automatic-setback thermostat	20–140	Up to 16 (night setback only)
Microwave oven	500	60–70
Drying control for dishwasher	475–555	30
Suds-saver washing machine	489–505	40
Flow-control shower head	15	50
Faucet aerator	2	60
Toilet-tank water saver	8	50
Energy-efficient refrigerator (17 cu. ft.)	550	30

*Costs reflect top-of-the-line products.

crease in home value (considering only your own use), which grows with inflation and by the tenth year ought to approximate another $11,220 under the energy-value formula ($4,490 × 25% × 10 = $11,220 + cost of improvements in the tenth year); plus the inflated cost ten years from now for the improvements you made (let's say another $10,000 for $5,000 worth of improvements made today).

So here's the breakdown on a theoretical $5,000 energy-improvement investment package that cuts your usage in half.

Fuel savings over 10 years at 10% energy inflation	$31,333
Interest or other return on savings	10,000
Energy value of improvement in tenth year	11,220
Replacement cost in tenth year, adjusted for inflation	10,000
Return over 10 years on a $5,000 investment	$62,553

It sure beats Wall Street!

These collectors for a solar water heater are the external evidence of one of the best home investments you can make.

HOWARD BLUME

An energy-saving fireplace is one of the most wanted extras in American homes today. Note the simple but handsome use of brick, wood, and rug to highlight the total image.

HOWARD BLUME

A handsome woodstove can really cut down your heat bill.

10

DO IT YOURSELF OR HIRE IT OUT?

THE DO-IT-YOURSELF CRAZE

In the past five years, the number of people electing to do their own home improvements has doubled. About half the nation's home improvements are done by professionals and half by the homeowners themselves. Homeowners find they save if they themselves do interior and exterior painting, wallpapering, paneling and insulation installation, and even some plumbing and electrical work. Professionals are more often hired to install carpeting, roofing, siding, heating, and air-conditioning.

We know that the type of home improvement largely determines the value added to your home; some improvements instantly add value equal to or greater than their cost, while others never give even an equal return (see chapter 7).

Beyond making a wise decision concerning the kind of improvement to be made, your goal as a homeowner is to effect the changes as *inexpensively* as possible while still maintaining the *quality* of the improvement. With the right kind of quality improvement, you stand the best chance of getting the highest return on your investment in increased value to your home.

The decision to use your own time and energy must be a calculated one. My friend Ted Sneider spent two years working nights and weekends to renovate his kitchen, only to end up with kitchen cabinets that warped and would not close and a wife who threatened to move out because of the prolonged inconvenience. In a case like this the dollar savings should be seriously questioned. But there are many shorter-term improvements that can be done by an amateur at considerable savings in labor costs and with a minimum of inconvenience to the household. And the result can look just as good as if a professional had done the work.

THE PROS AND CONS OF DOING IT YOURSELF

The savings on do-it-yourself projects vary. Most pay off in the dollars you save in labor costs, as you will see by referring to Table 8 (page 190) in which are listed some common home-improvement projects along with their hire-it-out and do-it-yourself costs. However, there are four situations in which doing it yourself does not pay off:

1. *When skilled work is required and the time investment is great*; for instance, when it is necessary or desirable to replaster an old ceiling as opposed to putting up acoustical tile.

2. *When material cost accounts for the major portion of the total bill on a professional estimate.* Carpeting is a good example here: The cost of the carpeting is great and the installation charge is relatively small. When you also consider the cost of the tools you will have to rent or buy if you choose to do the job yourself, it makes better sense to hire someone else.

3. *When the possibility of losing valuable living time and incurring an enormous hospital bill is increased* by such unfortunate occurrences as falling off your roof, cutting your hand on an electric saw, or squashing your thumb under a hammer (the U.S. Consumer Product Safety Commission puts these accidents at the top of its list of dangers for do-it-yourself home improvers).

Other potential hazards to consider include harmful vapors, airborne fiberglass, toxic chemicals, electric shock, bee stings and spider bites, and broken glass.

4. *When the satisfaction level of the finished product may be decreased because of poor workmanship, which in turn can decrease your investment return.*

THE ECONOMICS OF SWEAT EQUITY FOR THE DO-IT-YOURSELFER

While the guy who does it himself is initially saving more money, he may still lose in the long run by getting caught up in what I call the Happy Hammer Cult. People in the Happy Hammer Cult seldom place any value on their own labor and almost never adjust their profits downward by taking into account the number of hours they have put into their investment. In addition, they tend to overlook how doing it themselves affects their tax bills. For instance, the Internal Revenue Service places no value on the homeowner's time as compared with the tax advantages given to homeowners who hire professionals.

A capital gains tax is figured on your profit from a sale: the difference between your cost and the amount you receive. But your own labor time isn't counted as a cost. If you buy a house for $80,000 and have $10,000 worth of work done by a contractor, your cost for tax purposes is $90,000. If you save cash and do the work yourself for $5,000, your tax basis (cost) is $85,000. At selling time, then, you will have to pay tax on $5,000 of profit if you do the work yourself. In effect, this ultimately reduces the actual cost of having work done by another.

There are two mitigating factors, though. First, capital gains taxes are quite low and are likely to go even lower, making this less of a burden (maximum tax is now 20 percent of profit). Second, if within eighteen months you purchase another house that costs as much as or more than the sale price of the house you sold, there's no tax due, so the issue becomes moot. If you own more than one property (a vacation home or investment houses), the tax consideration becomes, of course, much more important: You will then always pay tax on a sale.

Quality Control

Once you've considered all the factors—the scope of the job, the initial expense, the required skills, the amount of time necessary for completion, and the overall monetary advantages—you are ready either to begin the work yourself or to look for a professional to do the work. Perhaps the most important decision you will make at this point is your choice of the option that will ensure the *highest-quality results*.

Quality is important for two reasons: The future value of your house depends on it, and your working capital demands it. For instance, if the sidewalk you have just paid a bargain price for will need to be replaced in two years, the depreciation on the improvement will be large, necessitating further outlays of cash for repair or replacement. This amount added to your initial cash outlay will probably exceed the cost of a better-quality, longer-lasting sidewalk. *An appropriate, high-quality improvement is the best safeguard against a depreciated pocketbook and a decreased return on your investment.* The following example shows the importance of quality control.

Ed Murphy enjoyed doing things himself and believed in the financial advantages of his own labor. Two years ago, he painted the exterior of his house, and today it looks as fresh as it did when he had just finished it. The kitchen floor he laid and the wallpaper he hung throughout the house also reflect his craftsmanship and initiative—and surely contribute to the value of his house. But Ed made one error. He got in over his head by tackling a job that required knowledge he didn't have. He spent eight months renovating his basement, building two walls, framing out and hanging two doors, applying insulation and paneling, installing ceiling and floor tiles, and adding outlets and overhead lights. When he finished, the basement looked great.

But what Ed forgot to consider, and what would have been a professional's *first* consideration, was waterproofing the cellar. Ed thought that by painting the cellar walls with a sealer, the problem of leaking water would be corrected. Not until the paneling became stained and warped, the tile floor buckled from seeping moisture, and the unpleasant odor of mildew became ever-present did Ed realize he should have consulted a contractor. He would have found that the gutter drainage on the house was inadequate, bringing the water right down into the cellar, and that the lay of the land required digging out the area around the foundation and installing a drain system. His shortsightedness cost $4,000, since the basement was rendered unusable and the furniture in it was damaged. The labor involved in removing the walls and floors, replacing the furniture, and redoing the room from scratch, if calculated reasonably at from $5 to $10 an hour, would have more than covered the expense of hiring a professional to waterproof the basement.

Quality demands knowledge, and your job as a homeowner is to assess properly the requirements of a job and your own ability to handle it. Many homeowners, with a few books and a lot of questions asked of the right people, can successfully improve their homes themselves. Others, who lack the time and necessary skills, will do better in the long run to hire professionals. Then the question becomes, How to find the right professional for the job—at the right cost?

THE BUSINESS OF CONTRACTORS

BE AN EXPERT ON THE EXPERTS

We hear a lot about dishonest people in the construction business. It is true that there are a few in the trade, but one rotten apple shouldn't spoil the whole basket! Most contractors are honest, hardworking, and talented people who, given your expectations and promise of fair payment, will do their best to accommodate you. When there is a breach of contract or a dissatisfied customer, it is usually because of poor communication (which means a poor contract) or unforeseen delays that have lengthened the time initially expected for a project.

The files of the Better Business Bureau and of consumer-protection agencies throughout the country are filled with stories about unfinished and poor-quality work, extravagant promises (of both the contractor's abilities and the properties of the materials used), of disappearing contractors and traveling handymen who run away with your money after a slick sales pitch. Such reports can indeed be unnerving. The best way to safeguard yourself against the con man and the incompetent contractor is to arm yourself with knowledge of what to expect from the competent contractor.

You have the *right* to expect competent work within a reasonable time frame and at a reasonable price. In most instances, if you devote some time and energy to pursuing a good contractor, you will get quality work and be satisfied with both the price and the time the work took.

THREE STEPS TO SAVING DOLLARS BEFORE THE CONTRACT

STEP 1: FINDING A CONTRACTOR. The majority of problems in the remodeling business occur when customers fail to investigate contractors properly before hiring them. If you haphazardly hire the first contractor listed in the Yellow Pages because you are impatient to get a project finished once you've decided to undertake it, you may well end up dissatisfied. The best way to find a competent contractor is to get his name from friends, neighbors, personnel at local home centers and supply houses, and your local utility company. The National Association of Home Builders has local chapters around the country, and a call to the nearest one will produce a list of member contractors in your area. This doesn't mean, however, that nonmembers should be eliminated from bidding your job, only that those member contractors listed have proven records for good performance.

It is wise to select at least three contractors initially and then to contact the licensing bureau (if licensing is required in your area) or the local consumer-protection office to see if there are any complaints against the contractors in question, the nature of the complaints, and their resolution. (A competent contractor may have had one or two complaints filed against him over a period of years; depending on their nature, he should not be automatically disqualified from bidding your job. It's the contractor with the string of complaints that you are interested in screening out.)

Don't be afraid to call up those homeowners you know have had work done by the contractor you're considering. Sometimes the contractor will provide a list of names for you; but of course he's not going to list an unhappy customer. So ask around. If the work has been satisfactory, you will find homeowners more than willing to spend a little time recommending "their" man or woman to you. Satisfied customers serve as a continual advertisement for a good contractor.

If the work has been unsatisfactory, the homeowner will be just as willing to tell you why and save you similar exasperation and loss. The following questions should serve as a guideline in your interviews with former clients:

- Was the job started and completed on time?

- Did the cost exceed the estimate, and if so, why?

- Is the quality of the work satisfactory?

- Did the contractor stay around during the construction to supervise his crew?

- Has the contractor been willing to return to fix anything that wasn't right?

STEP 2: SPECIFICATIONS. You will often hear people in the trade refer to "specs" in reference to a job. "Specs" are specifications: the details of the project, such as the grade and size of wood to be used; the size, type, and brand name of the windows to be used; the amount and weight of the shingles.

Before a contractor comes to your house for the first time, sit down and make some decisions about the improvement you want to undertake. For instance, if you have decided to add on a family room, carefully consider the size you would like it to be and the purpose for which it will most often be used. Think about the amount of light you want it to receive, which will determine the number of windows and their placement. Consider furniture arrangement and traffic patterns in relation to door placement. Consider the finished product and how you want it to look, the quality of the paneling, the type of ceiling, the type of doors. Write down as many of these specifics as you can, even though you may not be sure about some of them. This serves your purpose in two ways: (1) it turns your thoughts and feelings about your project into constructive and useful expectations, and (2) it gives you and the contractor a good baseline from which to work.

Presenting your specs to the contractor enables him to know at the onset of his dealings with you what you want done. This avoids confusion and encourages accurate estimates of cost, which will be a major factor in your final choice among contractors.

STEP 3: ALTERATION AND REFINEMENT. During the initial visit from each contractor, it is wise to have paper and pencil ready in addition to your list of specifications. Many thoughts will be exchanged regarding possibilities for your improvement, and you should be ready to record the best ideas. Expect to alter and refine your list of specifications, but don't come to any conclusions yet. Listen and learn from the experts in the business, but don't be talked into agreeing to extra work you really don't want or need.

Some homeowners play a game with contractors at this point. It is worth mentioning in the hope that you will avoid it. One man I knew asked five contractors to come and bid a job. He spent about an hour with each, gleaning from the experts all sorts of valuable information and ideas that applied to the project he had in mind. He then proceeded to have his son-in-law do the work, a course of action he had planned on from the beginning. In effect he had used these contractors as consultants—at their expense—for he had no intention of giving even one of them the job. A contractor's time is valuable, just as his knowledge is valuable, and while most are willing to spend time with potential clients in hopes of securing a job, others who have had an experience like this will charge a consulting fee. You can ask upon first contact with the contractor whether his estimate will be free. It may be to your advantage to pay a small fee for consultation with a quality contractor.

THE ROUGH AND THE PRECISE ESTIMATES

The contractor's first visit may produce a rough estimate, a ballpark figure, which gives you some idea of the *range* of cost you can expect to pay. Surprisingly, these rough estimates can vary by thousands of dollars, depending on the size and the nature of the job. Don't place too much emphasis on the rough bid; wait until you have given your revised specifications to each of the contractors and received precise estimates.

When the precise bids come in, carefully read the contractors' workup sheets and note what is included, at what price. Also scrutinize what is *not* included. Each estimate should list the materials to be used by name or number or other identifying method, in sizes, amounts, and types, and should include reference to their intended uses. It should also include an estimate of the time required to complete the project.

Once all the bids are in, compare each against the others in as many ways as possible before making your final decision. Beware of bids that are markedly lower than the average. Quality work may not necessarily cost what the highest bid suggests, but a very low bid may suggest incompetence.

Remember that the bid submitted for your consideration is *not a contract*, but rather a calculated appraisal of the scope of the work to be done and the contractor's price for doing it. Once you have chosen a contractor, the process of arriving at a quality contract begins. This is where good communication and precise wording are essential.

THE QUALITY CONTRACT AND HOW TO WRITE ONE

All home-improvement jobs, even the small ones, should have a written contract. It can be handwritten or typed, on a special letterhead or following a special form, with a place for the contractor's signature and yours. *It should be considered only a starting point for negotiations.* Most contracts prepared by the contractor leave a lot to be desired from the homeowner's point of view because they leave a lot of room for misinterpretation. (This isn't necessarily intentional, nor does it always imply that a contractor is out to get you. He may not feel it's important to spell out every little detail to assure you of his intentions to do a good job, but remember that details are synonymous with a good contract; insisting on them won't injure a good contractor's ego for long.) A sample contract appears in Appendix 4 for your reference.

COMPLETE JOB SPECIFICATIONS. Now is the time to spell out specific brand names, colors, grades, styles, and model numbers for appliances and materials. It's much more to your advantage, for instance, to say "blankets of Owens-Corning fiberglass insulation, with vapor barrier, rated R-19, to be installed between joists in attic floor and between studs in knee walls of attic," than to say simply "insulate attic."

STARTING AND COMPLETION DATES. Not only do starting and completion dates tell you when the work will take place, but they also tell the contractor when he can expect payment. A contract should allow for what are considered *reasonable* delays, such as a spell of rainy weather that prevents workmen from laying roofing shingles, the delivery of materials that are faulty and have to be reordered, or the delivery of the contractor's first child. (Opening days of hunting and fishing seasons are negotiable.)

Besides simply stating the dates for starting and finishing, there are two clauses which, when added to the contract, reinforce your position. The first might read, "All time limits in the contract are of the essence of the contract." This works to keep the contractor on schedule and obligates you to pay the contractor on schedule if the work is going along satisfactorily. If the contractor uses subcontractors, he is responsible for their time and production in relation to the contract.

A second clause that keeps delays to a minimum gives you the right to withhold payment in the event that work is delayed for no apparent reason. This is a form of the holdback clause discussed on the next page.

SCHEDULE OF PAYMENTS. Most state laws that cover payment schedules for home construction leave the actual schedule to the parties drawing up the contract. California is one exception worthy of note. The law there generally limits down payments to $100 or 1 percent of the contract price, whichever is greater. It also states that any additional payments are to reflect the cost of the work that is actually done, not waiting to be done. (There's no reason you can't incorporate California's example into your own Michigan or Ohio contract.)

You should never let the contractor get ahead of you. Always pay only for what has been done by setting up payment schedules for specific amounts at specific points during the construction phase. For example, if the improvement you are making involves refinishing a basement, the first payment might come when the materials are delivered, the second when the wiring and insulation are in, the third when the paneling is on and the ceiling is in, and the fourth after the job is completed to your satisfaction.

Sometimes, the contractor will arrange for the financing on your improvements. If this is the case the contract then must conform to the truth-in-lending law, which gives you the right to cancel the contract at any time up to three business days after you sign it, without penalty if your house is being used as collateral for the loan. In addition, the contract must state the annual interest rate, the actual interest rate, the actual cash price, plus the finance charge and the amount to be paid at each payment.

MODIFICATIONS. This is an area where the dishonest contractor can stick you if you're not careful—by charging you for extra work that you neither wanted nor needed. It's wise to protect yourself with a clause that states that the contract can be modified *only* if the homeowner and the contractor sign a later agreement that sets forth the changes agreed to. In addition, the contract should state that if there are any work modifications, the resulting cost or credits to the homeowner will be included in the agreement.

HOLDBACK CLAUSE. As a contractor, I am not particularly fond of holdback clauses, simply because when the job is done I like to be paid. But for the homeowner's protection, I recommend including a holdback clause as part of the contract. It should state that the final payment is due thirty days after the contractor has completed his work. This allows you to live with the improvement for a month and gives the contractor every incentive to return to fix anything that may need to be repaired or replaced. It also works to protect you against any liens filed against your property because of nonpayment.

PROTECTION AGAINST LIENS. In the event the contractor does not pay his suppliers or subcontractors (even if you have paid *him*), a lien or liens may be slapped on your house. This means that the suppliers and subcontractors, through perfectly legal channels, have the right to take away some of your property as payment.

There are essentially two ways you can protect yourself against this. One is to hold up final payment to the contractor until he offers evidence that no liens can be filed against your property.

The National Consumer Law Center suggests the following clause. "Final payment shall not be due until the contractor has delivered to the homeowner a complete release of all liens arising out of the contract, or receipts in full covering all labor, materials, and equipment for which a lien could be filed."

The other possibility is to require the contractor to post bond that would protect you against any liens. Those homeowners living in Hawaii and Louisiana have the right to demand that kind of bond, since those states have laws that specifically cover liens in home-improvement contracts.

PERMITS AND VARIANCES. I recommend that you put the responsibility for permits, fees, and licenses on the contractor. The contractor, as a rule, is better informed in these matters than the homeowner since he deals with local laws all the time and can more expeditiously obtain the necessary approvals. I would also make it clear in writing that any legal matters arising from the location of the construction or the specifics of the construction will be handled by the contractor.

LIABILITY COVERAGE. Deal with a contractor who has adequate insurance to protect you, should claims arise. Some states, such as New York, require contractors to carry insurance to cover liability and workmen's compensation claims. The contractor and his subcontractors should be able to offer proof of such insurance. Make this a part of your contract requirements.

WARRANTY ON THE WORK. If you have hired a contractor because of his good reputation, you can usually be assured of the quality of his work and the fact that, should anything go wrong with the work, he will be there to fix it to protect his good reputation. Putting this in writing, however, offers you definite protection against any defects that appear during the progress of the work or for a period of months afterward. (The time is negotiable, but many contractors, including myself, feel that a year is not too long to guarantee materials and workmanship.)

The provision should also cover work that subcontractors do and work that will be done by the contractor's crew.

CLEANUP. Some contractors never mention cleanup. The homeowner simply assumes that the contractor and his crew won't leave a mess. Unfortunately, and all too frequently, the homeowner ends up with the broom and the problem of disposing of garbage cans full of scrap lumber, pieces of brick and mortar, bits of wire, and a collection of nails.

Unless you enjoy cleaning up after someone else, have a clause in the contract that puts the responsibility on the contractor. It should state that the site must be left in broom-clean condition.

CREDITS AND REFUNDS. If the contractor orders more materials than he ends up using, you shouldn't have to pay for his error. The materials should be returned to the supply house and you should be credited. Make sure there is a clause in the contract to this effect or you may be charged for materials that find their home in the contractor's garage.

CANCELLATION RIGHTS. It is wise to contact your local consumer-protection agency or your state attorney general to learn what laws cover cancellation rights on home-improvement contracts. Some states give you a cooling-off period that allows you a few days to review the contract and cancel it, if you wish, without penalty.

If you find it necessary to cancel after a cooling-off period has ex-

State Laws Regulating Home Improvements

Nearly all states have laws covering home-improvement contracts in one way or another. Typically, those laws govern financing by including home improvements in consumer-credit, truth-in-lending, or retail installment-sales statutes. However, fewer than one third of the states have other laws directed specifically at home-improvement contractors or contracts. Those provisions are outlined in the chart below. In addition, some cities and counties have their own laws, which are often stricter than state laws. While some statutes are more comprehensive than others, only Florida's laws cover all the points CU considers important in dealing with home-improvement contractors.

The chart, prepared with the help of the National Consumer Law Center, is meant to be a general guide only. Readers who need specific information on state and local laws should consult a consumer-protection agency, local licensing bureau, the state attorney general, or a lawyer.

STATE	REQUIRED CONTRACT PROVISIONS							OTHER STATE LAWS	
	DESCRIPTION OF WORK	STARTING AND COMPLETION DATES	SCHEDULE OF PAYMENTS a	COOLING-OFF PERIOD	LIMIT ON LIQUIDATED DAMAGES	PROTECTION AGAINST LIENS	PROOF OF INSURANCE	CERTIFICATES OF COMPLETION REGULATED	LICENSING OF CONTRACTORS
California	•	•						•	•
District of Columbia								•	
Florida	•	•	•	•	•	•	•	•b	•
Hawaii						•			
Louisiana						•			
Maine	•		•				•	•	•
Maryland	•	•	•					•	•
Michigan	•		•	•	•c		•		
New Hampshire									•
New Jersey	•		•				•	•	•
Pennsylvania	•		•	•	•		•		
South Dakota									•
Texas								•	
Vermont								•	
Virginia									•
Wisconsin	•	•	•		•	•	•	•	

aCalifornia law generally limits down payment to $100 or 1% of contract price, and regulates payment schedules as well. Other states require only that down payment and other payments be specified in the contract.

bCertificates of completion include a release of all mechanics' liens.

cMichigan law prohibits provisions for liquidated damages in home-improvement contracts.

Source: Consumer Report, Feb. 1978, p. 77.

pired, a penalty clause (called a liquidated-damages clause) in your contract can protect you against paying the full amount specified for the improvement.

If your state allows you to write such a clause into your contract, find out the specifics and try to make it as undamaging to you as possible by putting a ceiling on the amount you can be expected to pay. Remember that a contractor can sue for actual damages if you fail to meet your obligations as stated in the contract.

REVIEWING THE CONTRACT

Whether or not the provisions we've covered are required by law, it is in your best interest to include as many of them as possible in your home-improvement contract. Some contractors, particularly those who live and work in states that do not have many specific laws directed at home-improvement contracts, will resist detailed contracts and become indignant at your seeming lack of trust.

Remind them that you are hiring them because you trust them and that it is only good business to protect yourself against possible dollar loss, even if it's remote.

You may want to have your attorney review the contract before you sign it, simply to be assured that the wording is correct and that you have included all you can to protect yourself.

GOOD WILL MEANS GOOD WORK

Now that you have hired a contractor with a good reputation and armed yourself with a good contract, *relax!* By now, you have spent many hours planning for a possible incident between you and the contractor that would necessitate your using all your protective measures. Most likely, an incident will not arise. But you can rest assured that you have done your job. Now let the contractor do his, and be cooperative and supportive. The contractor has overhead expenses that continue every day; he is just as interested in working quickly and efficiently to meet these demands as you are interested in having him complete your job quickly and efficiently.

Remember that good communication is important for the best results. The contractor is there to give you an improvement that will bring you years of increased comfort and pleasure in your living environment as well as increased value to your home.

SOME COST-SAVING TIPS ON HOME IMPROVEMENTS

- You can usually get a better price on construction in the cold months when business is traditionally slowed.

- It is possible to save from 5 to 10 percent on materials by paying for them within ten days. If the contractor is low on working capital, you might get him to give over part of his contractor's materials discount if you bankroll him with speedy payments. This also serves to reestablish his own credit.

- To save on installation costs of plumbing later, install all plumbing lines to appliances that will need water (icemakers, toilets, showers, washing machines) now, during the construction phase, even if you will not be using them immediately.

FIGURING THE SAVINGS IN DOING IT YOURSELF: THE RUYR JOB-ANALYSIS TABLE

Being your own handyman offers many opportunities for savings by eliminating labor costs and materials markup, but *not always.*

Table 8 lists twenty-six home-improvement projects and gives a percentage figure for potential savings when a job is done by the homeowner. It enables you to see at a glance the potential savings to you if you eliminate professional labor costs.

While applying your own weatherstripping and caulking can save you a big 73 percent, installing aluminum siding requires a great deal more skill. Therefore, the approximately 50 percent potential savings must realistically be reduced unless you happen to possess the necessary skills (perhaps you're a retired sheet-metal worker).

The higher the skill level for the project, the less accurate the percentage of savings if you do it yourself; conversely, the lower the skill requirements for the job, the more closely your savings will match the figures in Table 8.

How TO READ THE RUYR JOB-ANALYSIS TABLE

The figures in Table 8 are compiled from the *Dodge Manual*, a handbook based on current computer data for building-construction pricing and scheduling. Its calculations are based on national averages and represent estimated mid-1980s prices.

PROJECT. Under this heading is listed a brief description of alterations to existing structures. All specifications for the jobs listed are given in the note at the end of the table.

TOTAL COST. This means the average cost to you if all the work is done by professionals; that is, the ordering of supplies and labor costs from the project's start to its completion.

LABOR COST. The total cost of each tradesman's labor time on the particular project listed is shown under "Labor Cost of Professional Job." The figures are based on hourly big-city union wages across the country and include base rates, fringes (minus travel expenses), insurance, and taxes.

Generally nonunion labor is cheaper, and it is less expensive to hire a plumber or a carpenter in a rural community than in an urban community. Keep in mind that the more you pay for labor, the more you'll save by tackling the job yourself. (But remember, your taxes on a later sale may be higher, since your own labor doesn't become a deductible cost.)

MATERIALS COST. The figures listed in this column refer to average retail cost of materials in the United States in 1980. Remember that a contractor usually adds 10 to 15 percent (sometimes more) to this figure as additional profit. (In 1979, only 7 percent of the nation's homeowners bought materials themselves, which were then used by a contractor; most contractors refuse to work this way because of the reduction in profit.)

Any discounts that result from early payment on accounts or professional gratis will reduce the cost of materials approximately 10 percent.

Special considerations, such as material shortages, site conditions, and weather factors, and the simplicity or complexity of the job, affect materials cost.

HOMEOWNER LABOR TIME. This means the length of time in hours that it takes a professional to do the project, times two. Where a common laborer is able to do the job, the homeowner's time is calculated to be the same.

No dollar figure has been assigned to homeowner labor. It depends upon how much your time is worth per hour. If you generally earn $30 an hour as a corporate executive, it will probably be cheaper for you to hire a carpenter for $17 an hour or an electrician for $21 an hour—unless you enjoy spending your free time at the sawhorse.

Homeowners earning $25,000 or more a year account for most structural improvements, and most improvements are made on houses worth $50,000 or more. If you're earning $10 an hour at your profession and it takes you 10 hours to put up aluminum downspouts, then your $100 labor "cost" has exceeded the $87 it would cost to have a carpenter do the job in half the time. However, if you can get a friend or relative to help you, and the work takes half the time, you are ahead of the game and your savings will be increased. If you're unemployed or retired, the full percentage of savings will be realized—provided you don't fall off the roof!

All this is simply to say that you need to evaluate your time carefully for the highest net return. Ask yourself the following questions:

- How long will the project take if I do it? If a professional does it?

- How much time do I reasonably have available for this project?

- How much skill is required to complete this job?

- Do I possess the necessary skills?

- How much will I save by doing it myself?

TABLE **8**

PROFESSIONAL VERSUS DO-IT-YOURSELF COSTS OF TWENTY-SIX HOME-IMPROVEMENT PROJECTS

PROJECT	TOTAL COST OF PROFESSIONAL JOB (DOLLARS)	LABOR COST OF PROFESSIONAL JOB (DOLLARS)
EXTERIOR		
1. Install 100-ft. basketweave redwood fence, 6 ft. high	1,151	351
2. Plant 10 spreading yews around house	391	111
3. Install 200-sq.-ft. patio of flagstones set in concrete	1,008	792
4. Paint siding and trim on average two-story house	1,170	575
5. Install 6-in. prefabricated chimney pipe in ranch-style house*	295	95
6. Install 100 linear ft. of aluminum downspouts	169	87
7. Lay asphalt shingles over existing roof on 30-by-50-ft. gabled house	1,036	601
8. Install aluminum siding on average two-story house		
Plain	3,660	2,040
Insulated	4,350	2,040

SPECIFICATIONS LIST

1. Specifications given in table.

2. Yews 18–24 in. high.

3. Flagstones of irregular shapes, $1\frac{1}{2}$ in. thick.

4. 3,500 sq. ft., wood and composition siding, brush one coat oil paint, all sheens.

*Homeowner installation not recommended owing to degree of technical knowledge required for code compliance and safety insurance.

MATERIALS COST (DOLLARS)	HOMEOWNER LABOR TIME (HOURS)	DO-IT-YOURSELF SAVINGS (PERCENT)	SKILL LEVEL NEEDED
800	30	30	Low
280	8	28	Low
216	70	78	Low to medium
595	70	49	Low to medium
200	12	32	Low to medium
82	10	49	Medium
435	72	58	Medium to high
1,620	200	55	Medium to high
2,310	200	46	Medium to high

SPECIFICATIONS LIST Cont'd

5. Specifications given in table.

6. Aluminum downspouts, 3 by 4 by ¼ in.

7. Asphalt shingles, #235/100 sq. ft.

8. 3,000 sq. ft., plain and insulated aluminum siding.

T<small>ABLE</small> 8 Cont'd

PROJECT	TOTAL COST OF PROFESSIONAL JOB (DOLLARS)	LABOR COST OF PROFESSIONAL JOB (DOLLARS)
9. Install aluminum/glass sliding door to patio	446	56

I<small>NTERIOR</small>

PROJECT	TOTAL COST OF PROFESSIONAL JOB (DOLLARS)	LABOR COST OF PROFESSIONAL JOB (DOLLARS)
10. Paint interior of three-bedroom, two-bathroom house	2,236	1,290
11. Wallpaper 10-by-12-by-8-ft. room		
36 sq. ft./roll at $3/roll	293	117
15-oz. vinyl wall covering	363	117
12. Replace ceramic tile in 10-by-12-ft. bathroom	581	313
13. Install acoustical ceiling tile on 192-sq.-ft. ceiling	146	63
14. Panel 16-by-20-by-8-ft. basement room	1,040	303
15. Lay new flooring in 10-by-12-ft. kitchen		
Vinyl-asbestos tile	121	42
Sheet vinyl	170	52
16. Install vanity-sink unit in bathroom	120	40
17. Resheetrock 12-by-14-by-8-ft. room; tape and sand	208	121

SPECIFICATIONS LIST

9. ⅝-in. insulated glass with thermal break, screen, and hardware, 6 ft. by 6 ft. 8 in.

10. 8,600 sq. ft., two coats latex, including openings.

11. Approximately 350 sq. ft.

12. Approximately 175 sq. ft., 2-by-2-in. glazed tile on mud set.

13. Acoustical ceiling tile, glued or stapled, 24 by 24 in., ⅝-in. fiberglass.

MATERIALS COST (DOLLARS)	HOMEOWNER LABOR TIME (HOURS)	DO-IT-YOURSELF SAVINGS (PERCENT)	SKILL LEVEL NEEDED
390	6+	13	Medium to high
946	160	58	Low to medium
176	14	39	Low to medium
246	14	32	Low to medium
268	37+	54	Medium
83	7+	43	Medium
737	35	29	Medium
79	5	35	Medium
118	6	30	Medium
80	4+	33	Medium to high
87	14	58	High

SPECIFICATIONS LIST   Cont'd

14. 576 sq. ft., walnut paneling, prefinished, $\frac{1}{4}$ in. thick, 4 by 8 ft., including furring and layout.

15. 120 sq. ft., vinyl-asbestos tile, 9 by 9 by $\frac{1}{8}$ in.

16. Vanity, plastic exterior finish, 30-in. base, white with molded doors.

17. 416 sq. ft., $\frac{1}{2}$-in. gypsum drywall.

TABLE 8 Cont'd

PROJECT	TOTAL COST OF PROFESSIONAL JOB (DOLLARS)	LABOR COST OF PROFESSIONAL JOB (DOLLARS)
18. Weatherstrip and caulk windows and doors on two-story house	256	192
19. Install 6-in. fiberglass insulation in 800-sq.-ft. attic	336	136
20. Build masonry chimney on ranch-style house	586	381
21. Install solar water-heating system in existing house*	3,576	820
22. Purchase and install woodburning stove into existing chimney with working flue*	758	75

CONVERSIONS

23. Remove plaster ceiling in 14-by-20-ft. living room and finish underside of roof to form cathedral ceiling	474	240
24. Build 16-by-10-ft. wall†	246	124

SPECIFICATIONS LIST

18. Oil-base caulking, ¾ by ¾ in., 266 linear ft.

19. Specifications given in table.

20. 160-sq.-ft. hollow three-core block, ½ yd. concrete, 8-by-8-by-24-in. flue tile, thimble, wall ties, flashing, and concrete cap.

21. 82-gal. tank, 74.4-sq.-ft. collectors, four panels.

*Homeowner installation not recommended owing to degree of technical knowledge required for code compliance and safety insurance.

†Electric and heating/cooling costs not included owing to wide variation in labor costs. Labor cost varies according to condition and location of existing structure, condition and age of electrical service and heating/cooling systems, code requirements, etc.

MATERIALS COST (DOLLARS)	HOMEOWNER LABOR TIME (HOURS)	DO-IT-YOURSELF SAVINGS (PERCENT)	SKILL LEVEL NEEDED
64	15	73	Low
200	8	40	Low
205	48 (1 man)	65	High
2,756	80+	23	High
683	4	11	High
234	29+	51	Medium to high
122	14+	50	Medium to high

SPECIFICATIONS LIST Cont'd

22. Two 36-by-48-by-¼-in. fireproof boards; sheet metal with mineral fiber interior and installation kit for wall surface.

23. 6-in. batts fiberglass insulation, ½-in. gypsum drywall, taped and sanded.

24. 6-in. batts fiberglass insulation, 2-by-4-ft. studs, ½-in. gypsum drywall, taped and sanded.

TABLE 8 Cont'd

PROJECT	TOTAL COST OF PROFESSIONAL JOB (DOLLARS)	LABOR COST OF PROFESSIONAL JOB (DOLLARS)
25. Convert 35-by-25-ft. attic into master bedroom with half-bath[†]	3,809	1,754
26. Convert garage into 18-by-20-ft. family room with cathedral ceiling[†]	2,700	1,108

SPECIFICATIONS LIST

25. $\frac{1}{2}$-in. copper tubing, hangers and solder included; cast-iron pipe, hubless type with fitting every 10 in., hanger and clamps included; lavatory, countertop type, enameled steel, 18-in. diameter; water closet, floor-mounted with flush valve, regular tank type; 2-by-4-in. studs, 9-in. batt insulation, $\frac{1}{2}$-in. gypsum drywall, taped and sanded; 1-by-6-in. plain pine baseboard molding; $2\frac{1}{2}$-in. pine around windows; prehung interior door, including frame, sill, and hardware; sheet vinyl flooring in bath; bedroom floor sanded and finished with two coats polyurethane; bedroom and bath painted with one coat latex, roller, including openings.

[†]Electric and heating/cooling costs not included owing to wide variation in labor costs. Labor costs varies according to condition and location of existing structure, condition and age of electrical service and heating/cooling systems, code requirements, etc.

MATERIALS COST (DOLLARS)	HOMEOWNER LABOR TIME (HOURS)	DO-IT-YOURSELF SAVINGS (PERCENT)	SKILL LEVEL NEEDED
2,055	165	46	High
1,592	127	41	High

SPECIFICATIONS LIST   Cont'd

26. Sliding vinyl-clad door, safety insulated glass, hardware, screen, weatherstripped, 6 ft. by 6 ft. 8 in.; 6-in. batt insulation; ½-in. gypsum drywall; interior paint with roller, one coat latex, including openings; nylon carpeting with insulating pad $12/sq. yd., uninstalled; baseboard molding, 1-by-6-in. plain pine; 2½-in. pine molding around windows and glass sliding door.

11

KNOWING WHAT APPRAISERS KNOW

A good friend of mine is an extremely competent and sought-after appraiser. He has a slogan I find much to the point for home improvers. *Always improve a house with the idea in mind that you may have to sell in six months.*

That may seem extreme, but it's really just a way of getting you to think about the *market* before you spend your hard-earned dollars, for the market is the ultimate judge of your efforts. RUYR-type decisions should be based on facts, not guessing, and you should have an appraisal so the facts are clear in your mind.

In this chapter you'll learn what an appraisal entails and *how to do one yourself* using all the criteria of a professional. Once you have a reasonably objective appraisal of the value of your house, you can proceed in a systematic and organized way to increase the value. You'll know your house's strengths and also its weaknesses—weaknesses you can usually remedy for a surprisingly small investment.

THE MANY FACES OF VALUE

Value goes by many names: fair market value, loan value, present value, scrap value, antique value, speculative value, replacement value, insurance value, and a multitude of other "values." Fundamental to them all is *market value*: the amount of money an average buyer would be willing to pay for whatever it is you're going to sell on the open market. Whether you end up making money or losing money on a real estate venture (and your *home* is a real estate venture) depends in part on whether you have an accurate estimate of market value. Whoever makes that estimate needs to be objective and must know the factors involved in establishing market value.

Judging the value of anything demands a certain sophistication, although there are clear-cut principles that operate. Of these the most obvious (and the most powerful) is the law of supply and demand. Those lovely old tin boxes you've been collecting for years and that add so much charm to your kitchen don't mean a thing to me (although I may think they look charming in your kitchen). I don't collect tin boxes, don't particularly want them, and haven't the space to display them. *But*, to you they're worth at least $300 (the total of what you paid for them over the years) plus a great deal more in sentimental value. Another collector might even pay you $500 for them, and you'd both be very happy.

Value is largely dependent upon demand. *Demand* (how many people *want* old tin boxes) measured against *supply* (how many people have collected old tin boxes and want to sell them) accurately establishes market value (in this case $500).

You may love your little Cape Cod; I may find it boring; and the guy down the street may have coveted it for years and march up to you one day with an offer of $75,000. At that moment you have established a market value of $75,000, even though you may have paid only $30,000 for your house ten years earlier. (This is assuming, of course, that there's some sort of *general demand* for a house like yours and the guy down the street isn't completely out of line with his offer of $75,000.)

THE PROFESSIONAL APPRAISER

You may want to seek the opinions of people in the general real estate field: salesmen, brokers, investors, subdividers and builders, mortgage lenders, tax assessors, and so on. It's been established that about 95 percent of all homeowners rely on the opinion of a particular broker to help them establish the market value of houses they are planning either to buy or to sell.

While certain information can be gleaned from experts, it's well to remember that virtually all of them have a *vested interest* in what the market value of your home is and will no doubt be influenced accordingly. The broker wants to list your house and get the commission. The mortgage lender wants to maintain an honest image in the community and profit from the interest rate on your loan. A tax assessor often reflects current political forces rather than the true market value of local housing. Subdividers and builders want to share in the profits to be made from building or renovating your home. These may be honest, well-meaning people, but they give *subjective* estimates because their survival as businessmen depends on you and your favorable response to their opinion of value.

A professional appraiser, on the other hand, also depends on you for his success in the business world, but he gains that success by his objectivity. He doesn't (or shouldn't!) have any motive but a desire to help you make a decision based on hard, cold facts that constitute a valid assessment of the market value of a particular property. He doesn't really give a damn whether you buy a specific house, sell it, live in it for 100 years, or destroy it.

Appraising is an opinion, but not a guess. Good appraising is always supported by careful analysis of relevant data. You can either hire someone to do this for you or learn to do it yourself. In this chapter I'll tell you how to find a good appraiser and what you can expect to get for your nickel. I will also tell you, based on a number of interviews with respected appraisers, how to save the nickel and do it yourself.

In most areas of the country, appraisers aren't licensed. Generally they'll charge around $200 for an appraisal on a residential property, but the figure can jump dramatically if a lot of paperwork is involved or if the property to be appraised is unusual (a seventeenth-century stone mansion, say, or a house designed by Frank Lloyd Wright). To protect yourself, you should seek an appraiser who has a professional designation from either the American Institute of Real Estate Appraisers or the Society of Real Estate Appraisers. Both confer professional designations based on education, experience, examination, ethics, and expertise.

You may find listings for appraisers in the local Yellow Pages, under "Real Estate" or "Real Estate Appraisers." If you can't find a listing under either of those headings, ask the loan department of a local bank for the names of several qualified appraisers in the area.

How do Appraisers Establish Value?

Appraisers arrive at value in three ways:

1. *Market approach*: by comparing the property with similar properties on the market

2. *Cost approach*: by figuring how much it would cost to reproduce a similar structure, minus any depreciation that results from deterioration and/or functional and economic obsolescence

3. *Income approach*: by computing value based on multiplying the real or potential income of the property by a factor generally accepted in the marketplace for that location

Most appraisers have found that the market approach to value is the most useful and accurate.

Appraisal Techniques

The procedure for appraising a one-family dwelling generally follows these three steps:

1. *Inspection*: The appraiser inspects the community, the neighborhood, the block, and the plot. He measures the building's ex-

terior and interior, examining the structure as he goes. He takes Polaroid snapshots of the house from the front, rear, and street.

2. *Research*: He collects information on the community and notes any economic conditions that may affect the value of the property. Relevant are such factors as community services, schools, tax assessments, and zoning regulations.

3. *Report*: He prepares a written report which may include plot plan, floor plan, location map, tables and graphs, photographs, and a fully detailed qualification sheet.

How detailed an appraisal do you need?

Appraisers generally provide three types of reports: a certificate or letter (often all that is given in a residential appraisal); form reports, such as those used by various government agencies; and a narrative report—the most detailed and therefore the most expensive. (Table 9, a table of contents from a typical narrative report, gives you an idea of what the appraisal covers.)

Appraiser L. T. Bookhout in Upstate New York told me that he generally arrives at an agreement with a client over the phone as to what type of appraisal is needed and what its cost will be. He then asks the client to send him a letter requesting his services. At the same time, he sends to the client a letter of contract stating the terms agreed upon. In this way, both parties are protected.

You probably won't need a highly documented written appraisal if you're simply interested in establishing a value for your home (whether for selling, financing, or simply satisfying your curiosity). It's useful to know the market value of your house so that you can anticipate any change in value that may result from improvements you're contemplating.

(There are, of course, other reasons to seek an appraisal, such as in the settlement of an estate, to establish just compensation for condemnation proceedings, or to establish a basis for taxes.)

An appraiser can provide you with an informal letter giving a range

TABLE 9

SAMPLE TABLE OF CONTENTS FROM AN APPRAISER'S NARRATIVE REPORT

TABLE OF CONTENTS

APPRAISER'S INFORMAL ESTIMATE OF APPROXIMATE MARKET VALUE RANGE

 L. T. Bookhout, Inc. *REAL ESTATE CONSULTATION & APPRAISING*

(914) 229-5367

P.O. Box 278
42 Albany Post Road
Hyde Park, N.Y. 12538

June 14, 1983

Mr. and Mrs. John Doe
1983 Miller Road
Upstate, New York

Dear Mr. and Mrs. Doe:

REFERENCE: Doe Residence
Miller Road
Town of Upstate
Grid No. 17-6568-00-701016

In accordance with your request, I have made a preliminary study of the above-referenced property as of June 8, 1983. This preliminary study consisted of:

--physical inspection and inventory of property
--deed and tax account research
--preliminary market approach to value through analysis of comparable sales in the area
--conclusion of the property's highest and best use and applicable market sector
--preliminary cost approach to value
--correlation of two approaches and estimate of value range

It should be clearly understood that an appraisal has not been made of the above-referenced property, and that this letter does not constitute an appraisal report, nor should it in any way be construed as same.

Based upon this preliminary study, it is the appraiser's belief that if an appraisal were made, the final market value estimate would be in the range of approximately $55,000 to $60,000.

It should be clearly understood that the range of value approximated herein is subject to adjustment upon completion of an appraisal.

Should you have any questions regarding this study or require additional information, please do not hesitate to contact me. Thank you for the opportunity to have been of service and best of luck to you in the future.

Very truly yours,
L. T. BOOKHOUT, INC.

C. Richard Tobias, Staff Appraiser

CRT:km
Encls.

of values based on whatever information he has at hand or can gather relatively quickly (see example on previous page). An appraiser who does most of his work *outside* your area will not have as much information readily available as one who works mostly *in* your area. To get that information will take time, and time is money. The appraisal letter will probably cost you about $150, depending on the area of the country in which you live. It will state that the appraiser has made a preliminary analysis and will list what has been done. The appraiser will state that although his letter should not be construed as a formal appraisal, it is his opinion that if a formal appraisal *were* done, the value or conclusion of that appraisal would probably fall within the range he has stated to you. That's enough to work with; you will have an idea of the approximate market value of your home—and from someone who's objective.

WHAT AN APPRAISAL DOES NOT DO

While there's much a professional appraisal can do for you, there are things it doesn't do.

An appraisal:*

- Does not serve as an offer to buy the property. (It can, however, serve as a basis for *making* an offer.)

- Does not guarantee the property will sell at a particular price. (While it's no substitute for good salesmanship, it can certainly help make a sale.)

- Does not serve as a loan commitment. (It can, however, serve as a *basis* for making a loan commitment.)

- Does not guarantee that any lender will make a loan of a certain amount on the security appraised. (Many lending institutions, however, will lend a certain *percentage* of the appraised market value.)

*Source: Walstein Smith, Jr., *Appraising for Probate and Estate*, rev. ed. Chicago: Society of Real Estate Appraisers, 1974, pp. 11–13.

• Does not guarantee the actual physical condition of the property or that every fixture or appliance is in good working order.

• Does not serve as a permanent certificate of value "good forever" after its date. (Both the property and its environs are changing all the time.)

• Does not constitute a recommendation to act or not to act in any certain manner. (If you want this sort of advice, go to a counselor or an economist.)

• Does not guarantee the satisfactory settlement of a dispute involving a difference of opinion regarding value. (It serves merely as a *basis* for negotiation and comparison.)

• Does not prove or disprove anything and is not capable of *being* proved, in the sense of scientific accuracy. (Appraising, the appraisers will tell you, is a judgment art, not a science.)

Marketing your house to the appraiser

Appraisers are human. If you have a special reason for wanting the highest possible appraisal on your house, there's no law against trying to give the appraiser a positive attitude.

Donald Garner, a business executive from Shreveport, Louisiana, has learned how successfully to apply marketing techniques to his personal real estate. He says, "I've been able to increase the value of several houses I have sold in the last twelve years by five or six thousand dollars simply by giving the appraisers a list of my homes' attributes." Garner includes such things as central humidifier, special insulation, design alterations that provide increased storage space, rustic fencing, high-quality carpet, high-quality grass in lawn, and similar RUYR-type features.

He gives a neatly typewritten list of such assets to each appraiser who is hired to affix a value to his house. At the bottom of the page he lists what *he* thinks the house is worth because of those features. (His asking price is admittedly above the price he expects to get.)

The appraiser is immediately presented with a formal and concise list of those features the homeowner feels contribute to the value of his house. While the appraiser's final report will take into account the many and varied objective factors that go into evaluating a house, this initial, subjective review provides a reference point that shows the house in the best possible light since all its best features are right up front.

To market *anything*, you want to advertise its strengths. And who is better qualified to expound the virtues of your house than the appraiser? Passing on a copy of the appraiser's observations provides an interested buyer with a ready reference sheet for comparative analysis. Buyers feel more secure in their investments if they have a list of the special features that justify their assuming thousands of dollars of debt.

Take the time, as Donald Garner does, to market your house to the appraiser. You'll end up with an increase in profits.

THE NITTY-GRITTY: DOING IT YOURSELF

If you decide that hiring an appraiser is an extra you'd rather not pay for, you need to know the process an appraiser uses and some of the factors to be considered in determining a price.

Before even looking at the property, an appraiser gathers information that has to do with the location of the property. Your home may be a perfect example of Carpenter Gothic, but whether it's situated on a farm at the edge of a historic village or in the middle of an urban slum affects its market value. All the following are determined by location, and all have some bearing on the price you can expect to be paid for your home.* They are listed in order of importance, economic forces being the most critical.

Source: American Institute of Real Estate Appraisers, *The Appraisal of Real Estate*, 5th ed. Chicago: Donnelley, 1976, pp. 1–2.

Economic forces

1. Natural resources—their quantity and quality, location and rate of depletion

2. Commercial and industrial trends

3. Employment trends and wage levels

4. Availability of money and credit

5. Price levels, interest rates, and tax burdens

6. All other factors which have direct or indirect effect upon purchasing power

Physical forces

1. Climate and topography

2. Soil fertility

3. Mineral resources

4. Community factors, such as transportation, schools, churches, parks, recreation areas

5. Flood control and soil conservation

Social forces

1. Population growth and decline

2. Shifts in population density

3. Changes in the size of families

4. Geographical distribution of racial groups

5. Attitudes toward education and social activities

6. Attitudes toward architectural design and utility

7. Other factors which emerge from man's social instincts

Governmental regulations created by political forces

1. Zoning laws

2. Building codes

3. Police and fire regulations

4. Rent control, national-defense measures, priorities alloca-
tions, and credit controls

5. Governmental housing and guaranteed loans

6. Monetary policies which affect the free use of real estate

WHERE DOES THIS INFORMATION HIDE?

Where, you may wonder, can you possibly find such facts? They're
hiding in all sorts of nooks and crannies. If you're willing to put in a
little time, you'll get your answers. Go to officials of the local planning board or to the chairperson of the zoning committee. Environ-
mentalists, tax assessors, brokers, town clerks, friendly appraisers
who will give you a few minutes of their time over the phone, neighbors who have recently bought or sold—all are people in positions to
provide you with relevant data.

You can find out a lot by taking a Sunday drive and noticing the
proximity of schools, churches, the fire house, the hospital, shopping
centers, and banks. When we look at houses, we all tend to respond
with our emotions, and of course it's important that we feel comfortable, even excited, about an investment as big and as personal as our
house. *But try to be objective*: You will be more satisfied, and so will a
buyer down the road, if the house and property offer *practical assets*
in addition to the extremely important emotional appeal.

Here is a checklist* many appraisers use to establish market value.
It will be enormously helpful for you to evaluate your home carefully
using this list, point by point. It will help you be objective. (Chapter 4
gives details on how to evaluate structural soundness.)

*Source: Samuel Barash, *Standard Real Estate Appraising Manual*. Englewood Cliffs, N.J.:
Prentice-Hall, 1979, pp. 62–65.

Inspection Checklist for Existing Buildings

The plot

- Community facilities, transportation, schools

- Area low, flood prone

- Ponding on block, inadequate drainage

- Is lot well drained?

- Does lot need fill?

- Do gradients permit access and function?

- Heavy, fast traffic

- Inharmonious onsite or offsite usages

- Zoning permits usage

- Landscaping, setting

- Usable yard areas

- No effluent visible in area of septic tank

- Potable adequate yield of well (if one exists)

- Erosion? Soils stable?

- All improvements within lot—any encroachments?

- Access to property safe, maintained?

Building exterior

- Worn, missing shingles on roof

- Flashing serviceable?

- Chimneys, fireplaces plumb, mortar okay, washcap all right

- Any dry rot in wood exterior? Check near grade

- Exterior paint hides all wood, well-caulked

- All exterior openings maintained, serviceable

- All grades drain water away from building

- Beams at low built-in garage to divert water away from garage

- No "swayback" roof ridge line

- Splash blocks under downspouts

- Adjustable vents for crawlspaces, louvers in attic

- Paved areas functional, safe. No trip hazards

- Exterior steps have uniform and proper rise–tread relationships

- Stair railings sturdy, not rotted

Basement (or crawlspace)

- Stairs safe, handrails available

- Light switch at head of stairs

- Basement floor serviceable, no settlement

- Dry basement

- If sump pump, where does it discharge? Does it recirculate back into basement?

- Is there adequate electric service, branches?

- Condition of heating equipment, flue pipes

- Condition of domestic hot-water supply

- Condition of plumbing

- Condition of walls, efflorescence, eroded mortar?

- Was basement dug out after house was built? Are footings undermined?

- All walls plumb; no structural thrust, failures

- Termite tubes, damage

- Dry rot in framing members

- Spliced, sawn, cracked, deflected beams, girders

- No floor insulation in electric-heated house

- Inadequate basement light and ventilation

- Low ceiling height in basement

- Less than 18-inch clearance in crawlspace

- Crawl floor reasonably smooth, has vapor barrier or concrete screed floor

- Crawlspace has vents, is insulated or has adequate heat pipes in space and is open fully to basement

- Crawlspace dry

- Crawlspace access openings adequate for inspection and maintenance

Building interior

- Size of rooms adequate for furniture?

- Width of doors, halls, stairs adequate for passage and furniture movement?

- Number and depth of closets (bedroom, guest, and storage)

- Privacy of living, occupancy unit

- Bathroom privacy

- Adequate storage space for bulky, exterior storage items

- Commensurate kitchen

- Sufficient windows

- Sufficient electrical outlets, switches operable

- Fireplace works

- Windows move freely

- Plaster, drywall free of excessive cracks, "nailpops"

- Locks work

- Sufficient insulation in attic

- Floor, wall finishes acceptable

- Bath fixtures operable, pressure okay, toilet-bowl seal not leaking

- Paint not peeling, flaking (may harm children)

- Ceiling leaks (evidencing roof and or plumbing leaks)

- If vacant, is building drained, secure?

Miscellaneous checklist

- Is garage long enough for modern cars?

- Garage doorjambs clear of dirt grade, not embedded in concrete, not rotted or infested

- Plumbing pipes insulated in built-in garages

- Is heating unit enclosed from garage?

- Firewall on common wall of attached garage

- Adequate insulation in built-in garage ceiling and in common wall of attached garage

- Pool in a maintained state? All equipment available and apparently serviceable?

- Condition of common lands (if any) of condominium or home-owners association

- Condition of buildings or improvements owned in common by condominium or association (if any)

CONFORMITY PAYS!

As I've stressed, a house that's too different from others in its environs is a house whose market value is in serious jeopardy because the typical buyer doesn't want it.

We had such a house in Charlotte, North Carolina. It was the only white clapboard on a very long street of brick houses. We thought the white clapboard was charming. In the late sixties we were delighted to buy it for $18,000, a price about $1,500 lower than the typical brick houses on the same street. The owners of the white clapboard had had the house on the market for nearly a year, and even with the large addition on the back, they'd been unable to find a buyer. Little by little they'd reduced their asking price to far below the $25,000 they had estimated as the market value. Not then being particularly tuned in to the fine points of appraising, we thought we had a terrific find. We never bothered to check why the other houses on the street were thought to be more valuable. We snapped up our $18,000 "steal" and enjoyed living in it for three years without ever considering that someone else might think it a high-maintenance oddity. (That clapboard had to be painted every few years!)

When we needed to move, we sold the old white clapboard house to a couple who loved it—though not enough to pay a penny more than the $18,000 *we* had paid for it. And the house took six months to market! Had we invested in one of the other houses on the block we probably would have realized a profit. The *demand*—in that time and place—was for brick. Moreover, the addition our predecessors had built on the clapboard was an *overimprovement* for the neighborhood.

Once in a while a property may fetch a high price because it's non-conforming, but this is a tricky thing to judge in advance. If you want to speculate, speculate. Go after that mauve-and-putty-colored Victorian with the bubble skylight in the roof. But if you want to be *safe*, go for a real estate investment that will appeal to the largest possible number of potential buyers.

When All the Facts Are In

Accurately appraising can help you avoid costly mistakes in what is probably the biggest investment you will ever make. Many feel that a professional opinion is best. Not only will it save you a lot of time, but it may save you a lot of money as well because the appraiser is objective. He knows, for example, that homeowners in the neighborhood you're considering do their own gardening and that the people who would tend to move into that neighborhood are not likely to pay an extra penny for those day-lily borders you find so enchanting. So *you* shouldn't pay a penny extra. The extra $200 or so it will cost you to hire a professional may be worthwhile if it saves you from sentimental and emotional reactions that could alter the ultimate worth of your investment.

Market value is ever changing. An appraisal done a year ago may not accurately reflect the property's market value today. Keep this in mind and be aware of changes which may influence your property's value. Has a Little League field been established in the park across the street, inundating the neighborhood with the nightly noise of ballgames? Has the local sewer system been upgraded? Has the percentage of PCBs in the local water supply been high enough to trigger a front-page report in *The New York Times*? All these things have happened within the last year to friends who live in a small village only ten miles from us, and they have watched the market values of their little real estate gems rise and fall accordingly.

A house that is in demand stands the greatest chance of making a profit for its owners. Your task is to understand what features are in demand locally and what potential your house has for supplying them. Examine the property you own through the eyes of the market and strive to create a house that meets the needs in your area.

APPRAISAL REVIEW

Appraisers know that a house has maximum value if:

- It is *located* in an excellent neighborhood
- It *conforms* to the general architecture of the neighborhood
- It is *well maintained*
- It has *special features* in demand *in that* neighborhood
- It is fully modernized
- It makes good use of all *interior space*
- Its exterior *grounds* are well planted and cared for
- It is not exposed to *environmental problems* (noise, pollution, traffic)
- It is laden with no *idiosyncrasies* or features not wanted in the neighborhood

Is this your house? If not, bring it up to snuff!

12

How to Finance
Your Home
Improvements

Why You Should Get a Loan

Let's start right off with a key rule of real estate investment: *The longer you take to pay, the better off you are.*

This principle might well be called the rule of inflation or the rule of the declining dollar. The simple fact is that your income rises with inflation and so does the future cost of the improvements you make today. You pay for your improvements with "cheaper" dollars when you pay in the future. Meanwhile, your improvements are increasing in value because they would have cost you more later. Not only that, if you have cash now but don't use it all to pay for your improvements immediately, you can invest it elsewhere and make an additional return on your money.

Let's say I have $5,000 cash in the bank, and I want to make

$5,000 worth of improvements to my property. I *could* take the $5,000 out of my savings account and pay for the job. Then I'd have a more valuable piece of property, but no savings.

On the other hand, if I borrow the money, to be repaid over ten years, I'll *still* have a more valuable property that continues to increase in value with inflation. And I'll still have my savings, for extra investment income and to meet emergencies. At the end of ten years, in the first case, I'll get a return on my $5,000; in the second case, I'll *also* get a return on my $5,000 in improvements, but in addition I'll have doubled or tripled (at today's rates) my savings! The gain is much larger.

"Wait," you argue. "You had to pay interest on that loan." True, but there are two good answers to that objection. First, as the years go by I repay that loan in "cheaper" dollars, dollars that cheapen sufficiently to cancel the interest charges. Second, I get *two* investment returns: one on the investment (money borrowed) in the form of my improvements and one on the savings. Further, since I didn't invest any cash in the improvements, my *percentage return* on the investment has to be greater than if I'd put up cash. For example, if you earn $1,000 on an investment of $5,000 cash, you have a 20 percent return. If you earn $1,000 on only $1,000 cash plus $4,000 borrowed—after interest expense—you have 100 percent return! Moreover, the interest is tax deductible.

There's one fact of life you can count on. Improvements you make on your property in accordance with the principles set forth in this book will always earn you much more money than the interest you have to pay on a loan to finance them.

If nothing else, the return on improvements *compounds* through inflation, while interest on a loan stays level. Look at the example below. In the column headed "Cost of Straight Loan" I've assumed interest-only payments of 10 percent per year for five years on $5,000. In the column headed "Increase in Value of RUYR Improvement" I've assumed 10 percent inflation on the improvement money only—ignoring the combined increased value of the house *plus* improvements.

	COST OF STRAIGHT LOAN AT 10% INTEREST	INCREASE IN VALUE OF RUYR IMPROVEMENT AT 10% INFLATION
Year 1	$500	$500
Year 2	500	550
Year 3	500	605
Year 4	500	665
Year 5	500	732

As you can see, with each passing year you beat the bank on your improvement only. If you figured the real inflation increase on the total value of your home, not just on the improvements, your *profit on the loan* would be many thousands, not just hundreds. (And you'd still have your savings in the bank, collecting interest and compounding!)

I hope by now it's clear that you should borrow to make improvements whenever possible and that you should borrow for as long a time period as possible. *Get the real estate market working for you by borrowing.*

THE BORROWING ROUTES

Having established that it is prudent, even shrewd, to borrow money for your particular purposes, we need to explore how and where to get the money. There are many possible ways, and because you are borrowing the money for property improvement you *will* get it. A loan for property improvement is one of the most attractive types from the lender's point of view.

And rest assured that lenders *like* to be able to make a loan. All too often, clients of mine worry about whether a bank or other lender will "give" them a loan to make an improvement. These people are thinking of bankers as authority figures who are going to do them a favor.
· This is entirely the wrong attitude. Lenders don't "give" loans.

Nothing could be further from the truth. *Lenders are in business to make loans*; that's how they make money. They need you. They want you. You're a customer. Without you, a lender has no business.

You must understand this and arrange your financing with your head held high, not with your tail between your legs. Go with confidence. That very confidence will help you get the loan.

Home-improvement loans

The simplest and most straightforward loan for you is a home-improvement loan from your local bank. Banks like to make this kind of loan so much that they've set up a special category for it and called it by name. Interest rates are usually lower than for a car loan, for example, or for an ordinary personal "signature" loan. Home-improvement loans are available in most areas for up to $15,000 (depending on your income and the bank's policies), and time for repayment generally runs from three to ten years. *Take the ten-year payout.*

Bank loans are negotiable and banks compete. You don't have to take the first deal that's offered you. The best advice I can give, when dealing with banks, is to shop around. Remember, you're funding an investment.

Interest rates often vary by as much as 2 percentage points ($200 per year on $10,000!) within a single county. Maximum amounts available can vary by thousands and terms of repayment by years. Take a look at the loan application for one bank. Then type up a statement, a financial résumé of sorts, to take with you to each bank you visit. Since most banks make loans by formula, you'll get a fair idea on your first visit about whether you're eligible. This résumé will make it easier for you to get to as many banks as you can in a short time, and you owe it to yourself to do so. Include *all* your income, assets, and debts. Don't forget the value of your furnishings and collectibles as assets.

Banks like to make level-payment loans, in which you pay back a portion of the principal (loan amount) plus interest each month. This is the type of loan they'll offer you first. But don't just take what you're offered. Ask if you can pay interest only for the term of the loan, with a lump-sum payment of principal at the end. Or interest only for the first two years. Or any variation along those lines. If you can swing an interest-only loan, you'll cut your monthly payments considerably, and you'll *improve your percentage return on your investment.* (Remember, though, you'll still have to pay off the principal in a lump sum at the end of the term—or borrow again to pay the lump sum.)

Analyze the situation carefully. One bank may offer you a lower rate, but another may offer interest-only for a period of time. Interest-only is much better. One bank may have a prepayment penalty (for paying off the principal early); another won't. Try to get *all* the terms when you go shopping, so you've got a good basis for comparison and decision making (banks also have a nasty habit of leaving out the "minor details" until it's time to sign on the dotted line). The following information is what you need to know *before* deciding which bank is going to have the privilege of financing you:

- Interest rate (fixed or changeable over time)

- "Points"—fees for making the loan, to be paid at closing

- Term of years

- Amount of principal repayment

- Prepayment penalties (you'll want to pay off early if you sell your house before the loan is due)

- Extra requirements, such as keeping a checking or savings account at the bank, not increasing your present mortgage or taking a new one

You may find that the bank you choose isn't willing to lend you as much as you want. Here's a trick: Submit your loan application to two or more banks on the same day. Then when you get approval for two smaller loans at two different banks, take them both!

If you can't get a loan from a bank, you might try a finance company like Beneficial or HFC. But be forewarned that the interest rates from these lenders, who accept less credit-worthy customers, are substantially higher than those from banks. You'll also stand no chance of getting an interest-only loan from these sources. *Exhaust* your bank possibilities before going to a finance company or one of the outfits that advertise on television. ("Free money for homeowners" isn't free at all.)

SECOND MORTGAGE: THE WAVE OF THE FUTURE

When you borrow for your home improvement, you will be *personally liable* for the principal loan amount. If you lose your job or have a business reversal, you will still have to pay back the loan. But there *is* a way to get home-improvement money you won't have to pay back if fortune turns against you. In addition, this method of financing can often raise much greater sums than you can get with a personally guaranteed loan.

Large loans that don't necessarily require a personal guarantee (though some lenders may insist on it) are obtained through *second mortgages.*

A second mortgage is a loan that, like a first mortgage, uses the value of your home as collateral. The second mortgage lender stands second in line behind the first mortgage lender if you can't pay your loans and the loans must be foreclosed. However, if you don't pay the second mortgage lender and *do* pay the first mortgage lender, the second mortgage lender can still foreclose on the house. That's the dark side; nevertheless, negotiating a second mortgage is a useful way of borrowing.

Assume, for example, your house is worth $80,000 and you have a $40,000 first mortgage. You may want to take a second mortgage for $20,000 to fix up the house and make it worth $110,000. You'll probably get the second mortgage because you have so much equity (value less debt) in the house. Even if your fortunes should turn sour, a second mortgagee would be reasonably certain of getting his money back at a foreclosure sale. That's why your personal guarantee of the funds is often not required.

Second mortgages usually carry an interest rate 2 to 5 percentage

points higher than first mortgages. *But*—and this is a very big but—
the interest rate on your second mortgage may *still* be lower than the
interest rate on a personal home-improvement loan. It will certainly
be lower than the interest rate on a loan from a finance company. Of
course, the interest rate on any mortgage—first or second—depends
on general interest rates at the time you want your loan.

So, the first advantage of a second mortgage is that it may carry a
lower interest rate than a personal loan (you'll have to investigate
your particular case). The second advantage is that a second mortgagee will likely accept your home as collateral and not require your
personal guarantee for the loan. This will depend mainly on the value
of the house in relation to the amount of the first mortgage loan on it.

The third plus is that you're much more likely to get an interest-
only arrangement with a second mortgage. After all, the second mortgage lender knows that if you don't pay off the lump-sum principal at
the agreed time, he'll have your house as security. For that reason,
his terms for repayment are often easier. Second mortgages can run
from one to thirty years, so you can also get a *longer time* to repay—
while your house grows in value.

Recently, two huge federally backed corporations have taken steps
to make second mortgage lending more attractive. As a result, second
mortgages are easier to get than ever before. The Federal National
Mortgage Association and the Federal Home Loan Mortgage Corporation have entered the "secondary market" for home-improvement second mortgages. They'll *buy* the second mortgage from your lender, so
your lender does not have to have funds on hand to make you a loan.
The two companies will purchase second mortgages up to $30,000
and for terms up to thirty years—just like first mortgages.

This means not only that you will have an easier time getting a second mortgage, but that the rate will be lower because the loan will
come from a bank or savings and loan institution. Previously, most
second mortgages were made by individuals and private companies,
who charged higher rates because there was little competition. That
may be one reason you haven't heard much about second mortgages
before.

First, consult your local banks and savings and loan institutions to see if they will give you a second mortgage on your house. If there are no such lenders in your area, check the Yellow Pages under "Financing" or "Real Estate" to find the private companies that make these loans. They often advertise in the real estate sections of local newspapers as well.

A NEW FIRST MORTGAGE

Many people who have stayed put for five or ten years find that their houses are now worth two, three, even five times the amount of their mortgages. One way to gain money for home improvements at reasonable cost is to refinance your home; that is, to take out a new first mortgage. In a way, this is like making a partial sale to reap some of the profits on your home investment without actually having to sell and without becoming liable for capital gains taxes. Your monthly mortgage payments will increase, but you'll get cash to improve your property—or to do with as you wish.

My father had a house in Connecticut worth about $100,000. With artful landscaping and other touches similar to those that graced the other houses in his neighborhood, his place could have been worth almost $150,000. Since Dad had lived in the house a long time, his first mortgage was a paltry $32,000. His approach to home-improvement financing was to go to the bank and get a new first mortgage in the amount of $62,000. He could still easily afford the new, higher payments, and after paying off the old first mortgage he was left with a tidy sum of $30,000 in cash, *plus* his house.

He spent over $20,000 on improvements. Shortly after the improvements were finished, he received an unsolicited offer of $158,000 for his house—even more than he'd hoped for! A pretty good deal, I'd say. Not only that, he still had $10,000 in cash left over. With that he bought a new car. This is the only way I know to get a thirty-year car loan!

The new-first-mortgage route is a good one, but it's not too good to be true. The money is not free, of course; you still have to pay it back. Too, my father's original first mortgage was at only 5 percent interest. So in addition to the 11 percent interest he's paying on his fresh $30,000, he's paying an extra 6 percent on the old, cheaper $32,000 of the original first mortgage. Some banks will give you an average rate between the old and new mortgage rates to encourage you to wipe out the old mortgage, but Dad's bank didn't offer that.

Obviously, you've got to put pencil to paper to figure the exact consequences of new-first-mortgage financing in your particular case. It's going to cost you the interest on your "new" money plus additional interest over and above what you were paying on your old first mortgage. It could boost your monthly mortgage payments higher than is financially wise. (Most financial experts say housing should not exceed 25 to 30 percent of net income.)

You may well do better by adding a new second mortgage to your old first mortgage—to get an "average rate"—instead of taking out an entirely new first mortgage. (Of course, if you can get a new first mortgage at a *lower* rate than your old first mortgage, *do it fast!*)

Special Energy-Improvement Loans

Energy-saving improvements are a national priority as well as a sure-fire investment. Most utilities, in conjunction with the federal government, have now made energy-saving improvements all the more attractive.

One of my carpenters, Walter, had our local utility do an energy audit on his house (see chapter 9 and Appendix 3). After he received his computer printout he discovered he could make substantial savings by installing a setback thermostat and additional insulation. But he was really surprised when Central Hudson Gas and Electric's representative informed him he was eligible for a 9 percent eight-year energy-improvement loan of up to $4,000. His personal credit, he was told, had nothing to do with eligibility and would not be examined. All he needed to do was show up at the affiliated bank with his audit and an improvement estimate from a contractor (me, of course!). I don't have to tell you that Walter got his loan, saved enough on energy costs to pay for it in two years, and boosted the value of his house as well.

If you are contemplating adding insulation, storm windows, thermostats—any energy-saving measure whatsoever—*call your local gas or electric utility first*. You may be in for a pleasant financing surprise.

Some Slick Tricks for Financing

If none of the above routes is open to you, or if you don't choose to use any of them, consider some unusual alternatives that can and have worked well for people I know.

CHARGE CARDS. June and Bill planned to sell their house and move out of the area. They needed to upgrade it to get a good price, but they had borrowed to the limit at three local banks. Using a little creative financing, they charged all the needed materials on their VISA and Sears charge cards. Their labor costs weren't high because they did much of the work themselves. A broker estimated that when June and Bill sold the house—only six weeks after the fixup—they made two times the cost of the materials they'd charged.

SALVAGE MONEY AND YARD SALES. June and Bill also knew they'd have no use in their new home for any of the old fixtures they replaced (cabinets, a toilet, two windows) and they didn't want to move all their accumulated junk with them when they left. After ripping out everything usable that they were going to replace, they held a huge attic-and-salvage sale and included all their miscellaneous unwanted items along with the cabinets, windows, and so on. They made enough to pay for the plumbing, electric, and minor carpentry work needed for their improvements.

BARTER. Barter can be an effective way of adding value to your investment at zero dollar cost. It's worth thinking about what kind of services you might offer to finance your improvements. Charlie Bush is an accountant who lives alone in a small, adorable "doll house" in our village. He was put off by the price I quoted him to install a greenhouse. "Listen," he said, "you put up a greenhouse, including the materials, and I'll do your taxes for five years." I hesitated. It was a new one on me. "Personal *and* business taxes," he said. Quickly I figured that five years of his services were worth as much as, if not more than, the greenhouse—plus I have the advantage of getting a discount on materials. "You got it," I said. We were both pleased as punch.

So you see, your imagination's the limit in financing home improvement. Talk to your local brokers about it. You may be surprised to find you live in a historic district and are eligible for special loans. Or you may be in a rehabilitation area that qualifies for a HUD grant. The possibilities are countless; you owe it to yourself to find out about them. You've got an investment—your house. You've decided to make it grow.

Now pull out all the stops.

13

TIME TO SELL
(OR WHAT TO DO BEFORE THE DOORBELL RINGS)

Imagine that you're out with your favorite realtor in his new Volkswagen Rabbit. As you pull into the driveway in front of the For Sale sign (which, incidentally, has been half-destroyed by a monsoon or else the house has been on the market for eight years), your head abruptly bounces off the car roof from the impact of the potholes in the once-smooth asphalt surface. Before you've fully recovered, you notice, with rapidly vanishing enthusiasm, that one curtain in the front window has come down, allowing the morning sun to catch a very dirty window. You see a three-year-old with jam all over his face peering out at you, and suddenly you're imagining the Sheetrock disaster within. You look up and notice that the soffits are gray with mildew and that the roof is a mishmash of three different kinds of shingles, some of which are broken and some of which are missing entirely. Besieged by a mixture of curiosity (can the inside top the outside?), repulsion (how can they live this way?), and compassion (poor widow, poor favorite realtor), you smile as the head of the household (cigar in mouth) opens the front door.

Your tour is as brief as you can politely make it. Nevertheless, you can't avoid noticing the grease stains, peeling paint, worn wallpaper, leaky faucets, loose tile, gobs of caulk, eroded doorknobs, and squeaky stairs. Someone with a lot of imagination might buy this house, but it sure ain't gonna be you!

The importance of *condition* when selling a house cannot be over-emphasized. The house may have been built with the finest materials available at the time, but if the exposed surfaces are not consistently maintained, the overall appearance soon becomes rundown.

"They're asking *sixty thousand dollars* for *that*?" you exclaim in disbelief. Inwardly, you may be contemplating an offer of $45,000 and figuring the best place to buy materials, but if so, you're one of those rare persons who can envision what the rundown house will look like *after* it's been renewed. Most people, be advised, lack both your imagination and your inclination to work.

Now, take that same house and imagine a different situation. The owner, desperate because his house wasn't selling, decided to analyze how he might improve the situation. He took a critical look at his unkempt lawn, the peeling paint, the waterlogged cellar. Although he had been reluctant to put much money into improvements (after all, he was moving), he began to realize that a cash investment of under $1,000 would not only improve the marketability of his house but could also help him turn a profit. Many improvements would cost little more than his time and energy.

At the closing, several months later, this fellow ended up with a net profit of $15,000 in his bank account. But that's not all! In addition to the profit, he could also plan on deducting the amount he had spent for improvements on next year's capital gains tax. (Generally, only permanent capital improvements are allowable as deductions on capital gains taxes; routine maintenance is not. But all cleaning, painting, and repair expenses incurred within ninety days of the sale can be treated as deductible sales expenses, provided they are paid for within thirty days of the sale.)

Some people live in such an orderly way that they can put the house on the market at any given moment without having to make a single improvement. If you're one of these people, you can skip the rest of this chapter. However, for those of you who are busy with things other than the house, the following suggestions will help you realize the greatest possible profit from your real estate investment.

Before you begin scheduling appointments with potential buyers, take a merciless glance around your yard for stray pieces of paper, old tools, dog bones, rusty bicycle parts, leftovers from last fall's Thanksgiving dinner that the dogs got into, and deposit these in your nice, neat garbage can (you *do* have one with a working lid, don't you?). Is that stone wall you so painstakingly hauled rocks for still a wall, or has it deteriorated into a jumble of unrelated stones? Are there boards off the wooden fence that surrounds the yard? Does the fence need repainting?

Depending on the season, mow the grass, rake the leaves away from the foundation and out of the gutters, shovel the snow off the sidewalk (never use salt on concrete unless you plan on replacing it in a year or two), weed the shrubbery, clip the tall grass from around the big tree in the front yard. Spend several minutes at the roadside inspecting your property. If it helps, pretend your mother-in-law is coming to visit for the first time, or your boss, or photographers from *House and Garden* magazine.

Complain if your realtor has hastily tacked a flimsy cardboard sign out front that is within range of the neighborhood dogs. The For Sale sign is the very first thing the buyer sees, and it makes an impression. It's up to you whether that impression is good or bad. If you're selling your house yourself, take the time to space the letters properly so the sign is legible from a distance. Construct it carefully so it will weather well. The sign not only represents your intent to sell, but it implies something about who you are and how you take care of things.

The condition of your driveway contributes a great deal to the overall first impression people receive of your home. Strive for a clean, even edge and smooth surface. You won't need professional help unless the ruts are so deep and the holes so big that to start over with a brand-new driveway is the easiest—although costliest—solution. (See chapter 3 for suggestions on cheap ways to renovate your driveway. You'll be surprised how little effort it takes to produce big effects.)

Whatever type of siding you have, the outside of the house will probably need to be washed or touched up in areas where peeling and fading have occurred; or it may need to be totally repainted, restained, or resided. Think carefully before deciding just how much renewing you're going to do. It may be financially unwise to repaint or reside the whole house when some scraping and touching up of small, damaged areas will create a consistent color that looks good enough to the buyer. These final touchups are like the styling after the haircut. What a buyer sees on the outside determines, to a surprising degree, how he or she will feel about the inside.

Check the roof for damage and appearance as scrupulously as a buyer will. Repair or replace any loose shingles. Rejoin gutters and downspouts if they've become separated. Repair broken or cracked windows and damaged screening. Remove all items from the front porch except, perhaps, an attractive lawn chair or couch that would suggest functionality in good weather. Make sure all outside lights are working. (Yellow bulbs lend a softer, more attractive glow.) Give one of the kids a clean rag and some brass polish and offer a small reward for renewing the front-door handle and knocker. And while he or she is doing that, find your all-purpose oil and lubricate the hinges. Check the doorbell. The realtor is sure to try it.

Kids are great (I have four in my house), but when they run to the door fighting over who's going to answer the bell, the visitor—in this case the *buyer*—is likely to feel that the property and his life are in jeopardy. Try to have the kids playing *quietly* outside or occupied with a relaxed game in their room.

Stale smoke and unpleasant odors can be a real turnoff. Air the house out well before showing it, even in the middle of winter. It takes only a few minutes to exchange old, stuffy air for fresh. Boil some cinnamon and cloves on the stove, bake some brownies, or better yet, pop a loaf of fresh bread in the oven. If you show the house in the morning, brew fresh coffee and after the aroma has permeated your cozy abode, offer the buyer some.

Turn off the TV, but have some pleasant, soothing music playing in the background. Open the curtains. You might want to consider offsetting the curtain rods—that is, extending them beyond the window frames—to allow the maximum amount of light to enter the house and to enhance the proportions of the windows if they're skimpy. Turn on all the lights (the more light, the better—even in broad daylight).

Spaciousness, or at least a *feeling* of spaciousness, is crucial to most buyers. Take this hint. Let the buyer enter the rooms first; don't you take up space, especially when the room is small.

Remember to set the heat at a comfortable temperature. *Now* is not the time to cut your fuel expenses. If it's chilly outside, start a cozy fire in the fireplace. In summer, clean the exterior bricks or stones of the fireplace with a wire brush, but leave the black carbon deposit on the interior; it indicates a working, well-used flue.

Cleanliness Is Next to Godliness, the saying goes, but I have a better one when it comes to houses: Cleanliness Is Next to Financial Productiveness! Gather all the cleaning supplies you can find and see how "like-new" you can render things. This means *everything*: the ceilings, the walls, the woodwork, the floors, the windows, the mirrors, the light fixtures, and Aunt Tillie's oriental rug (although you're taking it with you). Removal of cobwebs and fingermarks should be first on the list of priorities. Then you can tackle the more difficult problems such as the stained carpet and the damaged wallpaper. It can be rewarding work, both immediately (look at the difference!) and later, when a buyer has been willing to pay a lot for your sparkling, well-maintained house.

There are two critical areas where improvement may make the difference between a quick sale and a financially draining long sale. These are the kitchen and the master bathroom. This is not to say that the rest of the house need not be in tiptop condition. A water-damaged floor in the bedroom or a leaky cellar will make any buyer think twice. But a kitchen and main bathroom that are attractive and well appointed do a great deal to offset any flaws your house may have.

Aspects of the kitchen in which buyers will be particularly interested are lighting (both natural and artificial), an efficient work area, and adequate counterspace and storage. Before you begin scrubbing and polishing, clear the clutter off the countertops, stash away dishes and utensils that are infrequently used (this will make cupboards appear larger), defrost the refrigerator (even if it will not be included in the sale), and let in every available bit of natural light by removing screens, trimming shrubbery away from the windows, and, of course, *washing the windows.* Newly laundered curtains contribute to the fresh, bright feeling you're trying to achieve.

If the cupboard doors stick, repair and oil the hinges. If handles or knobs are missing, replace them. Unless your cabinets are really horrendous, you'll never be compensated for the cost of adding new ones. (One exception might be the addition of a cabinet to enclose an open space below a sink.) Renewing the old cabinets with a fresh coat of paint will keep your expenditures to a minimum while creating effective buyer appeal.

Wash everything thoroughly and touch up with paint where it's needed (porcelain and chrome spray paints are available for appliances). Be especially attentive to odors; *track them down and eliminate them.* Don't leave any dirty dishes out and be sure to put away all pots and pans. Wash and wax the floor. If the area near the sink is worn or damaged, repair it or put down a nonskid rug instead of replacing the entire floor. (You won't get your money back unless the entire floor is a mess.)

The bathroom, especially the master bathroom, should look as clean as the kitchen—and smell as good, too. Scour the sink, tub, and fixtures. Retouch porcelain fixtures if they have chipped. Remove all the accumulated clutter, especially outdated medicines in the medicine cabinet. Use your skills to repair leaky faucets and clogged drains. A smart buyer will test all of them. Replace any raised tiles around the toilet, tub, or sink, trying to match the new tile with the old. Recaulk around fixtures and in seams of the tub or shower stall.

Hang out fresh towels that coordinate with the color of the wall or shower curtain and moisten some scented soap or put out some potpourri. (*Don't* use air freshener in tight spaces; some people hate it so much it will make your whole house suspect.) The conscientious buyer is going to ask to use this room, if only to check the plumbing.

Bedrooms seem to be collection stations for books, worn toys, parts of games, vacation souvenirs, extra change, old toothpicks, last year's Burpee Seed catalogue—important things to you, maybe, but clutter that's distracting to the buyer. Find a box or a drawer and store your valuables in there, leaving the dresser tops and bedside stands polished and free of clutter. Thoroughly clean and dust. If need be, repair surfaces of walls and floors. A clean bedspread over a carefully made bed, as well as clean curtains or drapes, make the room look inviting.

Again, remove excess furniture to make the room appear larger. Be sure the curtains are open to allow maximum light, and open the windows for that all-important air exchange. Pay special attention to the kids' rooms—the crayon marks, sticky woodwork, and peanut butter on the carpet. If you have an infant, see to it that the lid is secured on the diaper pail well before the arrival of your buyers.

Just a word about the attic. A messy pile of boxes and stored odds and ends makes some people think *fire*, especially if the attic is not vented properly and the climate is predictably warmish. The presence of attic vents is of interest not only to pyrophobics but also to energy-conscious buyers. Houses stay a lot cooler in hot weather when there is air movement under the roof. Also, roofing materials with an asphalt base do not deteriorate as quickly when the temperature is maintained at a lower degree. Be sure to share this information with the buyer. He'll be impressed with your knowledge and concern.

Stairways that jeopardize safety with loose treads, rotting boards, and missing or rickety rails should be high on your list of things to fix. Squeaky stairs can be remedied by counternailing from below, or, in some cases, by applying talcum powder or WD-40 (a silicone spray) to joints. Evidence of hard use is apparent in worn carpet, chipped paint, dirty walls and rails. Elbow grease will do a lot to brighten the staircase. A coat of paint or a new rug will do more. (Remnants can be bought from a rug wholesaler at considerable savings, and you can take the rugs with you on moving day.)

Every stairway should have a railing for safety. (A long, straight young tree, stripped of its bark and branches, works well secured to cellar steps.) Braces at key points can be countersunk for appearance and are often all that is needed to strengthen loose rails.

You can blow all the time you've spent renewing the upstairs by having a wet, musty-smelling cellar. A soggy basement can reduce the sale price of your home by 5 percent or more. There are several techniques to remedy a moisture problem. The most common is to use one of the special masonry paints that can be applied to a damp surface. These not only provide a moisture barrier, but lighten and brighten the whole cellar. It's important to vent the clothes dryer outside, wrap cold-water pipes so they don't drip from condensation, and unclog any drains that are plugged. You can rent or buy a dehumidifier to reduce excess moisture. Often the cause of water seepage can be traced to blocked gutters or downspouts, so be sure to check these before investing a lot of money in an elaborate drain system.

If the laundry area is in the basement, clean it up and brighten it with extra lighting. Wash off the washer and dryer tops and stack the cleaning products neatly on a shelf or table. Put away all the clothes.

By opening the windows and promoting good air circulation, you can make your basement appear light and airy. Be sure to provide additional light throughout to avoid a dark, dingy feeling. People absolutely *hate* going into moldy basements. Spend time with the kids organizing and discarding your accumulated items so that the cellar appears useful and attractive. Clutter on the steps invites accidents and possible lawsuits; so be careful!

Take a critical look at the inside of the garage. Store the excess items in a friend's garage temporarily. Organize the remaining tools and gear. Hanging related items near one another helps you find them and gives the buyer the pleasure of fantasizing similar discipline. Sweep the floor and remove grease and oil spots. Replace 60-watt bulbs with 100-watt bulbs. Unless you have a shiny new Mercedes, remove the car to increase the feeling of spaciousness inside the garage. And don't forget to touch up the garage door with the oil can and some paint. Any other outbuildings should be freshened and cleaned; otherwise buyers may view them as liabilities.

By now, you're probably saying to yourself, "Wow, that's an awful lot of work!" It is indeed, but before you give up, bear three things in mind.

First, unless your house is like the derelict one I described in the beginning of the chapter, you will probably have to concern yourself with only a few of the areas mentioned. Your bathroom probably looks just fine and your cellar is probably dry and functional, so you'll only concentrate on some cleaning and touching up in other areas. It won't take as long as you think.

Second, you'll have increased your awareness level and will be better able to scrutinize other houses you may consider buying in the future. You'll also know how long and how much money it will take to repair and renew areas of a house that are in poor condition.

Third, and most important, you will reap the benefits of your efforts in an obvious way: money! Not only will your house sell faster, but you may increase the selling price by as much as 10 percent. That means as much as $6,000 to $7,000 considering today's average resale price. Certainly that's worth a little scrubbing and polishing!

Good luck as you reap the rewards of your home investment!

14

RICHES-UNDER-YOUR-ROOF WINNERS AND LOSERS

The chart of winners and losers (Table 10) details a wide variety of possible improvements and the investment implications of each.

Your investment strategy should focus first on being sure your home is up to market. Are your prime surfaces prime? Are your bathroom and kitchen equal to those of similar houses in your neighborhood? Are your structure and mechanical systems sound and working well?

If your house is up to market, by all means add extras. Be sure to maintain and create a strong house image—simple and conventional, but interesting. Remember not to overimprove; you can increase the value of your home up to the top of your local market, but not beyond. Talk to local realtors. Be sure you know what people want in your area before you take the investment plunge.

The buyer-preference scale and the estimated five-year returns shown in Table 10 are not strictly scientific, but I think you'll find them sound, educated estimates. My own experience and wide contacts with builders and brokers, as well as national studies, have contributed to the buyer-preference ratings. Whatever improvements you make, try to pick them from the top of the buyer-preference ratings.

TABLE 10

RICHES-UNDER-YOUR-ROOF WINNERS AND LOSERS: HOME IMPROVEMENTS THAT WILL AND WILL NOT INCREASE YOUR SELLING PROFIT

FEATURE	BUYER PREFERENCE: WILLINGNESS TO PAY MORE (SCALE OF 1–5, 1 HIGHEST)	COST RANGE (DOLLARS)	ESTIMATED 5-YEAR RETURN	COMMENT
Brick and stone exterior	2	4,000–6,000	×2.2	Do if common in area, especially in better neighborhoods
White-painted exterior	2	500–1,800	×2.5	Conventionality Plus
Shutters	2	800–5,000	×3.0	Paint dark, sober colors
Tile or fancy shake roofing	1	1,500–5,000	×3.0	Quality much wanted today
Blacktop or concrete driveway	1	500–2,000	×2.2	House *must* have good driveway to be up to market
Carport	4	1,500–4,000	×1.6	Not anymore
Detached garage	3	2,000–4,000	×1.8	Must have space for two cars plus some work area
Detached workshop or office	2	2,000–5,000	×1.9	Only if *you* can really use it
Front porch/ vestibule	1–2	800–2,200	×3.4	Adds interest to exterior
Sun or screened porch	2	1,000–4,000	×2.4	Combine with passive solar heating

TABLE 10 Cont'd

FEATURE	BUYER PREFERENCE: WILLINGNESS TO PAY MORE (SCALE OF 1–5, 1 HIGHEST)	COST RANGE (DOLLARS)	ESTIMATED 5-YEAR RETURN	COMMENT
Flagstone or brick patio with grill	1	400–800	×3.0	Pleasant and worth paying for
Shade trees	1	10–100	×6.0	Loved by all
Fruit trees	2	5–100	×6.0	Dreams of Eden, good for image
Bushes along house	1	10–100	×4.0	Can cover an ugly foundation
Bushes in yard (walks, driveways, etc.)	2	10–200	×4.0	Add elegance to *any* house, even the humblest
Perennial flowers	2	1–300	×2.0	Can really help at selling time; read a good book on gardening first
Organic garden	2	30–200	×2.5	Coming on strong, but tuck it away at yard's edge
Detached greenhouse	5	To 10,000	×0.5	Perish the thought
Solar greenhouse window	2	400–600	×2.3	Plus your energy savings
Attached solar greenhouse	2	1,000–4,000	×2.5	Plus your energy savings
Split-rail fencing	1	8/ft., installed	×3.0	Nostalgic and glamorous, but don't be only one on block

TABLE 10 Cont'd

FEATURE	BUYER PREFERENCE: WILLINGNESS TO PAY MORE (SCALE OF 1–5, 1 HIGHEST)	COST RANGE (DOLLARS)	ESTIMATED 5-YEAR RETURN	COMMENT
Picket fencing	3	8/ft., installed	×1.6	Questionable
Stockade fencing	4	8/ft., installed	×1.5	Questionable
Gazebo	2	800–3,000	×2.7	Must be solidly built
Above-ground pool	5	500–1,500	×0.2	Leaks sooner or later
Below-ground pool	4 (2 in Sunbelt)	2,000–10,000	×0.8 (×2.0 in Sunbelt)	Only in wealthy and warm areas
Tennis court	5 (1 in Beverly Hills)	8,000–20,000	×0.8	Join a club
Swings and gym	3	75–300	×1.5	High quality
Basketball pole and area	3	100–300	×1.0	In family area
Night lights in yard	3	200–600	×1.5	Especially if well land-scaped
Heavy insulation	1	1,000–2,000	×4.0	Costs increas-ing rapidly every year
Weather-proofing	1	10–500	×4.0	Saves you energy
Double- and triple-glazed windows	1	300+	×3.0	Bound to make money

TABLE 10   Cont'd

FEATURE	BUYER PREFERENCE: WILLINGNESS TO PAY MORE (SCALE OF 1–5, 1 HIGHEST)	COST RANGE (DOLLARS)	ESTIMATED 5-YEAR RETURN	COMMENT
Brick-and-tile chimney	1	2,000	×2.6	Traditional and durable
Metal chimney	3	1,200	×1.9	Will rust and corrode (also cost more every year)
Cinder-block chimney (for woodstove)	3	1,500	×1.6	Tacky; enclose in brick or wood
Energy-efficient fireplace	1	1,200	×4.3	Most wanted luxury extra nationwide, even Sunbelt
Brick hearth for wood/coal stove	1	500	×3.8	Masonry never gets cheaper
Wood/coal stove	2	700	×2.6	Trend to coal now; get glass doors
Energy-saver furnace	1	2,500	×3.0	Good for you and house
Multifuel furnace	2	3,300	×2.9	Be ready for anything
Heat pump	1	1,000–3,000	×3.0	Best bet, especially where air conditioner wanted too
Solar hot water	2	3,000–5,000	×2.9	Plus tax credits; plus energy savings; big gains possible

TABLE 10   Cont'd

FEATURE	BUYER PREFERENCE: WILLINGNESS TO PAY MORE (SCALE OF 1–5, 1 HIGHEST)	COST RANGE (DOLLARS)	ESTIMATED 5-YEAR RETURN	COMMENT
Central solar heat	2	3,000–4,000	×2.0	Plus your own savings and tax credits; becoming more popular
"On-call" tankless hot water	3	900	×2.2	Return will improve as device becomes better known
Picture windows	1	400–1,500	×3.3	People *love* lots of window area
Skylights (energy efficient)	1	300–1,200	×3.1	Uncommon, but always glamorous
Dormers (only if space added)	3	1,000–3,000	×2.0	Only if attic needs headroom
Interior shutters	4	200–600	×1.4	Add *only* if common in your area
Cathedral ceilings	3	1,500–5,000	×1.9	In warm climates
Exposed beams	1	800–2,000	×3.0	Only if real and part of original house
Wood paneling	2	5/ft., installed	×2.4	Careful, careful; go for high quality
Synthetic paneling	3	3/ft., installed	×2.0	Don't you dare in an old house
Washable wallpaper	2	400–1,800	×2.3	Avoid offbeat designs

TABLE 10 Cont'd

FEATURE	BUYER PREFERENCE: WILLINGNESS TO PAY MORE (SCALE OF 1–5, 1 HIGHEST)	COST RANGE (DOLLARS)	ESTIMATED 5-YEAR RETURN	COMMENT
Finished hardwood floors	2	10/sq. ft., installed	×2.5	Last well; no one hates them
Wall-to-wall carpet	2	300–1,000/ room	×2.2	Especially in bedroom; risky elsewhere; wears out
Parquet floors	3	14/sq. ft., installed	×1.9	Only if wanted in your area
Stone floors	5	18/sq. ft., installed	×0.8	Have a *cold look*; warm with rugs or avoid
Track lighting	4	150–800	×1.1	Kitchen okay; elsewhere poor
Recessed lighting	3	150–800	×1.6	Kitchen okay; elsewhere poor
Dimmers, timers	2	60–300	×2.3	Add if *you* like them
Enlarged living room	2	800–4,000	×2.7	Aim for spacious feeling at low cost
Window seats	3	200–1,000	×1.8	Built-ins can be a problem
Wall organizer	2	300–1,000	×2.6	Don't go hog wild
Bifold doors	1	500–2,000	×3.0	Can work magic on total home value
Wainscoting	5	2,000–5,000	×0.8	Those days are gone
Built-in bar	5	900–3,000	×0.5	Big mistake

TABLE 10 Cont'd

FEATURE	BUYER PREFERENCE: WILLINGNESS TO PAY MORE (SCALE OF 1–5, 1 HIGHEST)	COST RANGE (DOLLARS)	ESTIMATED 5-YEAR RETURN	COMMENT
Built-in home enter-tainment center	4	500–1,500	×0.9	Avoid built-ins here
Separate dining room	4	1,000–2,000	×1.0	Do only in wealthy areas
Separate master bedroom/ bathroom suite	1	500–4,000	×3.0	Studies rate high; develop-ers use as selling point
Closets	1	74–300	×4.5	A must
Walk-in closets	1	200–800	×3.0	Nice luxury touch for unused corner
Cedar closets	2	200–800	×2.5	Sell the nose
Extra bedroom (beyond three)	2	500–4,000	×2.9	Combine with guest
Second bathroom	2	700–5,000	×2.6	Yes in most areas
Third bathroom	4	700–5,000	×1.8	Only in luxury areas
Bathroom modernized	1	500–5,000	×3.0	Good return *only* on low-cost job
Combination tub/shower	1	300–1,000	×3.0	Covers entire market
Fancy bathroom fixtures	3	80–500	×2.0	Quality and plain are better
Old-fashioned bathroom fixtures (claw-foot tub, wooden seat, etc.)	2	80–500	×2.8	For old-fashioned home; antiques good

TABLE 10 Cont'd

FEATURE	BUYER PREFERENCE: WILLINGNESS TO PAY MORE (SCALE OF 1–5, 1 HIGHEST)	COST RANGE (DOLLARS)	ESTIMATED 5-YEAR RETURN	COMMENT
Built-in bathroom closets	2	75–100	×2.8	Good if space allows
Large bathroom mirrors	1	100–500	×3.8	Vain notion
Built-in bathroom heat lamps	3	150–500	×2.1	Can't really hurt
Sauna	5	900–3,000	×0.8	Sorry
Modern kitchen	1	1,000–50,000	×3.0–0.5	A must, but the more you spend the less return; aim to spend less than 5% of home value
Full eat-in kitchen	1	1,000–10,000	×3.0	Do if you can; current trend
Breakfast nook	2	500–3,000	×2.6	Make it easy to maintain and away from cooking area
Separate pantry	2	700–2,000	×2.5	Good to cut off a clumsy corner
Work island	1	800–2,000	×3.0	Much sought after today
Extensive kitchen cabinets	1	500–2,000	×3.0	Custom-made can be too expensive
Butcher-block counters	1	200–800	×3.8	Good-looking and simple

TABLE 10   Cont'd

FEATURE	BUYER PREFERENCE: WILLINGNESS TO PAY MORE (SCALE OF 1–5, 1 HIGHEST)	COST RANGE (DOLLARS)	ESTIMATED 5-YEAR RETURN	COMMENT
Tile counters	4	400–1,000	×1.1	People won't pay extra
Vinyl-tile kitchen floor	1	350–1,000	×3.3	Popular for good reason— low mainte-nance; buy good quality
Ceramic-tile kitchen floor	3	1,000–3,000	×2.3	Beware of cheap "bargain" tiles and seconds; have spares
Double sink	1	250–600	×3.0	A must, now
Microwave oven	3	450–800	×2.0	Less valuable as used appliance
Finished basement	5	2,000–5,000	×1.0	Passé
Basement workshop	3	500–1,500	×1.6	Less passé
Organized basement workshop	3	200–1,000	×1.9	Good for all
Fancy-finished laundry room	1	400–2,500	×3.6	She'll fall in love
Attached two-car garage and organizers	2	2,000–6,000	×2.5	Studies show high demand
Automatic garage-door opener	2	300–600	×2.8	Nice touch

The five-year return is based on the cost of the improvement. For example, a flagstone or brick patio has a five-year return estimate of ×3. This means that you can expect an $800 investment in a patio to be worth $2,400 in five years. This figure includes increased value for the patio itself and for the house without patio. As we've stressed throughout, inflation compounds; your return multiplier increases as the years go by.

FEDERAL AGENCIES AND COMMERCIAL INSTITUTIONS THAT OFFER FINANCIAL ASSISTANCE FOR INSTALLING ENERGY-CONSERVING MEASURES

AGENCY	TYPE OF FINANCING	REPAYMENT TERM
Local utility company	Loan financed by Energy Conservation Plan. Minimum loan: $200/eligible customer. Maximum loan: $1,500/single-family home; $2,500/two-family home; $3,000/three-family home. Note: Installation of approved energy-conservation measure must provide an estimated payback period of 8 yrs. or less.	Varies; generally 1–7 yrs.
Community Action Program (CAP) agency	Community Services Administration (CSA) winterization program for low-income families. Maximum grant: $350.	Grant; no repayment
	Department of Energy (DOE) winterization program for low-income families. Maximum grant: $400, to be used exclusively for materials.	Grant; no repayment
Farmer's Home Administration	Weatherization program for rural families. Maximum loan: $1,500.	5 yrs.
	Grant 504: winterization program for rural senior citizens. Maximum grant or loan: $5,000.	Loan varies; grant requires no repayment
Commercial bank, savings and loan, or mutual savings bank	(1) Home-improvement loan (2) FHA/HUD Title I loan Note: Maximum amount that can be borrowed under Title I is $10,000. Terms of home-improvement loans and HUD Title I loans are similar. Title I loans are guaranteed to the lender.	Varies, up to 10 yrs.
Your credit union	Depends on credit union, but usually includes Title I loans (see above).	Varies with type of loan

STATE AGENCIES THAT PROVIDE INFORMATION ON ENERGY CONSERVATION

Director
Alabama Energy Extension Service
Auburn University
Auburn, AL 36830
(205) 826-4718

Coordinator
Alaska Energy Extension
Division of Energy and Power Development
Mackay Bldg., 7th Fl.
338 Denali St.
Anchorage, AK 99501
(907) 274-8655

Director
Energy Policy and Conservation Programs
Office of Planning and Economic
  Development
Capitol Tower, Rm. 400
1700 West Washington
Phoenix, AZ 85007
(602) 255-3632

Arkansas Department of Energy
3000 Kavanaugh
Little Rock, AR 72205
(501) 371-1379

Senior Staff Analyst
Office of Appropriate Technology
1530 Tenth St.
Sacramento, CA 95814
(916) 445-1803
(916) 322-8901

Director of Community Programs
Colorado Office of Energy Conservation
1600 Downing St.
Denver, CO 80218
(303) 839-2507

Assistant Director of Program Operations
Office of Policy and Management, Energy
  Division
180 Washington St.
Hartford, CT 06115
(203) 566-5803

EES Program Manager
Delaware Energy Office
114 West Water St.
Dover, DE 19901
(302) 678-5644

Program Analyst
Office of Planning and Development
Energy Unit
Jackson School
Avon and R St., N.W.
Washington, DC 20007
(202) 727-1804

Governor's Energy Office
301 Bryant Bldg.
Tallahassee, FL 32304
(904) 488-2475

Office of Energy Resources
270 Washington St., S.W.
Atlanta, GA 30334
(404) 656-2000

State Energy Office
1164 Bishop St. Suite 1515
Honolulu, HI 96813
(808) 548-4080

Acting Bureau Chief
Bureau of Public Affairs
Office of Energy
Statehouse
Boise, ID 83720
(208) 384-3800

Institute of Natural Resources
325 West Adams, Rm. 300
Springfield, IL 62706
(217) 785-2800

Department of Commerce Energy Group
440 North Meridian St.
Indianapolis, IN 46204
(800) 382-4631

Director
Conservation Division
Iowa Energy Policy Council
Lucas Bldg. 6th Fl.
Des Moines, IA 50319
(515) 281-6681

Assistant Director
Conservation and Solar
503 Kansas Ave.
Topeka, KS 66603
(913) 296-2496

Department of Energy
Capitol Plaza Tower
Frankfort, KY 40601
(502) 564-2500

Research and Development Division
Louisiana Department of Natural Resources
Box 44156
Baton Rouge, LA 20804
(504) 342-4498

Extension Agent
Maine Office of Energy Resources
55 Capitol St.
Augusta, ME 04330
(207) 289-3811

Acting Conservation Chief
Maryland Energy Policy Office
Department of Natural Resources, Energy,
    and Coastal Zone Administration
301 West Preston St., Suite 1302
Baltimore, MD 21901
(301) 383-6810

Assistant Director for Public Affairs
Massachusetts Office of Energy Resources
73 Tremont St.
Boston, MA 02108
(617) 727-4732

Michigan Energy Administration
Michigan Department of Commerce
P.O. Box 30228
Lansing, MI 48910
(517) 373-9090

Minnesota Energy Agency
980 American Center Bldg.
150 East Kellogg Blvd.
St. Paul, MN 55101
(612) 646-3052

Director
Mississippi Office of Energy
Department of Natural Resources
455 North Lamar, Suite 228
Barefield Complex
Jackson, MS 39201
(601) 961-5099

Planner I
Missouri Department of Natural Resources
Division of Energy
1014 Madison, P.O. Box 176
Jefferson City, MO 65101
(314) 751-4000

Coordinator, EES
Department of Natural Resources
Energy Division
32 South Ewing
Helena, MT 59601
(406) 587-3780

Manager, IBGP
Nebraska Energy Office
P.O. Box 95085
Lincoln, NB 68509
(402) 471-2867

Nevada Department of Energy
1050 East William St., Suite 405
Carson City, NV 89710
(702) 885-5157

Governor's Council on Energy
2½ Beacon St.
Concord, NH 03301
(800) 852-3466

Director, Conservation
Department of Energy
101 Commerce St.
Newark, NJ 07102
(201) 648-3290

New Mexico Energy Extension Service
525 Camino de los Marquez
Santa Fe, NM 87503
(505) 827-5860

Director, Conservation
New York State Energy Office
Agency Bldg. 2
Rockefeller Plaza
Albany, NY 12223
(518) 474-2121

Energy Division
North Carolina Department of Commerce
P.O. Box 25249
Raleigh, NC 27611
(919) 733-2230

EES Coordinator
Office of Energy Management and
  Conservation
1533 N St.
Bismarck, ND 58501
(701) 224-2250

Ohio Department of Energy
State Office Tower
30 East Broad St., 34th Fl.
Columbus, OH 43215
(614) 466-1805

Oklahoma Department of Energy
4400 North Lincoln Blvd.
Oklahoma City, OK 73105
(405) 621-2995

Conservation Administrator
Oregon Department of Energy
Labor and Industries Bldg., Rm. 111
Salem, OR 97310
(503) 378-8445

Acting Deputy Director for Grants
  Management and Administration
Governor's Energy Council
1625 North Front St.
Harrisburg, PA 17102
(717) 783-8610
(800) 822-8400

Senior Planner
Governor's Energy Office
80 Dean St.
Providence, RI 02903
(401) 277-3370

Governor's Division of Energy Resources
SCN Center, Suite 1130
1122 Lady St.
Columbia, SC 29201
(803) 758-7502

Director
EES Office of Energy Policy
Capitol Lake Plaza
Pierre, SD 57501
(605) 773-3603

Tennessee Energy Authority
226 Capitol Blvd. Bldg., Suite 707
Nashville, TN 37219
(615) 824-5495

Texas Energy and Natural Resources
  Advisory Council
411 West 13th St.
Austin, TX 78701
(512) 475-5407

Director
EES Utah Energy Office
231 East 400 South
Salt Lake City, UT 84111
(801) 533-5424

Deputy Director
Vermont State Energy Office
State Office Bldg.
Montpelier, VT 05602
(802) 828-2768

Planner
State Office of EES
310 Turner Rd.
Richmond, VA 23225
(804) 323-2897

EES Program Coordinator
Washington State Energy Office
400 East Union, 1st Fl.
Olympia, WA 98504
(206) 754-1351

Assistant Director
Fuel and Energy Office
1262½ Greenbrier St.
Charleston, WV 25305
(304) 348-8860

Department of Administration
State Energy Office
One West Wilson St., Rm. 211
Madison, WI 53702
(608) 266-8234

Assistant Program Administrator
P.O. Box 3965
University Station
Laramie, WY 82071
(307) 721-2011

Deputy Director
Territorial Energy Office
Government of American Samoa
Pago Pago, AS 96799
633-4115 (via Overseas Operator)

Guam Energy Office
Chase Bank Bldg., Rm. 402
P.O. Box 2950
Agana, GU 96910
(via Overseas Operator)

Energy Project Coordinator
Commonwealth of the Northern Mariana
  Islands
Saipan, Mariana Islands 96950
7174 or 6114 (via Overseas Operator)

Acting Director, Office of Planning and
  Statistics
Office of the High Commissioner
Trust Territory of the Pacific Islands
Saipan, Mariana Islands 96950
9429 (via Overseas Operator)

Director, Conservation
Office of Energy
P.O. Box 41089, Minillas Station
Santurce, PR 00940
(809) 721-1212

Energy Director
Virgin Islands Energy Office
P.O. Box 2996
St. Thomas, VI 00801
(809) 774-1252
(x 249, 251, 252)

SAMPLE ENERGY AUDIT

Con Edison

ENERGY AUDIT

Part 1

1.1

Customer Name __Mr. Barry Ex__

Acct # __12 3456 7890 0001-9__

Mail Address __123 100 Street__

__Queens Village, N.Y. 11428__

Service Address __same__

Customer Telephone __(212) 123-4567__

Type of Home __1__

Prepared by: __J. P. Feehan__
NAME

1 FAMILY (1)   2 FAMILY (2)   3 FAMILY (3)   4 FAMILY (4)

CSR Telephone __(212) 670-6369__ Date __02/13/81__
MM DD YY

Control # __Q 00213__

Location: __1__
NYC=1; Lower West.=2; Upper West.=3

Heating Fuel: __3__
Gas=1; Elec.=2; Oil=3; Coal=4

Water Heating Fuel: __1__
Gas=1; Elec.=2; Oil=3; Coal=4

Annual Fuel Usage: __1000__
ccf or kwh or gals. or tons

Central A/C: __O__
none=0; Gas=1; Elec.=2

A. CEILING INSULATION (SEE ATTACHED SKETCH)

Area	Roof Code	Sq. Feet	Floored Y/N	EXISTING INSULATION			RECOMMENDED ADDITIONAL INSULATION	
				Type	Thick	Est. R.	Type	Rec. R.
A1	4	476	N	1	4"	11	1	19
A2	4	136	N	O	O	O	3	19
A3	4	136	N	O	O	O	3	19
A4	O							
A5								
A6								
A7								

Roof Codes: Gable=1; Hip=2; Flat=3; "Cape Cod" (Expanded Attic)=④

B. WALL INSULATION

CONSTRUCTION CODE		SHEATHING CODE		POSITION CODE		INSULATION TYPE CODE	
Shingles, wood or asbestos	1	Wood/plywood	1	Above grade	1	Glass fiber	1
Clapboard	1	Insulating	2	Below grade	2	Rock wool	2
Siding, aluminum or vinyl	2	None	3			Cellulose	3
Siding, asphalt	3	Firred (1 x 3)	4			Foam	4
Veneer, brick or stone	4	Studded (2 x 3)	5				
Stucco	4						
Solid Masonry	5						
Unfinished Frame	6						
Unfinished Frame requiring access holes	7						

Area	SQ. FEET (Gross)	SQ. FEET (Net)	CONST. CODE	SHEATHING CODE	POSITION CODE	EXISTING INSULATION Y/N	RECOMMENDED ADDITIONAL INSULATION	
							Y/N	Type
W1°	O							
W2	1098	936	3	2	1	N	Y	3
W3	810	720	1	2	1	N	Y	3
W4	O							
W5								
W6								
W7								

*W1 IS ALWAYS BELOWGRADE WALL AREA; IF NONE, ENTER "ZERO" AT W1, GO ON TO W2.

Con
Edison

ENERGY AUDIT
Part 1 (continued)

1.2B
Control # Q 0023

C. FLOORS OVER UNHEATED AREAS (SEE ATTACHED SKETCH)

	Area	Square Feet	Temperature exposure F H*	Joist Size	Type	EXISTING INSULATION Thick	Est. R	RECOMMENDED INSULATION Y/N	Rec. R
FLOORS WITH CLOSED JOISTS (FC)	FC 1	6/2	H	2"x 8"	0	0	0	4	
	FC 2	0		2"x "					
	FC 3			2"x "					
	FC 4			2"x "					
	FC 5			2"x "					
	FC 6			2"x "					

	Area	Square Feet	Temperature exposure F H*	Joist Size	Type	EXISTING INSULATION Thick	Est. R	RECOMMENDED INSULATION Y/N	Rec. R
FLOORS WITH OPEN JOISTS (FO)	FO 1	136	F	2"x 8"	0	0	0	4	19
	FO 2	0		2"x "					
	FO 3			2"x "					
	FO 4			2"x "					
	FO 5			2"x "					
	FO 6			2"x "					

*F = surface is directly exposed to outdoor temperatures (unheated garages are considered to be at outdoor temperature)
*H = surface is not directly exposed to outdoor temperatures

D. ACCESS HOLES FOR REACHING CEILINGS AND FLOORS TO BE INSULATED

How many access holes are needed? Ceilings __0__
Floors with closed joists (FC): __2__; Floors with open joists (FO): __0__

E. VENTS FOR CEILING AREAS TO BE INSULATED

AREA	ARE VENT AREAS ADEQUATE? Y/N	HOW MANY EXISTING VENTS HAVE TO BE REMOVED?	WHAT KIND OF VENTS ARE RECOMMENDED? G/GE*
A1	N	0	G
A2	N	0	G
A3	N	0	G
A4			
A5			
A6			
A7			

*VENT CODE: G = GABLE VENT
GE = GABLE AND EAVE VENT

ENERGY AUDIT
Part 1 (continued)

1.3A

Control # _Q 00213_

(F) WEATHERSTRIPPING, (G) CAULKING, (H) STORM DOORS, (I) STORM WINDOWS

Door No. (see attached sketch)	Caulking (good, fair, poor)	Weatherstripping (good, fair, poor)	Is there a Storm door or window?	Recommendation
1 (Front)	Good	Poor	Yes	None
2	Good	Poor	Yes	None
3				
4				
5				

Window No. *(list picture windows first)* *(see attached sketch)*

1 to 14	Good	Good	Yes	None

GOOD CAULKING: Caulking and putty are intact and no drafts can be felt.

FAIR CAULKING: Caulking and putty which are old and cracked or missing in places; minor drafts can be felt.

POOR CAULKING: No caulking at all; the putty is in poor condition; noticeable drafts can be felt.

GOOD WEATHERSTRIPPING: Weatherstripping which is intact throughout; no drafts can be felt.

FAIR WEATHERSTRIPPING: Weatherstripping which is damaged or missing in places; minor drafts can be felt.

POOR WEATHERSTRIPPING: No weatherstripping at all; noticeable drafts can be felt.

Con Edison

1.4

ENERGY AUDIT
Part 1 (continued)

Control # _Q 00213_

WEATHERSTRIPPING, (G) CAULKING, (H) STORM DOORS, (I) STORM WINDOWS

(Cont'd.)

Summary

DOORS		Good	Fair	Poor
	Re-Caulk:	XXXXX	O	O
	Install weatherstripping:	XXXXX	O	2
	Install storm doors:	O *Good	O *Fair	O *Poor

PICTURE WINDOWS		Good	Fair	Poor
	Re-Caulk:	XXXXX	O	O
	Install storm windows:	O *Good	O *Fair	O *Poor

WINDOWS		Good	Fair	Poor
	Re-caulk:	XXXXX	O	O
	Install storm windows:	O *Good	O *Fair	O *Poor

(*Condition of weatherstripping:)

J.   THERMOSTATS

As this house is now controlled, what is the existing setback?_____ $O°$ °F

What setback do you want to use?___ $10°$ °F ___ (not more than 10°F)

How many new clock thermostats do you want?___ I ___

Operating voltage:___ I ___
low (1) or line (2)

Reason for the thermostat replacement: _Automatic setback_

Are thermostats properly located?___ 4 ___ Y/N

K.   WATER HEATER INSULATION BLANKETS

FUEL	Size (Gallons)	Number of Water Heaters	External Insulating Blanket		
			Existing Y/N	Recommended	
				Materials Only	Materials & Labor
Gas	40	I	N	I	O
Electric	40 gals.	O			
	52 or more gals.	O			
Oil	O				

<table>
<tr><td>Con Edison</td><td>ENERGY AUDIT
Part 1 (continued)</td><td>1.5
Control # <u>Q 00213</u></td></tr>
</table>

1. Existing insulation installed incorrectly in area 1 of ceiling. (vapor barrier reversed.)

2. Drapes blocking radiators should be shortened for unrestricted air circulation.

3. Air conditioners in windows should be removed in winter or covered with plastic to stop cold air infiltration and warm air loss.

4. Water heater temperature should be set down from 180° to 120°.

5. Water saving showerheads should be installed in shower outlets.

6. Hot water pipes in basement should be insulated.

ENERGY AUDIT

Sketch

Customer Name _Mr. Barry Ex_   Control # _Q 00213_

Address _123 100 Street_

Prepared by _J. P. Feehan_

Date _02/13/81_

Indicate Street Side or North

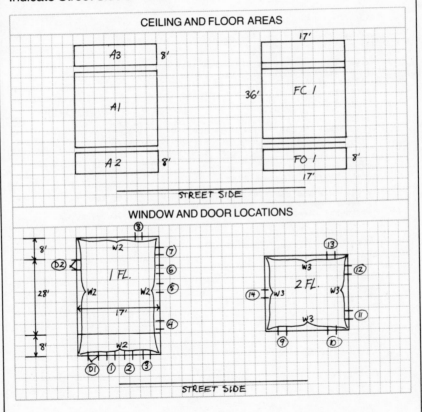

40-22 College Point Blvd.
Flushing, N.Y. 11354   212-670-6369

March 25, 1981

Mr. Barry Ex
XXX-XX 207 Street
Queens Village, NY   11428

Dear Mr. Ex :

We have completed the Energy Audit of your home.
The results are enclosed.

As you can see, the report shows that our estimate
of the cost of installing the conservation measures
will be recovered within seven years. They would,
therefore, be eligible for financing through
Con Edison.

You can install the measures yourself or have the
work done by a contractor. If you prefer to pay
cash for materials or work you can do so directly
with the materials supplier or your contractor.
If you wish us to arrange the financing, please
submit your contractor's bid or a building supply
house invoice for our review.

If you have any questions about your Energy Audit Report,
please phone me at the number shown above. If I am
not there, please leave a message. I will call you back.

                              Sincerely

                              J. Feehan
                              Queens Commercial Services

enclosures
ea/g

Con Edison

40-22 College Point Blvd.
Flushing, N.Y. 11354

ENERGY AUDIT REPORT

CONTROL NUMBER
Q00213

CUSTOMER NAME Mr. Barry Ex

ADDRESS   **XX-XX** 207 Street

Queens Village, NY   11428

TELEPHONE NO.   212-**XXX**-9311

ACCOUNT NO.   26-**XXXX**-3195-00-01-9

INSULATION COST AND SAVINGS SUMMARY

ITEM	ESTIMATED COST FOR ITEM (DOLLARS)	CUMULATIVE ESTIMATED COST (DOLLARS)	ESTIMATED ANNUAL SAVINGS (DOLLARS)	CUMULATIVE ESTIMATED ANNUAL SAVINGS (DOLLARS)	PAYBACK PERIOD (YEARS)	CUMULATIVE PAYBACK PERIOD (YEARS)
DOOR WEATHERSTRIPPING	52	52	43	43	1.20	1.20
CEILING INSULATION INCLUDING VENTS	663	715	371	414	1.78	1.72
WATER HEATER INSULATION	32	747	15	429	2.13	1.74
THERMOSTAT INSTALLATION	137	884	41	470	3.34	1.88
FLOOR INSULATION: OPEN JOISTS INCLUDING ACCESS HOLES	181	1065	46	516	3.93	2.06
WALL INSULATION	1875	2940	324	840	5.78	3.50
FLOOR INSULATION: CLOSED JOIST INCLUDING ACCESS HOLES	507	3447	69	909	7.34	3.79

ELIGIBILITY FOR FINANCING

THIS COMBINATION IS ELIGIBLE; MAXIMUM AMOUNT IS $ 2500

PREPARED BY

J. Feehan
Commercial Service Representative

TELEPHONE 212-670-6369
DATE   02/13/81

APPENDIX 4

SAMPLE CONSTRUCTION CONTRACT

CONSTRUCTION CONTRACT

The parties agree as follows:

Date

June 16   1983

Parties

Owner   Nancy Marsh
Address   1234 Main Street
           Barrytown, NY
Contractor Jim Belliveau
Address

Work Site

1.   1234 Main Street
          Barrytown, NY

Description of Work

2. Contractor will construct and complete with good and sufficient materials and in a good and workmanlike manner, the following construction:

Blankets of Owings-Corning Fiberglass insulation, with vapor barrier, rated R-19, to be installed between joists in attic floor and between studs in knee walls of attic. Cover floor with number 2 one-by-twelve yellow pine; finish corners with quarter-round molding. Sand and poly-urethane floor, three coats of Varithane.

~~Architect~~ ~~Architect~~
~~Address~~

~~3. The construction shall be under the direction of, to the satisfaction of, and in accordance with the drawings and specifications of the Architect. The Architect has no authority to bind the Owner except as stated in this Contract. All services of the Architect shall be paid for by Owner. The Architect shall furnish all detail drawings or additional specifications that may be necessary for completing the work. The parties agree to accept them. All instructions to Contractor shall be delivered by the Architect.~~

Drawings and Specifications

4. The drawings and specifications signed by the parties are part of this Contract.

Time

5. Construction shall start on   July 1   1983 and be completed on or before July 15   1983 which is the Completion Date. All times specified in this contract are of the essence.

Contract price	6. Owner will pay Contractor for the satisfactory completion of the construction fifteen hundred dollars ($1,500.00).

Payments

7. Contractor will be entitled to payments for materials used and work completed as follows:

$500 on signature of contracts; $500 on completion of work; $500 thirty days after completion of work. Final payment shall be less cost of any materials not actually used for work.

Owner's ~~Architect's~~ approval

8. ~~Contractor shall request approval from the Architect for each payment. The request shall be in writing. When the Architect gives written approval, payment will be made. Final payment shall be made within ___ days after the Architect gives written approval that the work has been satisfactorily completed.~~

The ~~Architect~~ Owner may inspect the work at any time. The ~~Architect~~ Owner may reject work or materials that do not meet Contract requirements.

Changes in work

9. Changes in the work may be made only by written order of the ~~Architect~~ Owner.

Additional work, etc.

10. Orders for additional work or additional materials must be given in detail in writing by the Architect to Contractor. The order must contain the price and time of payment. Owner and Contractor must agree on the price of the additional work or additional materials before additional work is started or additional materials supplied.

Contractor to supply labor, materials, services,

11. Contractor shall supply and pay for all labor, equipment, tools, transportation, heat, water, electricity, utilities, or other facilities and services needed to do the work.

Permits, etc.

12. Contractor shall obtain all necessary permits and pay fees and taxes in connection with the work and materials.

Contractor shall furnish suitable materials for performing this Contract. The materials shall be new, unless used materials are permitted by this Contract or the specifications. The materials shall be of good quality. Upon request Contractor shall furnish samples of the materials for approval. The materials furnished shall be exactly like the approved samples.

Contractor shall keep a competent foreman, necessary assistants, and a sufficient number of skilled workmen and laborers to properly and promptly perform the work. The foreman shall represent the Contractor, and in the absence of the Contractor, all instructions and notices given to the foreman shall be binding on Contractor. Upon request of the foreman or Contractor, instructions or notices shall be in writing.

Rubbish, etc.

13. Contractor will not allow rubbish to accumulate. Contractor shall remove unused and discarded materials and equipment and leave the work site in clean condition when work is finished.

Delay, liquidated damages

14. If the work is not completed by the Completion Date Owner shall be entitled to damages. The damages shall be $200.00.

It is agreed that the amount fixed as damages is reasonable considering the losses Owner will suffer if there is a delay. This amount has been chosen because it is difficult to determine the exact amount of damages that may be caused by delay.

The time to complete the work may be extended by the ~~Architect~~ Owner if the work is delayed by: (a) any act or neglect of Owner or Architect or other contractor employed by Owner, (b) changes ordered in the work, (c) labor strikes or lock-outs, or (d) fire, unavoidable casualty or other causes beyond the control of Contractor. An extension for a period greater than 7 days must be in writing and signed by the ~~Architect~~ Owner.

Waiver of claims

15. With certain exceptions, Owner waives all claims against Contractor by making final payment. The exceptions are: (a) unsatisfactory work or materials discovered after final payment, (b) unpaid liens, and (c) failure of the work or materials to conform to this Contract.

The Contractor waives all claims by accepting final payment, with the exception of those claims that have been submitted in writing to the Owner and have not yet been settled.

The Contractor shall warrant all labor and materials to be

Liens	satisfactory for one year. 16. Contractor must give to Owner a release of all liens or evidence of payment for all labor, materials and equipment which might give rise to a lien. Alternatively, Contractor may give to Owner a bond protecting Owner against any lien.
Insurance	Before work starts, Contractor shall furnish Owner with documentation that contractor holds 17. ~~Owner shall purchase and keep~~ fire, extended coverage, vandalism and malicious mischief insurance upon the entire work. The policies are to cover full insurance value of all work and materials at the work site. The policies shall cover the parties and subcontractors as their interest may appear, subject to terms of Mortgages on the work site. ~~Owner shall give Contractor copies of all policies before work starts.~~ The parties waives all rights they may have against each other for damages covered by this insurance. The Contractor shall obtain from subcontractors waivers to the same effect.
Arbitration of disputes	18. Any disagreement, dispute, controversy or claim rising out of or relating to this Contract or the breech thereof, shall be settled by arbitration in accordance with the Construction Industry Arbitration Rules of the American Arbitration Association. Judgment upon the award rendered by the Arbitrator(s) may be entered in any Court having jurisdiction thereof.
Successors	This Contract is binding on all parties who lawfully succeed to the rights or take the place of the Owner or Contractor.
Marginal titles	Marginal titles are for convenience only.
Signatures	The parties have read the contract. They have received a completely filled in copy and acknowledge receipt of copies of the drawings and specifications. They have signed the contract as of the date written at the top.

OWNER

....

....

WITNESS:

CONTRACTOR

....

....

....

Bibliography

Adams, J. T. *The Complete Home Electrical Wiring Handbook*. New York: Arco, 1979.

Albright, Roger. *Five Hundred Forty-Seven Ways to Save Energy in Your Home*. Charlotte, Vt.: Garden Way, 1978.

American Institute of Real Estate Appraisers. *The Appraisal of Real Estate*, 5th ed. Chicago: Donnelley, 1976.

Barash, Samuel T. *Standard Real Estate Appraising Manual*. Englewood Cliffs, N.J.: Prentice-Hall, 1979.

Becker, Norman. *The Complete Book of Home Inspection*. New York: McGraw-Hill, 1980.

Better Homes and Gardens Complete Guide to Home Repair, Maintenance, and Improvement. Des Moines: Meredith, 1980.

Browne, Dan. *Multiply Your Living Space: How to Put an Addition on Your Home at a Cost You Can Afford*. New York: McGraw-Hill, 1978.

Clark, W. *Energy for Survival*. Garden City, N.Y.: Doubleday (Anchor Books), 1975.

Conran, T. *The House Book*. New York: Crown, 1976. Upscale decorating and improvement ideas.

Consumer Guide Editors. *Your Home Is Money*. New York: McGraw-Hill, 1978. Tips on cost-efficient repair, maintenance, and improvement.

Cotton, Lin. *All About Landscaping*. San Francisco: Ortho Books, 1981.

Crockett, James U. *Landscape Gardening*. New York: Time-Life Books, 1971.

Daniels, George, et al. *Home Guide to Plumbing, Heating, and Air Conditioning*. New York: Harper & Row, 1976.

"Finding and Keeping a Healthy House." Forest Service Misc. Pub. No. 1248. New Orleans: U.S. Department of Agriculture, Forest Service, 1974.

Gladstone, Bernard. *The New York Times Complete Manual of Home Repair*. New York: Times Books, 1979.

Hand, Jackson. *How to Repair, Renovate, and Decorate Your Walls, Floors, Ceilings*. New York: Harper & Row, 1982.

Harrison, H. S. *Houses*. Chicago: Realtors National Marketing Institute, National Association of Realtors, 1973. General guide to features that make for soundness and value. Viewpoint of real estate professional on marketing and the desires of buyers.

Hutchins, Nigel. *Restoring Old Houses*. New York: Van Nostrand Reinhold, 1980.

In the Bank ... Or Up the Chimney. Radnor, Pa.: Chilton, 1976. How to save energy.

Kramer, Jack. *Finishing Touches*. New York: McGraw-Hill, 1978. Tips on detail and prime surfaces.

Lees, Carlton, B. *New Budget Landscaping*. New York: Holt, Rinehart and Winston, 1979.

McGraw-Hill Cost Information Systems. *1982 Dodge Manual*, annual ed., no. 17. New York: McGraw-Hill, 1981. The formula-filled book that contractors use for estimating jobs.

McGuigan, Dermot. *Heat Pumps*. Charlotte, Vt.: Garden Way, 1982.

Meyers, L. D. *How to Do Your Own Home Insulating*. New York: Harper & Row, 1978.

Morrison, James W. *The Complete Energy Saving Home Improvement Guide*, 4th ed. New York: Arco, 1981.

National Association of Homebuilders. *Basement Water Leakage Causes, Prevention, and Protection*. Washington, D.C.: National Association of Homebuilders, 1978.

Reif, Rita. *Home—It Takes More Than Money*. New York: Times Books, 1976. Decorating ideas.

Reschke, Robert C. *Successful Roofing and Siding*. Milwaukee: Structures Publishing, 1977.

Socolow, Robert H. (ed.). *Saving Energy in the Home: Princeton's Experiments at Twin Rivers*. Cambridge, Mass.: Ballinger, 1978.

Sumichrast, M., and Shafer, R. G. *The Complete Book of Home Buying*. Princeton, N.J.: Dow Jones, 1979.

U.S. Department of Housing and Urban Development. *How to Insulate Your Home and Save Fuel*. New York: Dover, 1977.

Van Orman, Halsey A. *Estimating for Residential Construction*. New York: Van Nostrand Reinhold, 1978.

Watkins, A. M. *The New Complete Book of Home Remodeling and Repair*. New York: Charles Scribner's Sons, 1979.

Wolf, Donald D., and Wolf, Margot L. (eds.). *Interior Home Repairs*. New York: Delair, 1979.

INDEX

Note: Page numbers in italics refer to illustrative material.